Under the
WESTERN SKY

Under the WESTERN SKY

Essays on the Fiction and Music of Willy Vlautin

EDITED BY
NEIL CAMPBELL

UNIVERSITY OF NEVADA PRESS *Reno & Las Vegas*

University of Nevada Press | Reno, Nevada 89557 USA
www.unpress.nevada.edu
Copyright © 2018 by University of Nevada Press
Cover design by Lindsay Starr
Frontispiece photo by Dan Eccles

LIBRARY OF CONGRESS CATALOGING-IN-PUBLICATION DATA
Names: Campbell, Neil, 1957– editor.
Title: Under the western sky : essays on the fiction and music of Willy Vlautin /
    Neil Campbell [editor].
Description: Reno : University of Nevada Press, 2018. | Includes bibliographical refer-
    ences and index.
Identifiers: ISBN 978-1-943859-58-0 (pbk. : alk. paper) | ISBN 978-1-943859-59-7
    (e-book) | LCCN 2017036487 (print) | LCCN 2017041074 (e-book)
Subjects: LCSH: Vlautin, Willy—Criticism and interpretation.
Classification: LCC PS3622.L38 Z96 2017 (print) | LCC PS3622.L38 (e-book) |
    DDC 813/.6—dc23
LC record available at https://lccn.loc.gov/2017036487

The paper used in this book meets the requirements of American
National Standard for Information Sciences—Permanence of Paper
for Printed Library Materials, ANSI/NISO Z39.48–1992 (R2002).

FIRST PRINTING

Manufactured in the United States of America

CONTENTS

ACKNOWLEDGMENTS

This collection began its life at the Western Literature Association conference in Reno, Nevada, in October 2015, when we convened a panel to discuss the writing and music of Willy Vlautin. The four panelists—Neil Campbell, Susan Kollin, William V. Lombardi, and Stephen Tatum—who all appear in this collection, were joined by Vlautin, who had agreed to respond to the papers and to answer questions from the audience. Appropriately, all of this took place not in a tiered lecture theatre, but rather in the Sammy Davis Junior Showroom at Harrah's Casino. Reno is Vlautin's hometown and it seemed like the right place to discuss his work, with the blackjack tables humming outside and the waitresses refilling bourbon glasses at three o'clock in the afternoon. Thanks to the panelists who developed their papers into book chapters and to the others who kindly agreed to join the project before you. Thanks to Greg Allen and Nate Beaty for their willingness to get involved, supplying their images for the book, and taking the time to write about their memories of Willy and Richmond Fontaine. Also, thanks to Chris Metzler and Aaron Draplin at Decor Records for some last-minute help with the illustrations.

We would like to thank Justin Race at University of Nevada Press for his support for this project. In addition, all the contributors are active members of the Western Literature Association, whose annual meetings have been a source of strength and an academic "home" to all of us over the years, and so we extend our thanks to all our fellow travelers. Lastly, a huge thanks to Willy Vlautin and Richmond Fontaine for years of writing and playing, as well as supporting this project. Let's hope for much more to come.

Under the
WESTERN SKY

INTRODUCTION

Under the Western Sky:
Willy Vlautin's Geographies of Hurt and Hope

by NEIL CAMPBELL

He wrote books himself. Now that's something.

—WILLY VLAUTIN, *Northline*

Under the Western Sky develops interdisciplinary connections played out in the "regional" writing and music of Willy Vlautin, set in and around his hometown, Reno, Nevada (the "City of Trembling Leaves"), the desert Southwest, and his adopted Pacific Northwest. His published novels, *The Motel Life, Northline, Lean on Pete,* and *The Free* (2006–2014), chart the dispossessed lives of people struggling to survive in demanding political and economic times, within a US West traditionally viewed as mythic, affluent, and abundant, yet which Vlautin reveals as highly stratified, deprived, and troubled.[1] In addition to the novels, Vlautin is the songwriter and lead singer of the Americana band Richmond Fontaine, whose eleven studio albums since 1994 (see Discography) chart a related territory of blue-collar Western landscapes, with a strong emphasis on narrative and affective soundscapes, and evoke "a lost and spinning world full of unquestionable brutality," similar to that explored in his fiction ("Hope and Repair," *Lost Son* [1999]).[2] On one hand, Vlautin's work seems intensely local, and yet, as the authors argue throughout this collection, it is resonant and interrelated to wider social, economic, and cultural themes, ranging from unemployment, violence, war, and gender struggles to race hate, alcoholism, and the loss of opportunity and dreams. To date, one of his novels, *The Motel Life*, has been made into a film. Directed by Gabe and Alan Polsky, it won the Audience Choice Award as well as awards for screenplay and editing at the Rome International Film Festival (2012). A new Vlautin-related film, *Lean on Pete*, is due as of this writing from the British director Andrew Haigh.

This introduction is intentionally unconventional, focusing on Vlautin's writing through flexible framings that explore and provoke approaches, sources, influences, and connections: indeed, a whole forcefield surrounding and permeating the music and the novels he has produced. When I refer to "writing," I mean both fiction and songs, because, as these essays assert, there are complex and consistent relations across all this work, emphasizing Vlautin's central importance to a cross-disciplinary response to the American West. Points introduced here will, in turn, be picked up in the chapters that follow and, in particular, be reflected upon in the book's conclusion. To borrow the words of Stephen Muecke, these writings cannot be contained by simple generic labels, for "interruptions from outside the given discipline or field...are the taps on the shoulder that force the writing to write with new partners" (2012: 56). Vlautin's "new partners" create this cross-disciplinary response, coming from all over, but chiefly through his absorption of others' fiction, varied musical influences, film and contemporary popular culture, regional geography, and the social and economic history of the West. Together, as this book will demonstrate, such "interruptions from outside" construct the complex affective landscape of Vlautin's work, whether entered through his fiction or his music. Thus the subsections in this introduction provide a "fugitive dance," to borrow a metaphor from Vlautin's favorite novel, William Kennedy's *Ironweed*, moving *across* and *into* a very specific selection of these "partners": contexts of the American West, *Ironweed*, the work of Raymond Carver (via George Packer), and Richmond Fontaine's breakthrough album *Winnemucca*. These provide suggestive dialogues with the chapters that follow and will lead towards the conclusion's deliberative return to some of these matters, producing a roadmap to the range, depth, and importance of Vlautin's work, and offering arguments, theoretical frameworks, and inspiration for future studies.

It follows David Matless's advice: "To account for a region, move across its varieties" (Matless 2015: 8).

STORIES THAT FALL INTO YOUR HEART

Greil Marcus wrote that "what we get from music when we are closest to it" is a "whole sense of what it meant to live" (1977: 152). And the collected works of Richmond Fontaine, spanning the years 1996–2016, surely engage the listener with an emotionally charged sense of just what it meant to live in the USA *regionally* at a certain point in history. Emerging at the intersection of their music with Willy Vlautin's novels, this substantial body of work suggests recurrent themes and concerns relevant to the American West, but which articulate more widely an active and critical regionality simultaneously expressing globally relevant human stories.[3] There is, undoubtedly, a raw geography to these layered narratives. A whole pulsing, affective landscape emerges, of working, hiding, escaping, waiting, yearning, failing, loving, messing up, and caring. In assembling a type of complex regional world to drive each story, the works simultaneously stand alone and connect to an evolving regionality, from Richmond Fontaine into Vlautin's novels: from places like Winnemucca, the Fitzgerald, the High Country, or the Thirteen Cities of the Southwest into the very smallest spaces, such as "a broken pool that we'd sit next to" ("We Used to Think the Freeway Sounded Like a River"), Exit 194B ("Exit 194B"), or Turf Paradise ("I Fell Into Painting Houses In Phoenix, Arizona"). Wherever the songs and the novels take us, they create "stories that fall into you, into your heart," as Vlautin puts it (Bertheimer 2009), routing a multifaceted mapping of the West from rural backwaters, motels, homes, and truck stops to the throbbing casino cities of Las Vegas and Reno.

In the fragmented stories of lives breaking apart and coming back together, loss and pain, home and homelessness, love and longing, searching and disappointment, and fear and uncertainty, Vlautin's intense geographies of hurt and hope share much with all he admires in Bruce Springsteen's work. This is particularly evident in his "darker, more brooding ballads," with their "cinematic" quality, which makes you feel "You can live inside them" because "[t]here's a world going on in his albums...and each song lets you live in that world for three or four minutes" (Vlautin in Burke 2011: 192). This "world going on" constitutes a key element of *regionality* in Vlautin's writing, because from within seemingly local geographies and micronarratives of everyday working life emanate *worlds* of intensity, drawing us to those "stories that fall into you, into your heart." Worlding, in this sense, suggests multiple active presences constituting life and living, moving bodies and minds through space and time without settling for The World as some perfect, finished thing, within which we exist already, measured, anchored, and weighed down. Instead, worlds open up before us in the regional encounters and intimacies of Vlautin's work, something he has readily admitted:

> I've always been a big fan of songwriters who bring you into their world. Details for me bring me in. Whether a town, a street name, a table, a bar, the lighting, characters' names, posters. Whatever it may be. I always wanted to take people there to a different world. Sometimes it works and sometimes it doesn't. Once inside the world you tell a story or give a feel you hope makes sense to people. (In Sherez 2002)

Earl Hurley, the sage of used car sales in *The Motel Life*, spells it out when he tells Frank Flannigan, "There's a world out there. If you don't open your eyes you ain't ever gonna see it" (Vlautin 2006: 156). Whether embedded in the soundscapes of Richmond Fontaine or the images within Vlautin's novels, such details resonate and connect into a recurring swirl of affects, a territory of troubled times and yearning spaces. However, as Zeese Papanikolas reminds us, "The other side of our longing is our fear, and our contempt for the very things we have destroyed" (2007: 15). This is the world Vlautin takes us into.

Mikhail Bakhtin coined the term *chronotope* (time space) to express this fusion in which the "*sociohistorical heterogeneity* of one's own country...is revealed and depicted" (1990: 245—italics in the original), and Vlautin's work charts such a course through the heterogeneity of the West. "The chronotope," argues Bakhtin, "is the place where the knots of narrative are tied and untied" and "time becomes, in effect, palpable and visible...makes narrative events concrete, makes them take on flesh, causes blood to flow in their veins" (ibid.: 250). Vlautin's interest in the past, in change, journeys, memory, decline, and transformation, underpins this concern with time made palpable in people's lives, as does his comment, echoing Bakhtin, "I always try to write with blood...I always figured I wasn't that talented so I had to be honest" (Gibney 2015). Thus as events unfold in time within his regional West, Vlautin's writing produces worlds with depth and feeling from the knots of everyday narrative, resonating simultaneously with historical and cultural processes. It is not in the myths of official discourse that one finds real, lived humanity but in the seemingly small-scale, regional, and fugitive within Vlautin's work. And yet, this is never parochial, since, just as in Springsteen's songs, there remains a vitally productive dialogue with wider, global forces tasked "to open our eyes...[to] discover the immense human wealth that the humblest facts of everyday life contain" (Lefebvre 2000: 132). To borrow from Lauren Berlant, Vlautin's writing explores "crisis ordinariness" and is "about the ordinary as a zone of convergence of many histories, where people manage the incoherence of lives that proceed in the face of threats to the good life they imagine" (2011: 10).

Therefore, this introduction creates *flexible framings* to demonstrate and help to appreciate and understand the significance of Vlautin's work as he represents the various crises that are never exceptional, but rather "embedded in the ordinary that unfolds in stories" (ibid.).

EVERYDAY WESTNESS: "HARDER TO SEE BUT NO LESS VITAL."

Is it not in everyday life that man should fulfil his life as a man? The theory of superhuman moments is inhuman...If a higher life, the life of the "spirit," was to be attained in "another life"— some mystic and magical hidden world—it would be the end of mankind, the proof and proclamation of failure. Man must be everyday, or he will not be at all. (Lefebvre 2000: 127)

Vlautin's chronotopes understand the enduring power of Henri Lefebvre's "mystic and magical hidden world" of promise, bound up in the optimism of the American Dream, translated through Manifest Destiny into the West. Lefebvre calls this type of rhetoric "a bookish rehearsal of out-moded masquerades" (ibid.: 135), and Vlautin's writing shows how the shadow of such mythology risks obscuring the "every-dayness" of people's struggles and the small-scale actions through which real life is actually measured. Rather than the grand gestures and manifestos of such official myths, Vlautin's project is concerned with another "magic," to "open our eyes" to a different world, best defined by Deleuze and Guattari's notion of the "minor." This includes working like a foreign language within the dominant language, "to place it in a state of continuous variation (the opposite of regionalism)," creating a stammer or stutter that interrupts the major flow of rhetoric (and myth) by introducing fugitive elements from below, creating "knowledge and genuine thought...[to] pass methodically from the individual scale to the social and national scale" (Deleuze and Guattari 1996: 105; Lefebvre 2000: 134). As Lefebvre argues, "it is in the most familiar things that the unknown—not the mysterious—is at its richest" (ibid.: 132), and it is the duty of the writer to represent these details, however brutal they may be. Rather than dismiss the everyday, such writing demonstrates how, in each familiar action or concern (its regionality, we might say), there is "something enfolded within which hitherto we have been unable to see" behind the cloud of myth (ibid.: 134). Seeing the acute "contradiction" between the myth and the actuality of such ordinary lives, we face up to a "new imperative: the practical, effective transformation of things as they are," rather than as they are supposed to be (ibid.). Significantly, such an approach alters the mythic concept of nation building, such as in the Manifest Destiny of the West, since the "nation ceases to be an abstraction, a 'moral person'...or a (national or racist) myth," and is replaced by the idea of a nation built over time, "slowly shaped by centuries of work, of patient, humble gestures" (ibid.: 134); and it is here, with these individual and collective gestures, that resilience and greatness lie. Appropriately, Lefebvre admires American writers who, despite the presence of capitalism and imperialism, were "looking lucidly around them" and not becoming lost in a "distant vision," as many French writers were in the "unreal, the surreal" and "in abstraction" (ibid.: 235). Lefebvre mentions writers like John Steinbeck (one of Vlautin's favorites) because he was willing to analyze America's "contradictory aspects, poverty and wealth, weakness and power, blindness and lucidity, individuality and massiveness" (ibid.).

In this sense, Vlautin's writing responds to what George Packer calls *The Unwinding* of American everyday life (discussed more below):

> If you were born around 1960 or afterward [Vlautin was born in 1967], you have spent your adult life in the vertigo of that un-winding. You watched structures that had been in place before your birth collapse like pillars of salt across the vast visible land-scape—the farms of the Carolina Piedmont, the factories of the Mahoning Valley, Florida subdivisions, California schools. And other things, *harder to see but no less vital* in supporting the order of everyday life, changed beyond recognition.... The void was filled by the default force in American life, organized money. (2013: 3—emphasis added)

As Packer put it in an interview, "I didn't look for it, it was there every-where—the sense that not necessarily a wonderful life, but a decent life had been available to the majority, and it was gone. You could see its absence on these main streets. It was traumatic. It's become normal to people who live there, but you get people talking about it and there are ghosts everywhere. As one man said to me, if it had been a plague it would have been a historic event, but it was economic dislocation, so it's considered a natural process" (in Rowland 2013). Packer's language parallels Vlautin's own sense of the West's traumatic history rather than its supposed "wonderful life," stressing that people living today have inherited its "ghosts" from such a dark past, named by Papanik-olas an "American Silence": "a kind of longing, a sense of something lost, lost perhaps even at the moment of gaining it, and possibly irre-trievable. It was a myth as compelling as all of the myths of success you grew up with and believed, and perhaps inseparable from them" (2007: 19). Vlautin locates these contradictions and dislocations in the West's complex regionality, permeating the music of Richmond Fon-taine (from *Winnemucca* to *You Can't Go Back If There's Nothing to Go Back To*), and his own novels, whose journeys travel across states (Char-ley Thompson in *Lean on Pete*, from Oregon to Wyoming), or across imagined spaces such as those created in the drawings of Jerry Lee

Flannigan or Earl Hurley's "place that's good" in *The Motel Life* (Vlautin 2006: 81). It also exists as the New West of Nevada, in the detailed mappings of *The Motel Life* and *Northline*, where we follow characters along specific routes through Reno, from Fourth Street motels to the casinos on Center Street and the Basque restaurants downtown, to the casinos of Las Vegas, or the small towns and truck stops in between. And, crucially, regionality exists too in the remains of the Old West myths retaining power in the landscapes, stories, and memories of those who live and work in Vlautin's haunted West, where, to borrow from Packer, there are "ghosts everywhere."

The Free seems at face value to be the least "Western" of Vlautin's novels, and so I will use it to demonstrate the contextual resonance of everyday westness forming a significant presence in all his work. I have previously defined "westness" as "a mobile genealogy...a cultural discourse constructed through both national and transnational mediations, of roots and routes, with its territories defined and redefined (deterritorialized) from both inside and outside the USA" (Campbell 2008: 8). Set in "a town in Washington State" (Vlautin 2014: 2), *The Free*'s characters function in bas-relief to a system of westness existing as an uncanny presence, a cultural haunting within which they live their everyday lives. Traces of the West circulate in the novel as spectral points of reference, reminding us how the past lives on in the present, like the damaged patients in the hospital: "Donald, the thirty-five-year-old Indian...nearly catatonic staring at the TV," or Mr. Flory, ex-rancher, "a real cowboy...pretty tough" (ibid.: 7, 43). Equally, however, the mediated West acts as a constant, inescapable reminder of values and myths, with Leroy Kervin, the injured soldier, often watching Westerns on TV (see 23), or Freddie McCall, searching "through the channels until he found an episode of *Gunsmoke*" and later *Bonanza* and *Wagon Train* (ibid.: 34, 130, 232), as though such scripted rerun versions of the West offer solace in difficult times, presenting a simplistic resolved narrative in which the good guys always win and heroic action is rewarded.[4] These narrow, comforting Cold War images are replicated when Freddie gives Leroy one of his father's old postcards, showing a "pin-up girl, a redhead in a white cowboy hat...leaning against a wooden rocking horse in a tight cowboy outfit, smiling. Her large breasts, her slim waist and long legs. She had a silver pistol in each hand" (ibid.: 40). The gendered *and* mythic idea of the West as a sexualized fantasy of control (echoing Jerry Lee's drawings in *The Motel Life*) furthers the novel's use of the region as a pervasive, if outdated, optimistic discourse still active in the lives of Westerners today, even if at odds with a more diverse, problematic contemporary culture. After watching *Wagon Train*, for example, Freddie dreams of being momentarily rescued by its hero, Flint McCullough, until reality crashes into the dream, and "his face grew frantic and blood spewed from his mouth" (ibid.: 233), returning him to the here and now. Alongside the novel Darla reads her bedridden son, *The Burning Cliffs of Planet Ryklon*, the postcard and the TV shows function like forms of science fiction, presenting the mythic West as just as remote and unlikely as faraway worlds. Freddie's sense of war "like it was a sport, like an adventure story" (ibid.: 171), has its roots in this remote, nostalgic, simplistic myth of the gunfighter West: of cowboys and Indians, goodies and baddies, which can only be confronted, challenged, and critiqued by the experience of caring for those directly affected by the long-term consequences of patriarchal violence, like Leroy or Jo/Carol, the abused girl.

These uses of the West convey the deeper resonance of the Western dream of unending opportunity, family inheritance, and achievement, now turned sour in the reality of financial depression and subprime hard times: "His grandfather had built the house, and now Freddie was failing it. He was given it free and clear, and now it was mortgaged twice.... In the end he knew he was going to lose it all" (ibid.: 11). Similarly, when Pauline Hawkins goes searching for Jo, the homeless girl, she describes a rural West of decline and ruination, "living in the aftermath of loss," as Tatum terms it (2006: 127): "an old yellow dairy barn next to a white house...surrounded by acres of empty fields...its white paint faded and bubbled and cracked. It looked vacant but not derelict" (Vlautin 2014: 112–13). The homesteads of another, more hopeful era have failed and become neglected, an idea ironically underpinned by the "framed crochet picture that read *The Ranch Life Is the Good Life*" (ibid.: 114) hanging on the kitchen wall. Rather than the hopeful "good life" and its golden dream of the West, Pauline finds "thousands of people living on the streets" near Pioneer Square, Seattle, "staying under overpasses or sleeping in cars or worn-out old Winnebagos and camper vans, covered in tarps outside of closed businesses or sleeping in vacant lots or squatting in empty buildings" (ibid.: 234). The *pioneer* dream remembered in the name of the city square has dissolved into a dislocated world of dereliction and despair, with people disconnected from the yeoman life once associated with the frontier, again recalling the Flannigans, who, we are told, had "never seen a horse outside a parking lot, a rodeo, or a TV" (Vlautin 2006: 16).[5]

In many respects, the West "marks" Vlautin's characters like the people in the allegorical fantasy Leroy retreats into throughout the novel, setting people apart as if scarred by a shared heritage of values whose powerful afterlife haunts lives today. In Leroy's internal narrative, however, "The Free" are vigilantes fighting for what they see as the maintenance of real American values, appearing as a distorted and dangerous form of "westness":

> What you don't understand is that at one time we had the greatest country in the world. The greatest country that had ever existed. Now it ain't shit and it's people like you who've ruined it. People who don't stand up for the flag. Who don't take their hat off when the anthem plays. Who won't sacrifice. (Vlautin 2014: 189)

With echoes of Jimmy Bodie's racist politics in *Northline,* and foreseeing recent statements and policies of President Donald Trump, *The Free*'s limiting nationalism curbs difference, insisting on a narrow set of values defended through violence and intimidation. Vlautin understands this problematic tendency in American life:

> I think the idea of the West comes from movies and books and popular culture. So it can't help but seep into the thinking of everyday people who live in the West. Maybe we're all products of it to some degree. The idea of open land, freedom, a new start, danger, and adventure. You can re-write your past, head out West and all that. I fell for the romance of it. (Vlautin and Campbell 2013)

The consequences of this cruel optimism, as Berlant terms it, form the ghostly milieu for Vlautin's writing—of people still living with the aftermath of myths that predate it: "Both my mom's boyfriend and my father loved the West and had great stories about it.... So I have that side in me, the romance of small time Nevada, cowboy Nevada" (ibid.).[6] However, as his writings demonstrate, this "romance" is tempered by the harsh realities of living and surviving in the West today. An example is *Northline*'s Reno, a city in transition, where "the old Nevadans feel threatened, maybe they are threatened," and, as a consequence, people like Bodie cling to an imagined past, a "false reality, a reality where the West is white and free and un-crowded. Where you can find your own place, a place free of the city, of people telling you what to do, the factory life. That way of thinking in a lot of ways is a dream, a movie dream. It's just not true anymore if it ever was true" (ibid.). For Vlautin, "Bodie lives in the dream of the West," predicated on a distorted myth of an unchanging, ordered, white world threatened by a "fog," from which he must escape by following a "line" to another mythical region, "North": "You know we should move. Head up north.... Get a place in Montana," he tells Allison early in the novel (Vlautin 2008: 30).

Vlautin's West is scarred, like his characters, uncoupled from the good life optimism contained in the myths of Manifest Destiny, because the colonized continent, with its narrative of success and abundance, growth and progress, has become instead a fragile, broken space where lives splinter, collapse, and fall apart against this background of myth and expectation. It is a precarious post-West where the dreams of casino culture capitalism or corporate ranching unravel to expose a vulnerable, peripheral underclass strangely at odds with its presupposed system of opportunity and aspiration and its framing narratives of triumphal destiny and assured progress.[7] As Mike Davis comments acidly of Las Vegas, it's "...the terminus of western history, the end of the trail," which began in the optimistic scripts of Manifest Destiny and westward expansion and end somewhere between Fremont Street and the Luxor in Las Vegas (Davis 2002: 86)—or, from Vlautin's perspective, between the resort casinos on Center Street and the dive motels on Fourth Street, Reno.

Within Vlautin's *critical* regionality, however, there remains hope in the West: no longer in the questioned grand myths emblazoned on the Harolds Club mural described in the finale of *Northline* or sung of critically on *Obliteration By Time*,[8] but rather in the small acts of kindness still possible between people in their everyday lives. People like Allison Johnson and Dan Mahony remake their lives through interdependence, education, labor, and acts of mutual care and intimacy that begin to open up the tentative possibility of some new space for a different life in the West. Another example is Charley Thompson, whose bildungsroman *Lean on Pete* uncovers his immense resilience as he moves across the West from Portland, Oregon, to Rock Springs, Wyoming, in search of a new life "elsewhere." Like that of Vlautin characters, Charley's mantra is "I don't know" (see Vlautin 2006: 34; 2010: 193, 197, 198, 254, 270), and yet his journey across the West, like that of some reverse pioneer, brings at least tentative knowledge about decency, kindness, and the ability to survive. This hopefulness is there, spelled out in the novel's epigraph from John Steinbeck: "It is true that we are weak and sick and ugly and quarrelsome but if that is all we ever were, we would millenniums ago have disappeared from the face of the earth."[9]

So, even though the West is so often a "movie dream" in Vlautin's work, it still remains a place where people live, work, and try to carve out possible futures, and where, if they are able, they find some hope in each other and in the world. As Vlautin has said, "I think so many live on the fence between hope and kindness and then bitterness and disillusionment. Maybe if they get a little help, or accept a little help they'll fall on the side of hope and kindness" (Vlautin and Campbell 2013).

"FUGITIVE AND FALLEN DREAMS": VLAUTIN AND *IRONWEED*

William Kennedy's novel *Ironweed* has had a huge influence on Vlautin's fiction, something he has readily admitted in many interviews over the years. In one he said, "My greatest ambition would be to write *Ironweed* before I die, but I'm not that smart" (Tyaransen 2011), while in another he went even further:

I always read…*Ironweed*. I read it once a year. Kennedy is everything I wish I was: a really good stylist and a genius with language.
Real Irish at heart, dark, funny as hell, and romantic. And he's got
magic realism in his stuff. I've always been drawn to that both as
a fan and in my own work. (Blau 2014)

Like Vlautin, Kennedy wrote American working-class fiction
deeply rooted in place, but, and this is crucial, neither writer is parochial or inward-looking. "If Tom Waits wrote novels he'd write like
William Kennedy," Vlautin told the Australian Broadcasting Corpora-
tion's *The Book Show* in 2010, underlining the connections he has always
drawn between his "saints" (Kennedy, Raymond Carver, John Steinbeck, Leonard Gardner, Waits, and Willie Nelson), that is, the artists
he aspires toward.[10] Location is critically important to all his "saints,"
becoming a mechanism through which they articulate and delve into
the dark heart of the world along complex lines of realism and dream,
romance and tragedy. A clue to this sense of worlding regionality, as
defined above, is apparent in Vlautin's comment that "Kennedy embraces Albany, New York to the point Albany becomes its own character. When I was working on *The Motel Life* and *Northline* I was hoping
to do the same with Reno" (Cage 2008).

For Vlautin, the landscapes of Reno and the West become characters, haunted and haunting, stretching into every aspect of life and
death, past, present, and future, since, as Kennedy writes in *Ironweed*'s
opening paragraph, "the dead, even more than the living, settled down
in neighbourhoods" (1986: 1). The ghostly become what Kennedy calls
"the magical key to history" (ibid.: 144), opening up a whole deep,
layered geography where people, place, memory, and affect are in constant, uncanny dialogue. Vlautin sees this connection as vital to his
own writing of place: "His love for Albany resonated with me because
I was in love with Reno the same way. I was born to the right place…in
high school I realized the darker side of that town. I felt my true heart
and the town's darkness were the same…the world felt less lonely
when I knew that, when I admitted that" (Vlautin and Campbell 2013).
These relations of person, place, and memory further underscore

Vlautin's comment that "I try to write with blood…with the things that haunt me the most" (Cajoleas n.d.).

Set in 1938, around All Hallows' Eve when spirits walk the streets of Albany, Kennedy's geographic specificity draws the past and present of Francis Phelan into elaborate chronotopic folds through strata of stories, memories, dreams, and desires that interrelate and overlap to form the novel's intense mapping of regionality:

> Francis saw the street that lay before him: Pearl Street, the central vessel of this city, city once his, city lost. The commerce along with its walls jarred him: so much new, stores gone out of business he never even heard of. Some things remained: Whitney's Myers', the old First Church which rose over Clinton Square, the Pruyn Library…life aged, died, renewed itself, and a vision of what had been and what might have been intersected in an eye that could not really remember one or interpret the other. (Kennedy 1986: 63–4)

The naming of streets and landmarks, typical too of Vlautin's psychogeography, opens up places as layered sites for Kennedy's Albany palimpsest, akin to *Northline*'s final chapter where, in Reno, "All the old places…are disappearing. I guess nothing stays the same" (Vlautin 2008: 191), or the decaying city Pauline walks through in *The Free*: "she passed through downtown, and the blocks of struggling and empty stores" (Vlautin 2014: 81). *Ironweed* moves similarly through Albany's haunted haunts, from Colonie Street and Francis's old home, to its dive bars, flophouses, junkyards, cemeteries, and seedy hotels, to the penultimate scene in the "jungle" encampment of transients, "an ashpit, a graveyard, and a fugitive city" (Kennedy 1986: 208). Here amid the "haphazard upthrust of tarpaper shacks, lean-tos, and impromptu constructions describable by no known nomenclature," Kennedy creates a "visual manifestation of the malaise of the age and the nation," where broken people suffering the Great Depression found their "journey's end" in the "city of useless penitence" (ibid.: 208–9). In Vlautin's fiction, as I have shown, the "malaise" is more a consequence of a postwar mood of cruel optimism, where the expected dreams of Manifest Destiny and unending progress associated with the region have been interrupted by economic decline, rural change, population shifts, and uneven distributions of wealth and opportunity.

Ironweed's Francis Phelan is "a twofold creature" (Kennedy 1986: 222), an ex-baseball player and now a drunken bum, living with guilt for abandoning his family after the accidental death of his son. Sleeping rough in the "weeds," "in love with the fugitive dance" (ibid.: 215) like his friend Rudy, Francis is "simple, hopeless and lost...questing for the behaviour that was proper to their station and their unutterable dreams" (ibid.: 23). Like an anti-heroic Ulysses trying to find his way home, Francis is full of "fugitive and fallen dreams," circling in "random movements across the country and back," while knowing that "everything is easier than coming home, even reducing yourself to the level of social maggot, streetside slug" (ibid.: 160). As he tells his daughter Peg, he exists in "Nowhere," whereas she reminds him his old house is "somewhere...a home you didn't build" (ibid.: 178-9).[11] Such journeyings are everywhere in Vlautin's work too, as we shall see in the section on *Winnemucca* below, with characters circling around, trying to recover or find some semblance of home in a postwar world that seems evermore fragmented, transient, and disconnected from earlier dreams and expectations of stability. This tension is even echoed through the titles of his works, from *The Motel Life* right through to the final Richmond Fontaine album, *You Can't Go Back If There's Nothing to Go Back To.*

This terrible fusion of hope and hopelessness dominates *Ironweed*, for despite its desperation, poverty, and violence there exists within it a shadow of decent humanity and a trace of care in a world that seems careless and broken. Everyone is vulnerable in Kennedy's Albany, living precarious lives at the very edges of survival, and yet they carry on and somehow retain humanity and, to a degree, the *possibility* of grace. For example, Francis's companion, Helen, refers to the songs she loves as "about the everyday currency of the heart and soul" (ibid.: 54), and it is this type of exchange, this *currency*, that persists even where economics and society have failed and lives appear as ruined as the urban landscape itself. As Francis ponders the death of Helen late in the book, there is the sense of this terrible duality, of "the soul already purging itself of all wounds of the world, flaming with the green fires of hope, but keeping their integrity too as welts of insight into the deepest secrets of Satan" (ibid.: 222). Kennedy's characters struggle through: live, die, and survive in a world where hope and wounding coexist, providing "welts of insight" like "fiercely glistening scars" (ibid.). As with Frank at the end of *The Motel Life* after the news of his brother's death, there is always a sense of somewhere else, an "elsewhere" held in the resilient words that finish the novel, "I hoped. Because hope, it's better than having nothing at all," or similarly in Allison and Dan's "fear and hope and uncertainty" at the end of *Northline* (Vlautin 2006: 206).

In an escalating series of encounters paralleling Dante's journeys through Hell and Purgatory, Francis traverses a spectral landscape as the past constantly returns to challenge him, offering guilt and redemption, reconciliation and despair in equal measure, since "The dead, they got all the eyes" (ibid.: 223). Clearly, he is a flawed, weak man capable of terrible acts of abandonment and violence, and yet the novel creates some sympathy for him, allowing glimmers of kindness and reciprocity that construct Francis as "an apparency in process" (ibid.: 169). For, as Kennedy puts it, using a baseball metaphor, "The ball still flies. Francis still lives to play another day" (ibid.). Just as in Vlautin's writing, Francis is capable of redemptive moments of kindness, often displayed through acts of giving, such as when he gives up precious food to a starving family in "The Jungle": "The man accepted the gifts with an upturned face that revealed the incredulity of a man struck by lightning in the rainless desert" (ibid.: 213). Similarly, Helen, despite the grim and brutal reality of her existence, holds on to hope: "There are nice people in the world and sometimes you meet them. Sometimes" (ibid.: 128). One thinks of Allison, saved by the kindness of strangers in *Northline*; Charley in *Lean on Pete*, given a Wendy's meal by a man he "never saw…again" (2010: 218);, or Vlautin's description of Freddie's relationship to Maura in *The Free*: "Maura the donut lady, I love her, because sometimes it's the little things people do that get you through the day. Like someone giving you an extra donut in your order, sometimes that's all you need to think: 'alright, I'm going to get through this'" (Faber 2016). Understanding what it means to be fully human is critically important to the drama of Vlautin's work, and is perhaps best summed up by the advice given to Charley in *Lean on Pete*: "Kindness breeds kindness. To get you must give" (2010: 197). Vlautin regards this as fundamental to his worldview: "There's this famous old saying.... 'You have to remember to be kind to everyone you meet, because everybody you meet is going through a great battle.' And so remember kindness, kindness, kindness. I try to remember that in my own life, and so I think the characters really reflect that" (Cajoleas n.d.).

Kennedy has spoken too of this aspect of Francis in *Ironweed*:

> ...the idea that here was a man at the bottom of the world, and yet he is still witty, resilient in a way, ready to get up tomorrow and start over, but not in any way that moved toward personal redemption or success in any form whatever. The opposite really. He was driving obviously towards self-destruction. At the same time he was riding on a rainbow of hallucinatory, boozy arcs. Rising up, peaking, going down, depressed, drunk, getting up in the morning, rising up again. That was a remarkable thing, and it struck me, when I began to write it, that that's probably the way Francis lived. (Smith 1993)

This sensibility echoes across the layered landscape of Vlautin's work, with "resilient" characters who have hit bottom and yet are still "ready to get up tomorrow and start over," like the Flannigans, Allison Johnson, Penny Pearson, Dan Mahony, Charley Thompson, Freddie McCall, and Pauline Hawkins, who in differing ways are seen "rising up, peaking, going down, depressed, drunk, getting up in the morning, rising up again." "These are stories," Vlautin insists, "about decent people who just get overwhelmed" (Faber 2016), but for whom life chimes with Kathleen Stewart's comments at the end of *Ordinary Affects*: "The world is still tentative, charged, overwhelming, and alive. This is not a good thing or a bad thing. It is not my view that things are going well but that they *are* going" (2007: 128). The intensities in Vlautin's writing, as seen throughout *Ironweed*, are "ordinary" and "everyday," and yet this is what makes his work so powerful, recalling Lefebvre's "Man must be everyday, or he will not be at all." So rather than take us out of ourselves, he engages us with worlds of emotion and affect that are perpetually swirling around us, but which are often ignored, dismissed, or evaded, since, as Stewart writes, "What a life adds up to is still a problem and an open question; an object of curiosity" (2007: 129).

In *Ironweed*, as always, the landscape itself emphasizes a world "still tentative, charged, overwhelming, and alive," even when Kennedy plunges us into its dark recesses of the junkyard, his "cemetery of dead things," where, for Francis, "Gray clouds that looked like two flying piles of dirty socks blew swiftly past the early-morning sun" and, simultaneously, "the world shimmered in a sudden blast of incandescence" (Kennedy 1986: 91). So even in this "castoff world" of death, with its circular echoes of the cemetery that opens the novel, something remains strangely alive as Francis works the rag-and-bone route of Albany "through the bright streets of morning" (ibid.: 93). Laboring in such a place, Francis nonetheless "felt rich seeing the people of his old city *rising* for work, *opening* stores and markets, *moving* out into a day of substance and profit" and, alongside these feelings of social well-being amid the city's ordinary affects, stirs an "optimism" with "new visions of survival" (ibid.—emphasis added). In these moments of active association, Francis reacquaints himself with the rhythms of the ordinary not as things that are mundane and dull, but as resources for optimism and survival: for getting on with life instead of dwelling in death. Although Francis can never live for long within such moments, Kennedy recognizes this capacity for flourishing, as Vlautin does in his characters, for such attunements and the capability to see "lunar majesty, a chilling fusion of beauty and desolation" (ibid.: 103). This "fugitive dance" (ibid.: 215) of survival, despite the vicissitudes of being and the painful memories constantly alive within it, clearly affected Vlautin's work:

> He moves between the lightness and darkness of humanity while all I do is struggle to stay afloat. *Ironweed* is what I aspire to. Kennedy has a great understanding for people who are living the hard life. He has great romance and great tragedy to him, he writes with both love and pain. He writes like a good man who's been beat up a few times. (Vlautin and Campbell 2013)

Ultimately, characters in Kennedy's and Vlautin's writing are the toughest of "ironweeds," refusing to die out despite all that life throws at them; they are rooted in the soil of Albany, Reno, or the Pacific Northwest, persisting and resilient even when they are knocked back, as they so often are, living on and endlessly "trying to move back into the world" (Vlautin 2008: 166).

THE UNWINDING: PACKER, CARVER, VLAUTIN

One of the earlier sections of journalist George Packer's collage of contemporary American culture, *The Unwinding* (2013), focuses upon the writer Raymond Carver, which in the context of its 432 pages stands out as a significant excursion into the literary world.[12] This both helps in understanding *The Unwinding* and Carver's stories, but, most suggestively here, provides a further framing of Vlautin's writing. Through a brief examination of Packer's appreciation of Carver and an example of one story, "I could see the smallest things," this section fleshes out Vlautin's often-made comment that Carver inspired his writing career as another "chronicler of blue collar despair" (Packer 2013: 75). As Vlautin explains,

> I started writing fiction after listening to a Paul Kelly song... "Everything's Turning to White" based on the Raymond Carver story "So Much Water so Close to Home." I read the story and I was blown away by it and found Carver... [whose] stories seemed like my stories. I knew those stories and the people in them...his characters hadn't done anything great in their lives, they were just people trying to get by, and I really identified with that... (Blau 2014)

Carver "wasn't writing about wars or bullfighting or espionage or politics, he was just writing about hanging on. More than anything I wanted to do the same" (Faber 2008).

According to Packer, Carver came from a struggling family who "lived together like strangers," "began to wander," "had great dreams and believed that hard work would make those dreams come true" (Packer 2013: 71,72). Sounding like Vlautin characters, "[t]hey moved around the West and they never stopped" (ibid.: 72), taking menial jobs to make a living, but always restless: "Hard work, good intentions, doing the right things—these would not be enough, things would not get better.... And somewhere along the way, his dreams started to go bust" (ibid.). Packer's language situates Carver within *The Unwinding*'s central dilemma: caught "in the vertigo of [America's] unwinding," as the structures, industries, dreams, communities, hopes, and optimism conditioned into the nation were sapped away (ibid.: 3). From this experience, Carver forged, in Deleuze's term discussed earlier, his own minor literature as fragmented poems and short, short stories "about people who did not succeed…alone and adrift," living out their lives "nowhere in particular" with "[n]othing like religion or politics or community" surrounding them, only "the Safeway and the bingo hall" (ibid.: 73). In one sense, it is as if "[n]othing was happening anywhere in the world," except in the ordinary business of the "epic" everyday captured in Carver's stories, where the focus is always proximal and relentlessly small scale, as if "Ray left almost everything out" (ibid.). This capacity to empty out the superfluous until the stories become as honed and sharp as arrowheads means Carver interrogates life-worlds of people whose "lives were trembling over a void" (ibid.), through an absolute attentiveness to their unremarkable existence in all its ordinary brilliance.

Packer quotes Carver about his own work: "they've reached the point.... It doesn't add up any longer. The things you once thought important or even worth dying for aren't worth a nickel now. It's their lives they've become uncomfortable with, lives they see breaking down. They'd like to set things right, but they can't" (ibid.: 73). The stories' smallness works to magnify "the lives of marginal, lost people, people who scarcely figured and were rarely taken seriously," inserting their concerns back into the fictions of a postwar America dominated by the very different styles of John Barth, John Updike, Norman Mailer, and Saul Bellow (ibid.: 74). Carver knew, Packer asserts, "the country's future would be most unnerving in its very ordinariness, in the late-night trip to the supermarket, the yard sale at the end of the line" (ibid.). Packer admires Carver's persistent interest in these "people who scarcely figured," despite the "distractions" of the supposed boom years of Reaganomics, since "in the American din, that small thing was everything" (ibid.: 76). The "small thing," wherever we might uncover it, resonates throughout Vlautin's work too, always set against this "American din"—the noise of myth and sales pitch, bravado and the bottom line, the dream of success and the supposed good life of the American West. As Vlautin told Sean O'Hagan, "It wasn't until I read Carver's stories that I realised you could write about the lives of beat-up, working-class Americans like the ones I saw around me in Reno" (O'Hagan 2016).

Carver's story "I could see the smallest things" typifies this attentive enterprise, magnifying the everyday until it fills the page, drawing the reader into an alternative perceptual space: "There was light enough so that I could see everything in the yard—lawn chairs, the willow tree, clothesline strung between the poles, the petunias, the fence, the gate standing wide open" (Carver 1985: 204). The detail of the yard's everydayness becomes the stage for the story, without distraction, without unnecessary actions or intrusions: "But nobody was moving around. There were no scary shadows. Everything lay in moonlight, and I could see the smallest things" (ibid.). Here Carver strips back, decluttering the American din, to open up scenes of incredible lucidity where the senses fall on "the smallest things" in the sharpest focus, as if heightened by absence. In the story, Nancy, troubled by the open gate, wanders outside to fix it, and in so doing wanders into a strangely illuminated space: "The moon lighted up everything—houses and trees, poles and power lines, the whole world" (ibid.). Suddenly, Carver's story is not small at all, for it is "the whole world" lit like a theatre, in which Nancy is soon noticing, *attending to*, her neighbor Sam Lawton: his "silvery" hair, "long nose," "the lines in his big sad face," and the slugs he is killing on his roses (ibid.: 205). But simultaneously Carver makes us aware of this *whole world* of the intensely slow and local—like slugs on the ground—bound up with and intrinsic to all the forces that constitute existence. This is most evident in Nancy's thoughts: "A plane passed overhead. I imagined the people on it sitting belted in their seats, some of them reading, some of them staring down at the ground" (ibid.: 206).

In the curious exchange of ground and air, near and far, and high and low, Carver lessens distance and flattens out experience until everything matters and connects to something, rather like the "reassembled" notion of the social proposed by Bruno Latour as a "flattened topography" (Latour 2005: 174). For Latour, it is important "to sit beside the 'local,'" rather than simply "jump to the global" without seeing the relations between them, for in these moments of attention one notices the "entire topography of the social world" (ibid.: 174, 176). This is Carver's flattened "social world," in which "no place can be bigger than any other place" and "'above' and 'below' remain side by side and firmly on the same plane as the other loci which they were trying to overlook or include" (ibid.). Thus Carver's stories, like Vlautin's, are not engaged with the abstract or remote, but attend to the ordinary to reveal the richness of the world, just as Nancy sees the slugs on the ground and the plane in the sky, and imagines the thoughts and lives of those flying overhead, going somewhere else. These interactions and the relations they provoke as thoughts, feelings, memories, and actions create a world in which Nancy, Sam, and her husband Cliff move. As she gazes on Cliff snoring, Nancy "think[s] of those things Sam Lawton was dumping powder on," revealing perhaps her unhappiness and the sexual frisson with her neighbor, but most significantly, "the world outside my house" (Carver 1985: 207). Nothing is resolved here, nor any decisive action taken to move life forward; rather it simply goes on to the next thing: "I had to hurry up and sleep" (ibid.). As in Latour's work, Carver shifts the scales away from the "hierarchical assumption that a larger character must explain a smaller one," as Bingham and Thrift (in Crang and Thrift 2000: 286) put it, or the idea that the local can *only* be explained by replacing it within the global frame. Latour sums it up with eloquent ease: "A giant in a story is not a bigger character than a dwarf, it just does different things" (Latour quoted in ibid.).

Packer's use of Carver within the broader "network" of *The Unwinding* explains its construction as a type of Latourian "actor-network" within which small things, lives, actions, decisions, and places are shown connected, "as if a huge red pen was connecting the dots to let everyone see the lines that were barely visible before" (Latour 2005: 181). As Packer told Katherine Rowland,

> I wanted to do something full of juxtaposition, with connections that aren't made explicit, history as the throughline. Dos Passos

once said that he was writing history as it was felt in people's nerves, and that was exactly what I wanted to do. (Rowland 2013)

In *The Unwinding*, as in Vlautin's fiction, this "nervous" history of the everyday is not without hope, since, despite all the struggles and the "low-rent tragedies" (Carver 1985: 282) echoing Carver's stories, people find ways to make do, carry on, and, as Packer has said, "go on living their lives and trying to find answers where they live. Those are the sparks of hope in the book, and they're still out there, still breathing" (Tisdale 2013). As we shall discuss in the final section of this introduction, Vlautin's writing has, from its beginnings in the songs of Richmond Fontaine, traced a similar "throughline" of hope and hurt.

Drop Me Off in Winnemucca

In 2002 Richmond Fontaine released *Winnemucca*, initiating a more cohesive style and moving their music away from the angry country-punk of *Lost Son* to an alternative-country sound, or what Vlautin sometimes simply refers to as dressed-up "folk songs" (Berhorst 2002). Blending traditional country and folk musical styles, *Winnemucca* became their first "novelistic," cinematic album whose tracks meld into a narrative arc of regionality through Carver-like vignettes, drifting from "Winner's Casino" to the "Western Skyline," and moving spatially and thematically from the close-at-hand to the distant horizon. Looking into the struggles and inner lives of ordinary people, Vlautin, following his "saints," expresses "little worlds of identity and desire," as Kathleen Stewart might term them, drawing us into dramas of *everyday westness* (2007: 12). Musically, too, *Winnemucca* is carried by acoustic guitars, pedal steel, and subtle drumming that, together with Vlautin's plaintive vocals, begin to define the sonic landscape of Richmond Fontaine albums to come. The softer, country-inflected sound is vital to the album's force, providing a central *dislocation* within which its lighter rhythms serve only to heighten, through contrast, the dark, disturbing thematic threads weaving across the stories' fabric like "spreading lines of resonance and connection" (ibid.: 4). *Dislocation* takes us away from the expectations of location—the myth of the West

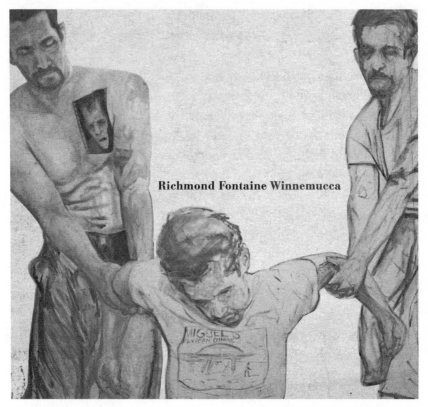

Richmond Fontaine Winnemucca

Greg Allen, "Winnemucca cover art." Used by permission of the artist.

and its people as good life "go-getters"—and plunges us into a different, murkier world of disappointment and loss, where characters are running *away* from something rather than *towards* its possibilities.

The album's disturbing, dislocative sensibility begins with its cover art by Greg Allen, portraying two men dragging a third, an image in tune with *Winnemucca*'s interest in struggle and troubled times: "The whole idea of that," says Vlautin, "is that there's always a part of you you're draggin' along. Maybe there's two-thirds of you...kickin' pretty good, and then maybe a third of you is on your back and you've got to carry it around" (Berhorst 2002). These motifs of burden and unease flow through the album's concern for people longing "to disappear for a while" and trying not "to look at [their] reflection in the window," and who would rather run away or hide from the world they fear. To this end, *Winnemucca* initiates Vlautin's fascination with restlessness and dread, or what Steve Tatum calls in this collection "vagabondage," drawing from its French meaning as "whatever strays" and "wandering about," but also the artistic quality of the unfixed and troubled imagination (see Vidler 1999: 209). In the spirit of vagabondage, *Winnemucca*'s characters are endlessly searching without any reliable home, work, or, in many cases, identifiable family and, although not necessarily criminals, they "might be in the future as a result of a wayward life" (ibid.: 210). As Nate Lippens suggests, "The men and women on *Winnemucca* drive away from places, and lives, but they are not driven. They are aimless and haunted; the ghosts they attempt to outrun may give them the appearance of forward momentum, but being chased by something you can't quite name and outrunning it is very different from having a sense of purpose and direction. Vlautin's narrators seek clarity even as it muddles before their eyes" (Lippens n.d.).

The second key to unlocking the significance of the album is the sample of Allison Anders' film *Gas Food Lodging* used on "Winner's Casino": "John, do we have the same last name?" asks Shade, to which a voice replies, "I'm him. I ain't shit but I'm your old man, darling." This is John Evans, the lost father, to his estranged daughter. He is a shambling Marlboro Man, no longer wrangling cattle or riding the range as his cowboy look might suggest, but barely surviving economically, delivering liquor for a local store and struggling to find $50 to help his daughter. And yet, we are told, "John's a big spender. Ladies' man." Vlautin admires the film, commenting that "that movie was a lot like my life growing up.... The whole story line is similar to mine...I was thinking a lot about that movie when I wrote this batch of songs" (Berhorst 2002).[13] The West that Evans represents is part of the "movie dream" discussed above, living, like so many of Vlautin's characters, in its aftermath despite being as disconnected from its mythology as John is from his responsibilities as a husband and father. The film shadows *Winnemucca* perfectly, portraying a static modern West hemmed in by economic and gendered parameters, despite the proximity of and potential still associated with the highway and the deserts beyond, promising something of the Western frontier dream. Richmond Fontaine's songs dramatize the tension between claustrophobic everyday life and the desire for escape and disappearance into a world beyond these boundaries. As Vlautin has said, contrasting it with their pre-vious release *Lost Son*, the "whole record is kind of about hiding out" (Lippens n.d.):

> I think it's kind of an answer to *Lost Son*, which was such a dark record. A brutal record. And I was feelin' that way when I wrote that record. And I think when I woke up from that phase of writin' like that, or feelin' like that, it's like when you wake up, you're really skittish. It's like if you get really drunk one night… you wake up the next morning and you just want to crawl in a hole. And never come out again, and just hide out. It's like you just got the shit beat out of you…you might not leave the house for a week after…. That's what I was trying to get at. That's why *Winnemucca*'s soft—it's like being scared, and all about hiding. It's not supposed to be in your face, it's supposed to be easy, slow. Like you are after some traumatic accident, or something. (Ber-horst 2002)

In many ways, the "traumatic accident" is Western history and myth, as discussed earlier, and his characters are living under its shadow and his writing is haunted by it. As a result, as in Vlautin's novels, the album's root is vulnerability and a deep sense of fear, as characters work through episodes of anxiety, isolation, and escape, beginning with "Winner's Casino," and its insistent pleading: "*All I ask* is for a little money and some time," "*let me* disappear for a while," and "*I just need* some time to drop below that line." This is a world of last chances with only the faintest hope that some of the "maybes" might just ease the pain: "maybe if I come back I'll be sane for a while," because "if I lose myself it'll be in a place that felt clear."

His characters are holding on despite living in an increasingly separated and isolating world, and they seek reassurance where they can: "Don't worry, no one knows where we are," so "Come back here I swear it'll be okay," the narrator of "Out of State" intones as he looks for somewhere "clear and safe," away from whatever it is that he fears outside. As Vlautin clarifies, "In that song, they're trying to hide out and she is uncertain, looking out the window like maybe someone's after them, but in the bigger scheme of things, maybe life's after them.

And they're just hiding and he's saying, 'Look, we're out of that state, for a while, out of our lives, out of whatever, so don't worry about it. You know, no one's gonna find us here, nothin' bad'll happen here, at least for a while'" (Berhorst 2002). As always in Vlautin's work, projecting forward to Allison and Dan in *Northline*, "in the bigger scheme of things" one cannot remain "out of state," hiding from the past, since to be human is to exist with others in time and within history or, as that novel puts it, to find ways to "move back into the world" (Vlautin 2008: 166).

Winnemucca's narratives maintain this strong sense of place and longing, characteristics Vlautin admires in many artists, notably Bobbie Gentry, whom he describes as "one of the best story songwriters I have ever heard. For me, 'Ode to Billie Joe' is one of the best songs ever written, let alone one of the best story songs" (Freeman 2016). As discussed earlier, he similarly admires Tom Waits' ability to transport the listener to other worlds within his songs and, perhaps most obviously, Bruce Springsteen's "dark romanticism," with its "cinematic" quality that wraps you up in a musical space "you can live inside." Because, as with Waits and Gentry, "there's a world going on in his albums," with each song adding to the next, constructing a powerful experience of working-class life "with little stability or hope or home" (Vlautin in Burke 2011: 192–3). *Winnemucca* builds in this way, with characters that are, of course, framed by an intense sense of the West and by the myths spelled out in its final track, "Western Skyline": "where golden light shines down upon everything and we will walk down the street under colored lights and we will walk arm in arm as beautiful women walk on by/beautiful women just so gentle and kind/under Western Skyline I swear you will be you'll be set free."

Measured against this romantic golden West with its promised visions of freedom, *Winnemucca* is populated by people leaving and coming home, escaping and returning or struggling with life's troubles: love, fear, disappointment, yearning, and loss. These are Vlautin's *post-western* folk ballads, which traditionally have within them what Bill C. Malone calls a "predilection for the mournful" (Malone 1985: 15), and it is these dark tales Vlautin continued to write from this point forward: "I always like the sad ballads…because those are the kind of songs that bring me comfort. So I've always written from that side...I try to write with blood, you know, with the things that haunt me the most" (Cajoleas n.d.). On *Winnemucca* one feels this haunting at work, carried by each twanged note on the pedal steel, like "dark swoonings" (Tosches 1977: 192), crying out alongside Vlautin's aching voice, working together to convey a country poetics of pain and yearning where human contact and connection seem on the brink of collapse and where "isolation is my biggest fear" ("Northline"). But, as Kathleen Stewart has argued of country music's "sad songs," there is also within them "a vision of life as a quest," conveyed like a "maze" through which people struggle so that their "essential narrative function" is "to hold open a space of suspense or desire" (in Lewis 1993: 221).

As Vlautin's characters move through his maze-like, disturbed landscape, like the characters in *Ironweed* they are suspended "in a dreamworld of floating extremes," caught between "wish fulfilment or sink[ing] into anxiety and nightmares" (ibid.: 222). Thus the possibility of human contact and communion, a key motif throughout *Winnemucca*, is fraught with obstacles like the separations resultimg from broken relationships ("Glisan Street") or imprisonment ("Santiam"), or the letters in "Northline," once exchanged but that "turned to postcards and then never appeared." And even where relationships exist, as in "Somewhere Near," they are fragile and tentative, as if they might dissolve at any moment at the approach of some unnamed dread: "And if it's somewhere near, I don't want to think about that right now. And if it's somewhere near, at least it's not here."

So *Winnemucca* creates its own geography of hurt and hope in a varied Nevadan landscape of deserts, casinos, warehouses, highway journeys, Greyhound bus rides, and city streets, brought to life with the regional details that would become a signature of Vlautin's writing. The climate varies, with the assumed desert heat and dust of the West growing wintry and unpredictable in the final tracks, "Somewhere Near" and "5 Degrees Below Zero," until snow and ice close in around its characters, ending in the "near dark" of "Western Skyline" where, under the shadow of death, a voice calls out "I can't see...where are we?" Repeatedly, Vlautin draws us into this world through detail and "the layered textures of a scene" (Stewart 2007: 4), such as in "Santiam," where we are told "the Highwaymen are playing quiet and low" while "my brother Harry's on the porch pacing and waiting, smoking Old Golds"; or in "5 Degrees Below Zero," a condensed drama of motion and stasis, where each moment is potentially the starting point for a whole unwritten novel: "A girl across the aisle is giving herself an ink pen tattoo/Her kid sits next to her and her kid is crying."[14] Equally, the confident language laced throughout "Somewhere Near" shows Vlautin's developing capacity to convey place and affect in compact images: "We didn't want or need to see it, not right now/With the street lights and the snow/it made the night time seem light."

However, alongside these particulars of place, the album explores the open vistas one associates with cinematic soundtracks, conveyed most convincingly, as Richmond Fontaine's Dave Harding argues, through the insistent pedal steel guitar that gives *Winnemucca* "that lush, huge sound...[so that] it feels like you're traveling through it" with the impression of a truly filmic, spacious, and sweeping experience. The two instrumental tracks "Twyla" and "Patty's Retreat" work in this way while enhancing the dislocative quality of *Winnemucca*, since the first has a distinctly countrified melody with a light, even hopeful tone, whereas "Patty's Retreat" is a piece of electronica building to a screeching, high-pitched crescendo through swirls of pulsing, jarring, and punk-discordant sounds. Like a Nick Cave and Warren Ellis soundtrack, such as the intertexts of *Hell or High Water* (2016), this creates a darker, harsher territory shifting us away from the calm of "Twyla," like a sinister preface to the album's final four songs. The instrumentals create breathing space within the narrative through which the listener adds to its story, imagining, as time passes, the lives of Vlautin's characters. Moving on from the last line of "Santiam" ("I hope it all feels the same when I get home again"), to "Glisan Street," with its ominous first line ("It's the middle of the night"), one finds within a heartbreaking story of the return of a lost love and a lonely man, "drunk from the moment that he heard she is back in town."

Throughout the album, Vlautin's voice echoes and vibrates, as in "Northline." Sometimes it cracks as it extends along poetic lines until they almost break (in songs like "5 Degrees Below Zero"), as if discovering some perfect yearning tone to equal the music's rhythmic frame, like a country and western heartbreak: "I knew that I could feel good but I just never thought that I would." As Stewart argues, country songs articulate an "excess of sensation that overwhelms 'the senses' (or ordinary sensibilities): there is too much pain, too much longing, too many memories, unforgettable sights, inescapable hindsight" and, as a result, the narrative is not "horizontal…driving us forward…but a vertical movement up and down between poles of good and bad or high and low…a movement 'down' to where the narrative speaks, as they say, 'from the heart'"(in Lewis 1993: 222). These postwestern ballads take us down, vertically, through their layers of sound and emotion to experience the vulnerability central to Vlautin's world: that is, until we reach "Ray Thaves" in "5 Degrees Below Zero," with nothing left to lose, trapped on a Greyhound bus, "swimming in a sea of rage," abandoning everything, and plunging out into the snowy Nevadan desert until "we can't see the city lights" or even the highway. Once again, Vlautin taps into a long tradition of "mournful" country music as "an indigenous music of loneliness and irremediable loss." These are songs whose mood and atmosphere "went beyond words" (Papanikolas 2007: 168, 179), creating a dynamic affective landscape that, although coming "from the heart," as Stewart writes, are "not just one man's private heart, but more like 'the heart of things'" (in Lewis 1993: 225). The West is never a local, inward place in Vlautin's work, but an arena for human struggles and global themes, getting at the very "heart of things."

Thus each of these songs suggests a story, offering an invitation to imagine lives in motion or suspension, as Stewart puts it, although often "compounded as much of silence as of words" (Papanikolas 2007: 185), with things unresolved and never fully expressed. In the silence between notes and between words, there is an intensity of meaning functioning "to hold open a space of suspense or desire." So "Santiam" tells of a man about to go to a prison, "leaving town, and…realizing that things are really beautiful here, and everything, even the warehouses, and stupid things, and the kids, and things he didn't like, he likes now, 'cause he's scared, and dreaming about a better [place]—this place that he likes. It's all…about hiding out in a place you like" (Berhorst 2002). Before he goes, he wants to fill up his memory with these places, captured here in a rare rhyming couplet: "Don't drive too fast, but don't drive too slow/I just want to memorize every street and club and restaurant I know."

So the "hiding out" in these songs is, in part, a recognition of a failure to achieve the presupposed dream of the West, of the stable community, reliable family, and good job, and instead to disappear into some timeless space like the curtained room in "Out of State" or the wild desert in "5 Degrees Below Zero." Appropriately, the album ends with "Western Skyline," with "glass and blood everywhere" as a man dies in the arms of another who makes a promise to him, in the comfort of a "drunkard's dream" (Sherez 2002) and the timeless solace of Western mythology, "where golden light shines down upon everything." "You'll be set free," he says to the dying man, but the ache in Vlautin's voice expresses the darker half of such promised freedom: indeed, how illusionary it can be, how lonely and disconnected the search for it can make you feel. But, of course, to offer only an illusion would be to fall back into the false promise of the West that Vlautin calls the "movie dream," so, equally important here, and central to the politics of Vlautin's work, is, once again, human contact and kindness. These are evidenced to a dying man in both the poetic rendition of the comforting dream of golden lights and an assurance of walking "arm in arm" in some imagined paradise, both examples of the kind of "hiding out" that punctuates *Winnemucca*. Yet, alongside these fantasies resides a genuine act of kindness, an offer of sincere comfort from one human being to another: "I held him in my arms," reaching out to him in the "near dark," despite there being "no one around for miles." As Papanikolas writes, "The wilderness still lived in the best of our songs, but it was no longer a wilderness of trees and prairies and great rivers, but that internal wilderness whose silence and sense of loss had been there even from the first" (Papanikolas 2007: 186). Just as Vlautin would explore explicitly in *Northline* (the seeds of which are sown on *Winnemucca*), to imagine the West as an ideal space was a deeply flawed notion, since "the place right over the hill was in fact a place in a mythical past, a nostalgia for somewhere that had never been" (ibid.). So Vlautin's songs tell of "something we were leaving, not some promise we were going toward, and if we were going home it was to someplace that would be changed by the knowledge of what

we had seen and that in leaving we would never be able to see again"
(ibid.). In the critical regionality of Vlautin's work, what people learn
through the kindness and contact of others enables a similar process
of leaving and going home to what Papanikolas sets out: a process no
longer about a mythical promise, but something more tangible, bound
up with an honest understanding of what it means to be truly vulnerable, open, and, ultimately, human.

NOTES

1. As of this book's publication, Vlautin is soon to publish a new novel, *Don't Skip
Out on Me*, about a half-white/half-Native boxer and ranchhand obsessed with Mexican prizefighters, set in Nevada and the Southwest.

2. Vlautin is not the only example among American musicians who have also
written fiction: see Steve Earle, *Dog House Roses* (2002) and *I'll Never Get Out of This
World Alive* (2012); Simon Felice, *Black Jesus* (2011); Josh Ritter, *Bright's Passage* (2012);
and Richard Hell, *Godlike* (2005); see also Julie Schaper and Steven Horwitz (eds.),
Amplified: Fiction from Leading Alt-Country, Indie Rock, Blues and Folk Musicians (2009).

3. Regionality here is an active presence, a *becoming* that deviates from the traditional model of regionalism and region with its tendency to fixity. Regionality is
always "more-than-representational": experienced, lived, performed, and felt. In this
sense, it cannot be fixed at all, since it *moves*, and *moves us*. It is a process, something
continuing and active, incomplete, and, therefore, intensely related to the world
around it. For more on regionality, see Neil Campbell, *Affective Critical Regionality*
(London: Rowman & Littlefield International, 2016).

4. See Susan Kollin, Chapter 8, for more on the use of TV and Westerns in
Vlautin's work.

5. This line first appears on the album *Lost Son* (1998), in the song "Fifteen Year
Old Kid in Nogales, Mexico," showing the interconnections between music and
fiction.

6. "A relation of cruel optimism exists when *something you desire* is actually an
obstacle to your flourishing...it might be a fantasy of the good life...they become
cruel only when the object that draws your attachment actively impedes the aim that
brought you to it initially" (Berlant 2011: 1—emphasis added).

7. The terms post-West and postwestern used in this book refer to a cultural
moment in which the past myths of the West persist alongside, and in critical dialogue with, an emergent New West. The "post" does not just mean overcoming the
"past," and so when it is used, as in the term "postwestern," it should be seen as dis-
engaged from the system of mythology it is in tension with, but understood with the
full knowledge that it is probably inescapably connected to that system as well. See
Campbell, *Post-Westerns* (2013).

8. The song "Harold's Club" contains the lyric, "They blow up pigeons/While
wearing cowboy hats/And adultery wears plaid in a motel room," further adding

to the critical regionality running through even the earliest songs. See Chapter 9's interview for more on this song.

9. "On Intent," in George Plimpton (ed.), *Writers at Work (The Paris Review Interviews, 4th Series)*, New York: Penguin, 1977.

10. Vlautin used this expression in the interview with me. "I have William Kennedy quotes all around my house, and I re-read *Ironweed* once a year or so. He's one of my saints. William Kennedy, John Steinbeck, Willie Nelson, and Tom Waits." Waits appears in the Hector Babenco film of *Ironweed* and wrote a song for it called "Poor Little Lamb." Waits said, "It's based on a poem [Kennedy] saw on the side of a bridge when he was a kid. 'Life is an empty cup' is one of the lines. It's like those nursery rhymes you may understand one way when you're a kid and another way later on, like 'Ring Around the Rosy' is about scarlet fever and when they all fall down, they fall down dead." (Source: Charles Champlin "Tom Waits: Eccentric in the Very Best Sense," *Los Angeles Times*, January 14, 1988.) The song appears on Waits' *Orphans* (2006).

11. See Chisum, Chapter 4, and Chaparro Sainz, Chapter 1, for more on these ideas of "here," "nowhere," and "somewhere" in Vlautin's work.

12. See Packer's articles for the *New Yorker*, (for example, http://www.newyorker .com/magazine/2016/10/31/hillary-clinton-and-the-populist-revolt), where his astute narratives resemble Carver's or, indeed, Vlautin's sensitive representations of working lives: "A few years ago, on a rural highway south of Tampa, I saw a metal warehouse with a sign that said 'American dream welding + fabrication.' Broken vehicles and busted equipment were scattered around the yard. The place looked sun-beaten and dilapidated. When I pulled up, the owner eased himself down from a front-end loader, hobbled over, and leaned against a pole. He was in his fifties, with a heavy red face, disheveled hair, and a bushy mustache going from strawberry blond to white."

13. For more on Allison Anders, see Campbell 2013 and Chapter 3.

14. As authors in this collection prove, the novels often emerge from the songs and the songs from the novels in Vlautin's work. In part, this is a natural product of the "world" he wants to immerse us in, the type of worlding he admires in Waits and Springsteen, as we have seen, but also present in the work of authors like Kennedy, Steinbeck, and Carver.

WORKS CITED

Anders, Allison. 1992. *Gas Food Lodging*. Film. Cineville Productions.

Bakhtin, Mikhail. 1990. *The Dialogical Imagination*. Austin: University of Texas Press.

Berhorst, Kim. 2002. "Country-Rockers Talk Gambling, New Album and More." *In Music We Trust*. http://www.inmusicwetrust.com/articles/48h06.html. Accessed October 15, 2016.

Berlant, Lauren. 2011. *Cruel Optimism*. Durham: Duke University Press.

Bingham, Nick, and Nigel Thrift. 2000. "Some New Instructions for Travellers: The Geography of Bruno Latour and Michel Serres" in Crang, Mike, and Nigel Thrift (eds.), *Thinking Space*. London: Routledge.

Blau, Jessica Anya. 2014. "Land of *The Free*: A Conversation with Willy Vlautin." In *The Nervous Breakdown*. http://www.thenervousbreakdown.com/jablau/2014/02/land-of-the-free-a-conversation-with-willy-vlautin/#more-115908. Accessed October 24, 2016.

Burke, David. 2011. *Heart of Darkness: Bruce Springsteen's Nebraska*. London: Cherry Red Books

Cage, Caleb. 2008. "Q&A with Willy Vlautin." *Nevada Magazine* (website), http://www.nevadamagazine.com/notable/read/qa_with_willy_vlautin/. Accessed October 29, 2016.

Cajoleas, Jimmy. N.d. "Don't Get Bitter: An Interview with Willy Vlautin." *Lent Mag*, n.d. http://lentmag.com/dont-get-bitter-an-interview-with-willy-vlautin/. Accessed October 29, 2016.

Campbell, Neil. 2008. *The Rhizomatic West: Representing The American West in a Transnational Global Media Age*. Lincoln: University of Nebraska Press.

———. 2013. *Post-Westerns: Cinema, Region, West*. Lincoln: University of Nebraska Press.

———. 2016. *Affective Critical Regionality*. London: Rowman & Littlefield International.

Carver, Raymond. 1985. *The Stories of Raymond Carver*. London: Picador.

Deleuze, Gilles and Felix Guattari. 1996. *Kafka: Toward a Minor Literature*. Minneapolis: University of Minnesota Press.

Faber Authors. 2008. "A Few Questions with Willy Vlautin." *Faber & Faber Blog*. http://www.faber.co.uk/blog/a-few-questions-with-willy-vlautin/. Accessed October 20, 2016.

———. 2016. "Willy Vlautin: *The Free*." *Faber & Faber Blog*. http://www.faber.co.uk/blog/willy-vlautin-the-free/. Accessed October 24, 2016.

Freeman, John. 2016. "Baker's Dozen: Escape to the Country: Willy Vlautin of Richmond Fontaine's Favourite LPs The Quietus." *The Quietus*, April 6. http://thequietus.com/articles/19996-willy-vlautin-richmond-fontaine-favourite-albums-interview. Accessed October 24, 2016.

Gibney, Cara. 2015. "Willy Vlautin: More the Aftermath than the Upheaval." *No Depression*, July 12. http://nodepression.com/interview/willy-vlautin-more-aftermath-upheaval. Accessed October 24, 2016.

Kennedy, William. 1986. *Ironweed*. Harmondsworth: Penguin.

Latour, Bruno. 2005. *Reassembling the Social*. Oxford: Oxford University Press.

Lefebvre, Henri. 2000. *Critique of Everyday Life, Vol. 1*. London: Verso.

Lewis, George H. (ed.). 1993. *All That Glitters: Country Music in America*. Bowling Green: Bowling Green State University Press.

Lippens, Nate. N.d. "The Great Escape: Richmond Fontaine's *Winnemucca*." *Bandcamp.com*, https://richmondfontaine.bandcamp.com/album/winnemucca. Accessed October 27, 2016.

Malone, Bill C. 1985. *Country Music, USA*. Wellingborough: Equation.

Marcus, Greil. 1977. *Mystery Train: Images of America in Rock 'n' Roll Music*. London: Omnibus Press.

Matless, David. 2015. *The Regional Book*. Axminster: Uniformbooks.

Muecke, Stephen. 2012. "Motorcycles, Snails, Latour: Criticism without Judgement" *Cultural Studies Review* 18, 1 [March]: 40–58.

O'Hagan, Sean. 2016. "Willy Vlautin: 'I had a picture of Steinbeck and a picture of the Jam,'" https://www.theguardian.com/music/2016/apr/24/willy-vlautin-richmond-fontaine-interview-delines.

Packer, George. 2013. *The Unwinding: An Inner History of the New America*. London: Faber and Faber.

Papanikolas, Zeese. 2007. *American Silence*. Lincoln: University of Nebraska Press.

Richmond Fontaine. 2002. *Winnemucca*. El Cortez Records.

Rio, David. 2014. *New Literary Portraits of the American West: Contemporary Nevada Fiction*. Berlin: Peter Lang.

Rowland, Katherine. 2013. "Freedom's Ill Fortunes. *Guernica*, September 16. http://www.guernicamag.com/interviews/freedoms-ill-fortunes/. Accessed October 24, 2016.

Sherez, Stav. 2002. "Richmond Fontaine: An Interview with Willy Vlautin." *Comes with a Smile*. http://cwas.hinah.com/interview/?id=114. Accessed March 23, 2016.

Smith, Tom. 1993. "Very Bountiful Bones: An Interview with William Kennedy." *Weber*, 1993. https://weberstudies.weber.edu/archive/archive%20A%20%20Vol.%201-10.3/Vol.%2010.1/10.1KennedyInterview.htm. Accessed October 20, 2016.

Steininger, Alex. 1999. "Vlautin Interview: Richmond Fontaine Alt-Country? Rock 'n' Roll? Call Them Anything, Just Listen to the Music." *In Music We Trust*. http://www.inmusicwetrust.com/articles/26h03.html. Accessed September 28, 2017.

Stewart, Kathleen. 1993. "Engendering Narratives of Lament." In *All That Glitters: Country Music in America*, edited by George H. Lewis (Bowling Green: Bowling Green State University Press), 221–225.

————. 2007. *Ordinary Affects*. Durham: Duke University Press.

Tatum, Stephen. 2006. "Spectral Beauty and Forensic Aesthetics in the West," *Western American Literature*, vol. 50, no. 2, Summer 2006: 123-45.

Tisdale, Sallie. 2013. "Interview with George Packer: The Unwinding: An Inner History of the New America." *National Book Foundation* website. http://www.nationalbook.org/nba2013_nf_packer_interv.html. Accessed October 20, 2016.

Tosches, Nick. 1977. *Country: Living Legends and Dying Metaphors in America's Biggest Music*. London: Secker and Warburg.

Tyaransen, Olaf. 2011. "The Loneliness of the Long Distance Writer." *Hot Press*. http://www.hotpress.com/Willy-Vlautin/music/interviews/The-Loneliness-Of-The-Long-Distance-Writer/8376949.html. Accessed October 24, 2016.

Vidler, Anthony. 1999. *The Architectural Uncanny: Essays on the Modern Unhomely*. Cambridge: The MIT Press.

Vlautin, Willy. 2006. *The Motel Life*. London: Faber and Faber.

————. 2008. *Northline*. London: Faber and Faber.

————. 2010. *Lean on Pete*. New York: Harper Perennial.

————. 2014. *The Free*. London: Faber and Faber.

Vlautin, Willy and Neil Campbell. 2013. Unpublished email interview.

CHAPTER 1

YOU CAN MOVE BACK HERE

A Literary Perspective
on Willy Vlautin's Songwriting

by Ángel Chaparro Sainz

> *I lose confidence when I go back.*
>
> —Willy Vlautin

I do not believe in fairy tales but I do believe in coincidence. Your whimsical choices may turn your life around. It was like that when I heard about Richmond Fontaine for the first time. I woke up too early on a rainy Sunday morning, and I went out for breakfast. Somebody had forgotten a music magazine on the table. I started glancing through it. In the new releases section one name caught my eye. Why? Who knows, but Richmond Fontaine was releasing *Post to Wire*, and I went back home and had nothing better to do than to go digging on the internet.

Still, it is weird to admit that when, on October 28, 2016, I happened to see PJ Harvey in concert with Willy Vlautin by my side, it was just because some thirteen years earlier I could not sleep and somebody forgot a magazine in a bar. But yes, Richmond Fontaine was touring Europe to say goodbye, playing a venue just a ten-minute walk from where I lived. A few weeks before, I had sent Vlautin an email: I was working on this chapter, and I could not find some of his old lyrics. Then, while PJ Harvey raised her shiny saxophone, Vlautin remembered that email and he apologized because he wrote back saying that he would send them and he never did. I told him not to worry, that I would not need them anyway, but he apologized again and, smiling, he said that it was hard for him to sing those songs again: "I lose confidence when I go back, you know."

Automatically, I asked him for permission to use that as a quotation for my chapter. Somehow, I knew that it would make sense with what I was writing on him. It was while seeing them on stage, singing "Montgomery Park" again, the first song I ever heard by Richmond Fontaine, that I realized why that negligible utterance would be just perfect to open this chapter.

After more than twenty years, Richmond Fontaine's musical career has been thoroughly covered in the specialized press. Interviews with Vlautin and other band members abound. Their albums have been reviewed and their music and songwriting extensively covered in publications from all around the world, such as *No Depression* in the United States, *Uncut* in the United Kingdom, and *Rockdelux* in Spain. It is difficult to bring something different to the table. Vlautin's songwriting, for instance, has already been compared to that of John Steinbeck and Raymond Carver a thousand times. More than once I have read about how he writes vignettes or snapshots. He has been interviewed on topics such as Western landscape, his musical influences, and the cinematic nature of the band's instrumentals. Of course, writing a scholarly chapter is different from writing a review or conducting an interview. I could have focused on stuff like the dialogues between music and literature and the constant interchanges between his songs and his books, and dressed it up with the proper scholarly critical framework. This is only one way I could have gone. There are many different themes, perspectives, or motifs I could have specifically chosen to provide a thoroughly and rigorously academic chapter: mobility, migration, borders, marriage, family, urban studies, class...

Still, when I wanted to make sense out of the data, notes, readings and rereadings, listenings and relistenings that had been piling up, none of those themes, perspectives, or motifs satisfied the personal concern that was gripping me. I needed another way to go. I had not known it beforehand, when I started researching. I knew it then, though, after that final gig, when I found fresh inspiration. Vlautin spoke that negligible utterance, and I realized the question that I wanted answered and how I wanted to do it.

My final question was and still is this: Why do I feel connected to these stories, to this music? Writer Bruce Robbins says, "We are connected to all sorts of places, casually if not always consciously, including many that we have never travelled to, that we have perhaps only seen on television" (1998: 3). I could understand why the American West was a familiar place for me, but why do I feel so close to the characters in Vlautin's songs? I needed to answer that question, and I needed to do it in a different way: a mixed way, half rigorously academic and scientific and half candid and personal. Vlautin himself writes with intensity and candidness, with undisguised and straightforward force: "I always try to write with blood, you know? I always figured I wasn't that talented so I had to be honest" (Gibney 2015a: n.p.). In a way, I share that concern about my own personal skills, and I wanted to write this chapter with the same probity and baldness. Boldness, if you wish.

This, I believe, is the proper tone to match the affective patina that my textual analysis will strive for. Steven Livingstone and William Thomson defined the notion of "affective communication," in which they talk about how "much of the arts is a motivation to communicate and engage affectively with others" (2010: 85). Music would thus be understood "in the desire of humans to understand and learn about the emotional states of others and themselves, and the ways in which this is communicated" (ibid.). I want to explore that "affective engagement." Emotion, affect, or what I here call affection will be my vehicle.

The answer to my earlier question, therefore, is that affection is central to providing a significant reading of Vlautin's literary songwriting. Affection should be at the heart (pun intended here) of any attempt to understand his universal appeal. As Tim Easton sings in "Broke My Heart": "There's only two things left in this world: love and the lack thereof" (*Porcupine*, 2009).

Affection, as a synonym for love, is too wide a concept to be used without further clarification. In the context of this study, Ted Gioia helps to define it when affirming that the love song "has demanded not only freedom of artistic expression, but other freedoms in matters both intimate and public" (2015: xi). Love as a musical trope goes beyond the popularized romantic standards that swamp commercial music. It is more than a simple cliché to fill in the blank lines before and after the instrumental bridge. Gioia explains that a love song

> brings people together on a more intimate level, but even here the diversity and range of its uses are remarkable, encompassing everything from purely procreative purposes to the most stylized forms of modern-day romance. (Ibid.: 1–2)

In many ways, the word *love* already encapsulates much of what I am arguing, but I have decided instead to use the term *affection*. The reason is twofold: On the one hand, it relates my analysis to the theories of affect; on the other hand, and this is the main reason, *love* is a tragically overused word that we associate too easily with notions of romantic love and sexual attraction. And here I mean to talk about connection, location, a rewriting of individuality: an attempt to redefine oneself by empathy, significance, humanness, and closeness, even tactile, physical, bodily connection.

Brian Massumi, for instance, says that his ideas on affect are also related to connectedness: "With intensified affect comes a stronger sense of embeddedness in a larger field of life—a heightened sense of belonging, with other people and to their places" (Massumi 2015: 6). This is what I try to encapsulate with my use of affection as a key word, to provide a thorough and all-encompassing analysis of Vlautin's lyrics. Affection then, in this context, can be related to family, friendship, and romantic love, but it also draws us toward notions of belonging and direction within place and within time.

In this manner, Vlautin has confessed that he has always been touched, personally and artistically, by the tension between notions of home and stability, and travel and experience. Extremes have been a constant tension in his writing. This can be connected, in part, to the tension between what he refers to as the "warehouse" life (stability) and the "disappearing" life (motion):

> So those two sides have always been battling inside me. The drifter side versus the pragmatic, gut-it-out-in-a-job-you-hate-'cause-you're-scared-you-might-end-up-living-in-your-car side. (Gibney 2015a: n.p.)

"The Warehouse Life" and "Disappeared" were both recorded for *The Fitzgerald*, and one perceives in these two songs not only the poetic and musical construction of that tension between stability and mobility but also the uncertain ramifications of making either of those two choices. The middle ground between those two available choices, then, is the natural zone in which Vlautin elaborates and evokes his concept of home. Thus, Vlautin's idea of home is never simply a "domestic retreat" (Mallett 2004: 69), but more complex, with images of home often related also to itinerant spaces (a mobile home, a motel, cars). He reveals through such ambiguity the necessary struggle to belong.

Shelley Mallett concludes that "home and more particularly being at home is a matter, at least in part, of affect or feeling—as the presence or absence of particular feelings" (2004: 79). That being so, Vlautin's complex images of home are always defined by the relationships taking place within them. In a way, he recalls Michael Jackson when he explains that "a sense of home is grounded less in a place per se than in the activity that goes on in a place" (1995: 148). Vlautin's characters exemplify a search for connection and affection represented not only by human interaction but also by an emotional location of their identity within a spatial dimension, the American West, in which fixedness and mobility play a key, contrastive role.

Affection then is related to human association *and* location within spatial coordinates but also, as suggested above, to an equation of time. As I explore in my analysis of Vlautin's lyrics, backwardness, looking back, the confrontation of memory and guilt, and the reconciliation and balance of time are also important ingredients in understanding the emotional and artistic profundity and significance of his writing. Mallett adds that searching for a home can be "a confused search, a sentimental and nostalgic journey for a lost time and space" (2004: 69). Time and space. Home and travel. Me and you. Words and music. All of these play out in Vlautin's songs and in my interpretations of them in the text that follows.

My affective reading of Vlautin's lyrics places them within the theoretical framework provided by Neil Campbell's concept of regionality, so that my observations on Richmond Fontaine's lyrics position my analysis within the wider context of the American West and Western American culture. Vlautin's lyrics relate to an American West (in terms of representation and revision) understood as a fluid and contested territory that he scrutinizes through the vivid perspective of his fictional characters: an American West that embraces complexity, failure, and conflict.

Lars Eckstein says that "musical meaning is an historically and culturally relative affair" (2010: 73), while Charles Hiroshi Garrett states that music has the power to "act as an essential bearer of social, historical, and cultural knowledge" (2008: 5). Through Richmond Fontaine's lyrics, and their ruminations on affection, place, and time, a social, historical, and cultural knowledge emerges. It's an awareness that proposes a different approach to the American West, one that contributes to Susan Kollin's idea that "the West is a multiply inflected terrain whose identity is always in flux and revision" (2007: xi), and it testifies to David Wrobel's statement that "the West in rock and pop music has a more interesting and complex past than the casual listener or the western scholar might initially expect" (2000: 96).

Traditionally, the West has been associated with images of conquest and individualism, the archetypal celebration of mobility as freedom, or with notions of spiritual regeneration and renewal. In fact, this perception of the West still pervades the imagination of both insiders and outsiders to the region. It seems ever more necessary today to underline that the West is complex and manifold and that it cannot simply be defined by its mythologies or its unquestioned tropes.

Thus, Campbell's recent studies on the distinction between regionality and regionalism prove useful for my dissection of Vlautin's depiction of the American West. My affective understanding of Vlautin's lyrics fits within Campbell's articulation of "minor" perspectives in the American West. Vlautin frames his lyrics within his own "minor" experience in a West that he does not understand as a region of "straight lines, neat borders, simple rootedness, or fixed points" (Campbell 2016: 2). Vlautin examines the relationships of characters moving around specific geographical areas and within a particular social and economic spectrum. His perspective proposes insights on a group of people whose categorization as "minor" comes from social or economic aspects, but also from this critical idea that their lives provide "alternative ways of thinking and being" in which the "mythic frame" is deconstructed and altered (ibid.: 3). In Vlautin's mobile, transient, complex, and personal perspective on the American West, I see that refusal "to allow the local to become static, nostalgic, or reductive" (ibid.), even more so when Campbell relies on a human dimension as central to his theory. To outline what he means by "affective critical regionality," Campbell proposes a tri-layered bedrock: the "redistribution of the sensible," "the radical potential of the 'minor,'" and "human relatedness" (ibid.). It is that third level that harmonizes with Vlautin's songwriting most strongly. In general, when Campbell talks about the "redistribution of the sensible," one recalls the snowed-in and urban Western landscape in "5 Degrees Below Zero," the solemn drumbeat in "Western Skyline" that modifies Western icons by adding the city's skyline, or the motorway as the main artery of the emblematic journey in *Thirteen Cities*. Campbell's focus on "affect" and place is related more to "experiencing" the place than to "representing" it. In the same way, Vlautin's perspective is progressive and human and it does not rely on direct critical statements; instead, it presents affective stories throughout his songs that engage the listener with regard to people and place. He hesitates, questions, and explores, but does not affirm or denote. Vlautin's encompassing of the West is born from personal experience rather than symbolic representation: his is a perspective of *affection*.

"The Water Wars" is a good example. In this song, the main protagonist keeps going ahead because there is no other way to go: getting cheap jobs, stealing money and cars from roommates. But, at the same time, Vlautin draws a poetic connection between him and a postmodern American West that is typified in the concatenation of sprawl and the perpetuation of water problems. There is beauty in how the main protagonist keeps ahead of a downward spiral, and his political and social consciousness seems to suggest that human progress parallels that same personal escape that he is experiencing. The song evokes how both the West and the main protagonist probably need to stop and look back, but that seems unfeasible.

THE BAND AND THE SONGS

I believe that with this broader and more holistic presentation, readers will better understand my analysis of transience and representational traditions. In any case, before I go ahead and start my exploration of Vlautin's fictional world, I also need to stop and look back. Before I do the whole set list and come to the encore, I need to introduce you to the band.

Willy Vlautin has recently gained recognition as a fiction writer, mainly in relation to his four published novels. His fiction has been highly praised, and he was recently inducted into the Nevada Writers Hall of Fame. Appreciation of him as a novelist, however, is almost always accompanied by a succinct reference to his simultaneously being a songwriter and the leader of the band Richmond Fontaine. However, music and songwriting were there before he started publishing books. In a 1997 review in *No Depression* of his band's album *Miles From*, the reviewer opens with an inspired prediction: "Don't be surprised to see a book on the shelves of your local bookstore penned by Willy Vlautin sometime soon" (Brannan 1997). Well, we had to wait ten years, but Michael Brannan was right to predict the literary skills Vlautin was showing from the very beginning of his musical career.

Occasionally, his literary work has been analyzed in combination with this musical dimension, from the most obvious connections to more complex and sophisticated approaches in which both his musical production and his novels are examined in conjunction. Justin St. Clair, for example, has studied the musical accompaniment that Vlautin has provided with some of his books, only to conclude that he enriches his fiction with "an extensive system of musical references and allusions" (St. Clair 2011: 92).

Vlautin's musical career grew from the foundation of his band Richmond Fontaine, formed in Oregon in 1994, following the path opened by bands such as the Blasters, Uncle Tupelo, and Jason & the Scorchers, which, in the second half of the twentieth century, extended the reach of country music. In 1999, Richmond Fontaine released *Lost Son*, rereleased in 2004: an album about anger and self-destruction, with shorter lyrics, louder soundscapes, and the obvious influence of their two first albums, *Safety* (1996) and *Miles From* (1997), both long unavailable. *Lost Son* reveals the punk and cowpunk roots of the band. (They rerecorded their favorite songs from those two early albums on *Obliteration by Time* in 2005 with the band's most solid and successful lineup: Willy Vlautin on vocals and guitar and Dave Harding on bass from the original lineup, Sean Oldham on drums, Dan Eccles on guitars, and Paul Brainard collaborating with pedal steel and other instruments.) They self-released their fourth album, *Winnemucca,* in 2002, a turning point for the band, and signed with Decor Records for management in Europe. *Post to Wire,* their next album, released in 2003, as Harding explains, "would open up new avenues and take us to places we had never been before" (Harding n.d.: 15). Here, Vlautin plays with the narrative possibilities of the album format, interspersing Walter Denny's story with a series of audio postcards. *Post to Wire* and its follow-up, *The Fitzgerald* (2005), were both "Albums of the Month" for *Uncut* and, in 2007, *Thirteen Cities* also earned excellent reviews, especially in Europe. That album was followed by the EP *$87 and a Guilty Conscience that Gets Worse the Longer I Go.* Both were recorded in Tucson, Arizona, using local but internationally renowned musicians such as Jacob Valenzuela, Howe Gelb, Joey Burns, and Craig Schumacher. Two years later, in 2009, they recorded *We Used to Think the Freeway Sounded Like a River,* and in 2011, *The High Country,* a concept album that they did not tour with extensively. It took five years before they recorded a new album. In 2016, they announced the release of the very last one, *You Can't Go Back If There's Nothing to Go Back To.* There was an important change in the credits that partly explained why the band had decided to take a long break: Harding is only mentioned as a collaborator on acoustic guitar, while Freddy Trujillo had taken his spot on bass. All albums since *Winnemucca,* by the way, were released by El Cortez Records, the band's own label.

Every song on Richmond Fontaine's eleven studio albums is attributed to the whole band, but Vlautin's writing of the lyrics has been declared and attested to more than once: "We all construct the arrangements together after Willy brings in the stripped down idea" (Gibney 2015: np), explained Freddy Trujillo. Despite Vlautin's role as dominant "author," what is interesting in the context of this study is to consider how genre conventions can determine what the audience expects from a lyric or how the listener judges the reliability of the voice delivering that song. Eckstein, for instance, explains that folk music is "essentially seen as the music of the people devoid of artistic pretension and commercial devaluation" (2010: 54). That is probably why Vlautin has talked about his music as folk music:

> My folk songs—I've been writing a lot of folk songs lately—they all come words first, and then I just try to find the right music to fit, trim the words, you know, make them fit the music. It all depends. I haven't written a rock song for more than six months. (Berhorst 2002: np)

He distinguishes between his rock songs and his folk songs since, in the latter, the narrative gains weight and the instrumentation is usually bare, a pattern that started to become important for the band after the release of *Winnemucca*. Richmond Fontaine's roots, however, are equally found in punk music, and here André Schlesinger's words come to mind when he talks about the punk subgenre Oi! and its similarities "with folk music," due to "its often simple musical structure; quaint in some respects and crude in others, not to mention brutally honest, it usually tells a story based in truth" (Schlesinger quoted in Glasper 2014: 314). Finally, Vlautin's songs have been placed within the genre of Americana or alt-country, which offers a more modern twist on another traditional music genre. One of the most important characteristics defining country music has to do with the content of its lyrics: "realism, sincerity, and frank depictions of everyday life are its most obvious stylistic marks" (Pecknold 2007: 2). Paul Kingsbury adds that, "Country music is simple music. It is music of nostalgia and sentiment" (Kingsbury 2004: x). Richmond Fontaine's music, however, while maintaining an interest in frankness and everydayness, complicates country's feelings of nostalgia and sentiment by creating a music whose simplicity belies an energy and depth.

In fact, in Richmond Fontaine I perceive a clear process of musical experimentation and development that took the band from its initial attachment to punk music to a more folky sound. However, throughout the band's musical career, genres such as punk, rock and roll, country and western, folk, and spoken word can be perceived in its compositions and performances. Still, the first-person pronoun "I" in Vlautin's songs needs to be framed and considered within those expectations that Eckstein, Pecknold, Schlesinger, and Kingsbury attributed to these musical genres:

> Also my songs are usually more personal, even if they just seem like a story. I started writing songs as a kid to help me get my head straight. I was too shy and insecure to talk or admit I was having a hard time, but for a while I had a hard time. So my songs always come from that side of me, even twenty-five years later. (Vlautin 2008: 10)

The voice in a song—its timbre and enunciation, as well as the persona and/or point of view—is important because it anticipates the audience's reaction. Vlautin combines the first-person and the third-person to write his song-stories, but in both instances, the tone of the songs and the fictional correlation between the singer and the speaking voice in his lyrics remain somehow intertwined. To say that his use of the first-person is a blend of what you expect from folk music, country music, and punk music speaks to how his songs are told with a consistent and natural candidness, straightforwardness, and asperity. Those same conventions that create expectations about musical genres, however, also shape the audience's reaction to themes and motifs. Of course, for bands like Richmond Fontaine, stereotypes and conventions are deliberately confronted in their lyrics and musical styles, offering musical deviations from the stereotyped or standard depiction of Western American motifs and imagery in country music. The cowboy myth, for instance, is neglected in songs that portray contemporary urbanites affected by unemployment, addiction, and issues of postmodern alienation and social incapacity. In fact, one of the most significant examples of such motifs and themes comes from the typical genre division between a rural setting (country music) and an urban setting (punk music), which does not apply coherently here. Richmond Fontaine rewrites genre definitions in its music by representing an urban and complex American West, rather than a more typical rural, country landscape. As Eckstein explains: "Rural and urban traditions have mutually influenced each other from very early on" (2010: 55). But alt-country bands, like Richmond Fontaine, renovated the genre conventions of country *and* rock and roll music to produce something different. Thus, the thematic content of Vlautin's lyrics is complex, contrasting, and unconventional while his musical composition helps to connect and hybridize those conventions that Pecknold, Kingsbury, Eckstein, and Schlesinger attributed to isolated musical genres.

AFFECTION, TIME, AND SPACE

The essence of Vlautin's songwriting is related to quests for affection through space and through time. In other words, if affection is understood as the emotional and transcendental urgency for a connection and an association that provides significance and purpose, its pursuit is sometimes expressed through movements that are desperate, circled, unsuccessful, anomic, or oblivious. The traveling experiences in Vlautin's songwriting swing between exercises of freedom and extensions of discomfort and that idea of the tension between staying and moving, routes and roots, home and road, love and the lack thereof, is at the heart of many of his songs. Precise geographical references, for instance ("Dayton, Ohio," "Willamette," "Laramie, Wyoming"), are contrasted with buses, cars, roads, and the vital search for something that, sometimes, transcends the physical journey to become strictly an inner trek toward self-discovery, concord, and acceptance of the past.

In what follows, I will divide my analysis in three ways: first, by focusing on the tension between ideas of home and movement; second, by focusing on affective relationships and how they can be observed in parallel to the previous focus on place; and finally, by examining how Vlautin (and his characters) deal with issues concerning the passing of time. These three aspects have to be examined in combination in order to support my thesis that affection is at the center of any attempt to explore Vlautin's songwriting, and even more so when all three are visibly blended in Richmond Fontaine's songs, from their first albums to the very end of their career. That is why, in order to examine and evaluate Vlautin's lyrics, I use songs from all the albums: to show that there is both a persistence of certain themes but also an evolution.

The tension between moving and a sense of home has always been a strong motif in Richmond Fontaine's musical repertoire. The myth of the open road and journeys as embodiments of freedom are rarely expressed in Vlautin's lyrics, where he prefers a more nuanced and complex attitude. In "Willamette," the main protagonist lives the consequences of his brother's travels. In "The Longer You Wait," the journey seems an escape from tension, a looking ahead to forget time rather than to move through space. In "Always on the Run," romantic visions of the road are reinterpreted as Vlautin sings instead about wrecks, abandonment, and arrests, while an unsuccessful journey frames the story in "The Janitor." "Exit 194B" refers to the exact place where the main protagonist once lived, close to a motorway exit, thus establishing a powerful contrast between the motorway and the house, the dynamic and the static, and elaborating an emotive discourse that goes beyond spatial issues. In fact, the story tells how a boy tries to cope with the death of his young brother by staying at that house even after his death. However, his brother's absence and the damaged relationship that he has with his cousin contribute to his inability to beat the "darkness in both of us" (*The Fitzgerald*). "Out of State" offers a metaphor for leaving and disappearance, a disappearance that becomes invisibility in "Song for James Welch," wherein a Native American soldier cries: "'How do you go back?' he said /'If there's no place from which you came? /And every time I try to leave /I always end up back at this place'" (*$87*). "Wilson Dunlap" offers a reflection on the idea of home as a physical space (both motels and houses or cars) and the human factor required for homemaking.

That exploration of the feeling of home is also present in "Westward Ho," where, amid a long list of motels, Vlautin shows how his sense of home is far from being romantic. It is, in fact, complex and ambiguous: "Motel life ain't much of a life, and a motel ain't much of a home /But I found out years ago that a house ain't either" (*Thirteen Cities*). "Capsized," wherein "I" is used twenty-one times, shows how the unromantic feelings of home in "Westward Ho" are paralleled by an obsessive journey that, in fact, discloses the same lacks and needs: "I drifted and I drifted ended up in..." (ibid.), Vlautin sings, while retelling a trip with a sense of compulsion and infinitude, providing no renewal or satisfaction, only dissolution and postponement. From Spokane to Walla Walla, then Stockton, Yuma, and Bullhead City, the list of cities reminds us of "Four Hours Out" (*Lost Son*), in which the main protagonist says that he has lived in thirteen different cities in seven consecutive years, conveying again how endless mobility is no solution to the bad experiences of home. In "Four Walls," the standard home of four walls becomes a positive image, oneirically evoked as a possibility for fixity, security, and happiness: "We'll just lay around and our hearts will sing like Mariachis" (*Thirteen Cities*). However, those positive feelings are conveyed by the company of a beloved somebody rather than by the protection and certainty provided by the place itself. In other words, such positive feelings are more about affection than about space. Precisely the same affective link can be found in "St. Ides, Parked Cars, and Other People's Homes," where that fixed, physical space we call home is related to feelings of loss and nostalgia: "staring at other people's homes" (ibid.). However, he is not staring with envy at other people's homes because he is missing his own; rather, he is missing those people associated with it. The sorrow and pain he feels are, in truth, related to time (dealing with the past) and affection (having lost a relationship): "Wasn't that supposed to be me and you?" (ibid.).

Ultimately, home in Vlautin's writing is an unsentimental and paradoxical ideal. It is related to and contrasted with drifting and movement. Neil Campbell states that "the desire for fixity, belonging, and integration has an impressive presence in the narratives of the West" (2008: 1–2), and that is perceived in Richmond Fontaine's songs. But, again, Vlautin elaborates on ideas of home, transfigured and adjusted by affect and time, and by its apparent opposite of movement and traveling, activities which, in fact, have always been an active part of any definition of home: "ideas about staying, leaving and journeying are integrally associated with notions of home" (Mallett 2004: 77).

Traveling is thus also represented with complexity and ambiguity. Journeys have overtones of psychological and emotional confusion and pursuit conferred upon them. Moving is not only physical. The characters in these voyages unveil a necessity for improvement and possibility, as in "Black Road," for instance, or in one of the band's first songs, "Miles From," a slow, inspiring, and reverberating piece of melancholia driven by the pedal steel and the solid drums, sketching a road that encapsulates the uncertainty and relativity of the myth of mobility: "Once there was a calmness but it/disappeared as soon as it was noticed" (*Obliteration*). Vlautin sings here about the idealization of departure and starting a new trip; yet, more than anything, movement, in Richmond Fontaine's songs, is related to affection, whether to escape from it or to search for it. Those affective explorations are usually connected to couples, but not exclusively. Affection is also about family, friends, place, and, as I have said before, time. The past casts a long shadow over the road at sunset.

In "Savior of Time," four minutes of electrical discharge that starts with a storm of fuzzy electric guitars and crazy drums, a boy picks his girlfriend up at St. Mary's Hospital after she attempts suicide. The song is constructed upon a highly rhetorical and metaphorical language in which religious images entangle a narrative that sways between feelings of abandonment and detachment. Only one lone line of dialogue exists within the intimate scene that delivers the story, and it has overtones of failed and desperate hope: "We're too far north" (*Lost Son*). Another tragic story can be found in "We Used to Think the Freeway Sounded Like a River," where basic instrumentation and a repetitive melody accompany a spare narrative of a couple that lives in a simple apartment near an overpass and an abandoned pool. One day someone breaks into their house. The soft drums and the piano cushion this recollection of a past time, which brings complexity to the simple narrative. The use of the past tense and the final, closing line tell about a search for identity located in a crossroads between the symbolic overpass, the broken-into apartment, and the passing of time: "We used to think it sounded like a river/but all that slipped away that day" (*We Used to Think*). In "Ruby & Lou," music is just the background for the story of a young couple that escapes to the West and rents a room in a motel, where a kid named Dallas blows his brains out with the couple's gun. They keep running somewhere else, while a dark feeling takes hold of them: "What if the whole world is cursed?" (*We Used to Think*). However, they keep heading somewhere, and they find release in a new destination: "Maybe it was just the West" (*We Used to Think*). In fact, hope and healing were not to be found in the temporary homes they found on their way, but in the fact that they stayed together, heading somewhere. This reference to constant movement as a positive solution, but qualified by attachment and empathy, is also to be found in "Give Me Time," where Vlautin sings, "Don't stop unless you have to/keep the line straight down…" (*Obliteration*). However, the final destination and the natural landscape of that journey end up in a redefinition of self that is determined by bodily connection: "I disappear into the slender of your back."

That human landscape is always the location for songs in which affection is celebrated or savored as a conduit for empathy and belief. "You Can Move Back Here," for instance, is upbeat, with a catchy riff and words like "here" and "please" that resound with the possibility of affection overcoming geographical distance. The bass and the guitars echo in the back, maintaining an atmospheric tension that disappears when the upbeat rhythm comes back and takes with it the promise of something better: in this case, an opportunity to "move back" to the "Western sky" (*We Used to Think*). However, the emphatic assertiveness of those lines is underscored by the fact that she or he is coming back to *somebody*, rather than to *somewhere*. In "Two Alone," a husband goes on a spree the whole night, only to dream of his wife in a bar and to find resolution and healing in the final instrumental part, more than two minutes of emotion in crescendo.

In "Somewhere Near," a couple is walking back home when they come across a car wreck and find refuge in a phone booth. The song is about how close tragedy can be when you are feeling safe. And the safety comes from a certainty that pertains more to kisses and bonding than to refuge and protection. "I kissed your freezing face and I held your frozen hand" (*Winnemucca*), Vlautin sings, picturing how the physical and affective connection locates his rewriting of individuality in a brief moment of intimacy in a telephone booth. The concept album *The High Country* tells of the unsuccessful marital life of a young couple. It has a tragic ending, wherein the inevitability of destiny seems to be clouded by the social circumstances that the band evokes with its recited lyrics and fleshly music. The only way out from despair is tunneling through affection, by breaking off the disconnection and seclusion represented by the cold silence of the forests and the simplicity of the musical structure. The same failed attempts at bonding and connection are channeled through another natural landscape in

"Cascade," "where rivers are like moving lakes," sings Vlautin with a plaintive voice. This time, however, the musical structure has a contrastive pattern, and dark memories are framed by the open wilderness and confronted by the vivid guitar and the vulnerable mandolin.

The search for affection, even when narrated through physical movement, is often temporally attached to Vlautin's sense of past, present, and future. Vlautin's songs can sometimes be read as creative dialogues or emotional negotiations, balancing the weight of past actions and memories. In his songs, the past is usually charged with moral and emotional agitation, and the present is related to urgency and immediacy. In fact, these issues of time and experience can be located as if on a map, since looking back is usually a physical destination that his characters try to avoid by moving or looking forward. Earlier, I analyzed how Vlautin's songs depict the tension between images of home and tropes of movement, but this tension is sometimes entangled within the dialogic concoction of past memories, present circumstances, and future dreams. Roads are connected to the future, and the present time seems to be frozen in a fixed moment and place (cities, casinos, motel rooms, apartments, and bars), usually in urban areas that are temporary or transitory. In "Winner's Casino" and, in fact, the whole city of Winnemucca, spaces provide a sense of repose and certainty; however, that certainty proves unreliable by the end of the song, a feeling driven by the agitation of internal exposition. In other words, when Vlautin confesses that this will last only "for a while," he is acknowledging that this clarity and certitude will only be temporary, because "it doesn't have to be that town" (*Winnemucca*). In fact, what he needs is "a little money and some time" (ibid.) an alternative that conveys an inner and personal renewal. In "Santiam," coming back is anticipated before it really happens. A downtempo song with a strong rhyme, it depicts the effort of memorizing an exact time and place because, when coming back, things will not be the same. "Moving Back Home #2" illustrates how coming back is not always a good choice. A radiant horn section and a solid drumming pattern open this song, in which Vlautin sets the story within one of his frequent urban landscapes, a local mapping of everydayness and working life: "I'm sitting in the vacant lot again/ staring up at those power line towers" (*Thirteen*). The vibrant music contrasts with the forsaken setting, creating a clashing but harmonious soundscape in which past and present emotionally converge on a single but mixed feeling. In "The Boyfriends," bygone echoes of guilt determine the present. "Making It Back," meanwhile, closes *The Fitzgerald* with a poetic portrayal of coming back home, where romanticism is overthrown by realism.

ON THE BUS

The equation among affection, movement, and time explored in this chapter is generally cast in a somber tone, one in which hope is hard to find. However, I wish to conclude this discussion of the search for affection by considering a perceived change or evolution in Richmond Fontaine's final album, *You Can't Go Back If There's Nothing to Go Back To* (2016). It marks for me a pronounced evolution in affection and bonding in Vlautin's songwriting. To start with, all the songs address somebody: liaison is at the heart of these songs. Ray, in "Wake Up Ray," is absent but he is addressed. In "Whitey and Me," Whitey has no say in the story but he is mentioned in the title. In "I Got Off the Bus," "Let's Hit One More Place," "I Can't Black It Out if I Wake Up and Remember," and "Don't Skip Out on Me," somebody is always invoked or insinuated. Even if these relationships are partial or defective, the shadow of a dialogue prevails as individual voices strive for connection and face their inner turmoil. "Easy Run" is the last song on Richmond Fontaine's last album, and even so, it seems to look back once more, with references to fictional characters that initiated Vlautin's literary career: significantly, Frank Flannigan and Annie James. Frank and Annie's presence here, ten years after the publication of *The Motel Life*, reveals how their story still looks (and sounds) fresh and contemporary. Musically, "Easy Run" echoes Tom Waits's "Christmas Card from a Hooker in Minneapolis," a favorite song of Vlautin's, depicting an imagined scene where "we're all together eating" (*You*), and Annie will hold his hand under the table. It is a profound and emotive longing for home, but specifically a home that encompasses an extended family gathering around a cluster of possibilities and questions in which pronouns are important: "Do you think someday that could happen for me?/Do you think an easy run will find me?" (*You*).

However, the most conclusive illustration of how the travel-time-affection formula has progressed and changed in Vlautin's last album can be seen if we take the (metaphorical) bus back home. In *Lost Son*, from 1999, "Ft. Lewis" portrays a man riding a bus with a pocketknife, cutting his hand while he listens to two women laughing. Nothing will happen on that bus, but he will keep hurting himself because there is no relief in the four days of crazy freedom that the song evokes, with its repeated patterns of distortion and ascending electric guitars. However, it is with two other songs from Richmond Fontaine's repertoire in which buses play an important role that we can perceive an evolution. When they are analyzed in parallel, "5 Degrees Below Zero" (*Winnemucca*, 2002) and "I Got Off the Bus" (*You Can't Go Back If There's Nothing to Go Back To*, 2016) reveal a marked progress in Vlautin's songwriting.

"I Got Off the Bus" is a narrative song with strong rhyme patterns and a steady structure, evoking a sense of inescapable continuity. That same sense of continuity is felt in "5 Degrees Below Zero," released fourteen years earlier, a song with a catchy mid-tempo beat, inviting drums, and a powerful refrain that Vlautin sings with a mellow timbre. The pedal steel never stops, and the song finishes with a prolongation of its melody, as if the story could continue even after its conclusion. However, there is narrative closure, whereas in "I Got Off the Bus," the concluding verses are a repetition of previous lines, as if to suggest that the journey is inconclusive and open.

Coming back is the backbone to both stories. In "5 Degrees Below Zero," Ray Thaves is moving back to Las Vegas because he has gambled and drunk away everything he possessed. But on the bus, he cannot help but stare at the passengers: somebody high on speed, a young girl tattooing herself while her kid cries, an old woman with metal braces on both her legs. He forces the driver to pull over and steps outside into the desert, walking away from the city even if he does not know where to go. Everything is dark and snowy: it is five degrees below zero, and he has nothing over his T-shirt. In "I Got Off the Bus," the journey is more located and framed in time, as its main character wanders around his old neighborhood in a search that can only be resolved as an emotional or moral lesson. It is a journey of self-discovery and/or self-acceptance: "I know what you abandon dies/what you leave leaves you too/I know you can't go back if there's nothing to go back to" (*You*).

The title of the album in this line offers an invitation to interpret it as a broader reading of the whole collection of songs. The "I know" discloses how this character is aware of the distance between the physical journey and the inner journey and so, even if we observe the same feelings of loss and failure found in other songs, this strong recognition and acceptance offers an opportunity for coping with the past that illuminates this track with a hopeful ending. In "5 Degrees Below Zero," the powerful image is that of Ray being unable to look out the window because it is so dark out there that he can see nothing. He does not want to see his own reflection in the window, and so he looks to the people inside and his fears and traumas spiral down within him until he snaps. The affection in both songs is centripetal and inward, but the affective determination that can be felt in "I Got Off the Bus," and in the whole album for that matter, is potent and revealing. Fourteen years after "5 Degrees Below Zero," *You Can't Go Back If There's Nothing to Go Back To* is an exercise in the same hope and determination that seemed crippled or vague in the previous albums. The characters in these songs do not hesitate to look back and assume their own failures and mistakes, even if partially and inconclusively; there is a general tendency toward self-acceptance. If still vulnerable and fallible, the characters in this album truly attempt to embrace an identity that emerges from facing their own past and relying on human connection. Thus, in "I Can't Black It Out if I Wake Up and Remember," the main character dives deep into his own memories and addresses someone, while facing his own past with an open heart and a determination to be brave and to give a name to those pains that somehow we tend to disguise or put aside. The physical journey back to a city where he finds lively memories full of moral recognition and emotional charge structures a song that concludes with a final confession, "I miss them all so much" (*You*), summarizing the frank determination and brave assumptions that inform the whole album. It is as if all the characters in this album *get off the bus* and walk back to face their own troubled memories. In conclusion, this last album reveals a fictional, musical, and personal development that both encapsulates and completes Richmond Fontaine's career.

Encore

At the end of *Northline*, Dan Mahony and Allison Johnson are witnessing the demolition of Harolds Club. Harolds Club is a symbolic location in *Northline*, but also the second track on *Obliteration by Time* and a significant but small detail in one of Nate Beaty's drawings for Richmond Fontaine's last album. In a way, it is a metaphor that binds Vlautin's creative world and his fictional American West. In the novel, Dan is taking pictures when he stops and says: "And now it's gone. All the old places from that era are disappearing. I guess nothing stays the same" (Vlautin 2008: 190–191). He is talking about Reno but also about the American West. Allison answers: "I guess people just need a place to live. Everyone does" (ibid.: 190–191). In a way, Allison is echoing what Vlautin sings in "You Can Move Back Here," as discussed earlier, that the importance lies ultimately in going back to *somebody*, rather than going back *somewhere*. We all need a place to live, as Allison puts it, but what we need, above all, is to live in connection, and with affection.

I have lived, from time to time, inside Vlautin's songs, lived with his characters. Like Ted Gioia, I also believe that "songs possess a force of magic, of enchantment, a metaphysical, quasi-spiritual dimension" (2015: x), within which time can be negotiated and we might connect and create ways to affect each other. In a way, this is the answer I discovered while Richmond Fontaine played "Montgomery Park" for the last time in my hometown: I had never been there, but I knew then that I could always go back.

This essay has been completed under the auspices of the research group REWEST, funded by the Basque Government (IT1026-16) and the University of the Basque Country, UPV/EHU (UFI 11/06). The research carried out for its writing was also funded by the Spanish Ministry of Economy and Competitiveness (code: FFI2014-52738-P).

Works Cited

Berhorst, Kim. 2002. "Interview: Richmond Fontaine: Country-Rockers Talk Gambling, New Album and More." *In Music We Trust*. http://www.inmusicwetrust .com/articles/48h06.html.

Brannan, Michael. 1997. "Richmond Fontaine—*Miles From*." *No Depression: The Journal of Roots Music*, October 31. http://nodepression.com/album-review /richmond-fontaine-miles.

Campbell, Neil. 2008. *The Rhizomatic West: Representing the American West in a Transnational, Global, Media Age*. Lincoln: University of Nevada Press.

———. 2016. *Affective Critical Regionality*. London: Rowman & Littlefield International.

Easton, Tim. 2009. *Porcupine*. CD. New West Records.

Eckstein, Lars. 2010. *Reading Song Lyrics*. New York: Rodopi.

Garrett, Charles Hiroshi. 2008. *Struggling to Define a Nation: American Music and the Twentieth Century*. Berkeley: University of California Press.

Gibney, Cara. 2015. "Freddy Trujillo on The Delines, Richmond Fontaine, and the Music of His Mixed Heritage." *No Depression*, August 16. http://nodepression.com.

———. 2015. "More the Aftermath Than the Upheaval." *No Depression*, July 12. http://nodepression.com.

Gioia, Ted. 2015. *Love Songs: The Hidden History*. New York: Oxford University Press.

Glasper, Ian. 2014. *Burning Britain: The History of UK Punk 1980-1984*. Oakland, California: PM Press.

Harding, Dave. N.d. "Somewhere Near: The Story of the Making of *Winnemucca*." richmondfontaine.com.

Jackson, Michael. 1995. *At Home in the World*. Durham: Duke University Press.

Kingsbury, Paul, ed. 2004. *The Encyclopedia of Country Music*. New York: Oxford University Press.

Kollin, Susan. 2007. "Introduction: Postwestern Studies, Dead or Alive." In *Postwestern Cultures: Literature, Theory, Space*, edited by Susan Kollin, ix-xix. Lincoln: University of Nebraska Press.

Livingstone, Steven R., and William F. Thomson. 2010. "The Emergence of Music from the Theory of Mind." *Musicae Scientiae*, Special Issue: 83-115.

Mallett, Shelley. 2004. Understanding Home: A Critical Review of the Literature. *The Sociological Review*, Vol. 52, Issue 1 (February): 62-89.

Massumi, Brian. 2015. *Politics of Affect*. Cambridge: Polity.

Pecknold, Diane. 2007. *The Selling Sound: The Rise of Country Music*. Durham: Duke University Press.

Robbins, Bruce. 1998. "Introduction Part I: Actually Existing Cosmopolitanism." In *Cosmopolitics: Thinking and Feeling beyond the Nation*, edited by Cheah Pheng & Bruce Robbins Minneapolis: University of Minnesota Press.

St. Clair, Justin. 2011. "Soundtracking the Novels: Willy Vlautin's *Northline* as Filmic Audiobook." In *Audiobooks, Literature and Sound Studies*, edited by Matthew Rubery, 92-106. New York: Routledge.

Vlautin, Willy. 2008. *Northline*. New York: Harper Perennial.

Wrobel, David M. 2000. "Western Themes in Contemporary Rock Music, 1970-2000: A Lyric Analysis." *The American Music Research Center Journal*, Vol. 10: 83-100.

CHAPTER 2

MELANCHOLY SOUNDTRACKS OF VAGABONDAGE

Four Riffs

by STEPHEN TATUM

> *Well, my heart has always been in the novel,*
> *but I like being in a band and writing songs.*
>
> —WILLY VLAUTIN, *The Observer*

RIFF 1

The band Richmond Fontaine was founded in 1994, during the early years of what eventually became known as "alt-country" music. Headed by singer-songwriter and guitarist Willy Vlautin, the band produced ten full-length albums before officially disbanding in late 2016 at the conclusion of the farewell tour that supported its final album, titled *You Can't Go Back If There's Nothing to Go Back To*. Though never as commercially successful and critically discussed as, say, such contemporary alt-country groups as Son Volt and the early Wilco, the band did enjoy critical acclaim in the alt-country and indie-rock listening community, especially in the American West and in Europe. With regard to the overall artistic trajectory of the band during its twenty-two-year existence, the year 2002 marks a watershed moment. For in that year the band started its own independent label, El Cortez Records (named after a casino in Reno, Nevada), and then—at regular intervals over the next seven years—released five albums: *Winnemucca* (2002); *Post to Wire* (2003); *The Fitzgerald* (2005); *Thirteen Cities* (2007); and *We Used to Think the Freeway Always Sounded Like a River* (2009).

These titles represent the quintessential Richmond Fontaine playlist, displaying the entire band's best work musically and Vlautin's most mature work as a self-described story-based songwriter, whose lyrics invariably center on "the places I was in love with…the West and the desert and Portland" (see Jarman 2016).

Whether appearing on pre- or post-2002 album releases, Richmond Fontaine's sonic landscapes and lyrical vignettes disclose various genealogical influences. There is Vlautin's longstanding interest in "movies and novels and records set in the desert." And there is his early interest in punk rock, both its affective force and themes: "I was into punk rock and I identified with the pain, and the songs about not fitting in and feeling dislocated" (Vlautin 2008; Walsh 2016). On the one hand, some Richmond Fontaine tracks seemingly desire to continue the legacy of L.A. cowpunk and post-punk groups from the 1980s, such as Green on Red, the Long Ryders, and Wall of Voodoo (especially its 1982 album *The Call of the West*). On the other, the spare instrumentals and tightly focused narratives of dislocation and loss on other tracks subtly evoke the haunting, resonant story- and place-based songs of such singer-songwriters as ex-Byrds member Gene Clark or Bobbie Gentry, and such prose fiction writers as Raymond Carver and William Kennedy (see introduction for more on this). Still, regardless of its musical influences, and even as its sonic approach incrementally evolved from the more straight-ahead urgency and raw grit of cowpunk to an eclectic blend of traditional rock, country, and folk sounds and themes, Richmond Fontaine's musical universe has certain features that have remained relatively constant. As we especially can recognize in the quintet of albums from 2002–2009, the band creatively experimented with the standard rock and country song structure, playing with and against the formulaic verse-chorus-instrumental break-verse format. And in a distinctive departure from several of its peers, the band continued to conceive of the record album as a song cycle unified by character, theme, setting, and—as illustrated by *Post to Wire* (2003)—by the inclusion of both instrumental tracks and spoken word vignettes, or "postcards," sent by characters in the songs (these narrated by Vlautin).

The period I am highlighting here in the band's second decade, of course, coincides with Vlautin's emergence as a novelist of note, beginning with the 2006 publication of *The Motel Life*, eventually made into a feature-length film. As he notes in a "Conversation" that accompanies the paperback edition of his second novel, *Northline* (2008), "[w]riting takes so long that I can't help but write tunes set in the world of my books." Indeed, as he concludes his commentary, "in my head the two forms are married. They both come from the same part of me, and my songs become stories and my stories becomes songs" (Vlautin 2008: 10). This interplay between songs and stories is attested to by evidence found in either Vlautin's prose or his song lyrics: *Northline* itself, for example, was published with an accompanying instrumental soundtrack Vlautin curated to convey the atmospheric "feel" of the novel, and for his 2010 novel, *Lean on Pete*, he created a companion CD titled *Motorcycle for a Horse*. Moreover, that the songs not only may be "set in the world of my books" but also can become the genesis of the novels is also evident in Richmond Fontaine's body of work. For example, the title and concept of Vlautin's second novel, *Northline*, appears initially in the song "Northline" from the *Winnemucca* album, while the novel's central character appears initially in the song "Allison Johnson" from the *Post to Wire* album. On *The Fitzgerald* (2006), the track titled "Laramie, Wyoming" sketches biographical details and the journey from Oregon to Wyoming of the youthful protagonist featured in the novel *Lean on Pete* (2010). The tracks "43" and "Letter to the Patron Saint of Nurses" from the 2009 album *We Used to Think the Freeway Sounded Like a River* conjure up two of the four main characters in Vlautin's fourth novel, *The Free* (2014).

"The characters, places, and references drift across his albums and books with such frequency," writes Gwendolyn Elliott, "that the songwriter and novelist has essentially created his own mythology" (Elliott 2016: 28). Indeed: With regard to Richmond Fontaine's final album, Vlautin states, "I wrote *You Can't Go Back*...to give an end piece for all the characters who inhabited the world of Richmond Fontaine over the years. Throughout the new record are hints of past Richmond Fontaine albums and nods to past locations that the characters had found themselves in, and always they're drifting and searching, hoping for a decent place to land" (Fluff and Gravy Records, 2016). "Wake Up Ray," the opening track in *You Can't Go Back*, for example, centers on updating the fortunes of the character Ray, first presented in the song "Always on the Ride" from the *Post to Wire* album. The tracks "I Can't Go Back" and "I Got Off the Bus" update the desultory vagabondages of a character in the *Winnemucca* album's track "Five Degrees Below Zero" and a character named Walter Denny in the *Post to Wire* album. So it is by design, then, that the evidence of such synergy between songs and stories solicits the listener of these assorted albums to establish a *synoptic* Richmond Fontaine, one whose emotional structure, lyrical repetitions, and core obsessions reveal what we might call the DNA of the writer and his musical collaborators. As an older Mexican man tells the young Texas cowboy Billy Parham in Cormac McCarthy's novel *The Crossing*, it is as if for Willy Vlautin and, by extension, Richmond Fontaine, the task at hand is or has been not that of choosing "his tale from among the many that are possible.... The case is rather to make many of the one" (McCarthy 1994: 143).

So how then to *articulate*—as in to give visible or concrete expression; as in to connect or join together disparate parts—that one "tale" or story out of which Richmond Fontaine has generated many variations? For starters, let us consider—out of the many possibilities—the track "The Kid from Belmont Street" from the *Thirteen Cities* album (2007), recorded in Tucson and featuring various musicians associated with Joey Burns and John Convertino's Calexico project. In this haunting song, Vlautin's lyric persona gazes from a distance at an anonymous, "mixed-up" street kid poised to get into a stranger's car. As this vignette of a Portland street scene unscrolls, the lyric persona reveals that he "has been there too," once upon a time in an unspecified place. And based upon his own past experience, he projects that the street kid he surveys is not yet experienced enough to know "what it means not to trust anyone," not yet aware of all those things and predatory people that "will haunt you and destroy you." So it is as if here—during this transitory sighting of a homeless, isolated, and younger "double" figure of himself—this lyric persona experiences the uncanny return to his consciousness of a repressed traumatic event, one that, heretofore, had been displaced or veiled by a protective screen memory.

With its flat tone and brittle phrasing of the plain diction, the delivery shaped by breaths seemingly restricted to only his mouth and throat, Vlautin's vocal seemingly wants to trail off into silence, not complete any thought prompted by the lyric speaker's projective gaze. It is as if the lyric speaker simultaneously wants to retrieve words and phrases even as they are assayed and tentatively uttered into the encompassing void that is the silence between words and musical chords. On one level, perhaps, this approach-retreat stance toward the crucial intersection of memory and desire can be explained by the lyric speaker's belated recognition of the inherent failure of language to either apprehend or comprehend the truth of experience. But on another level, as Greil Marcus has remarked about Stan Ridgway's voice in Wall of Voodoo's "Lost Weekend" track, it is also the case that, as "The Kid from Belmont Street" progresses through its duration, "You begin to hear panic behind the matter-of-fact plainness of the voice, then plain fact behind the panic" (Marcus 1999: 316). In this representative Richmond Fontaine track, the underlying "panic" seemingly centers on the dilemma of *ambivalence*, whose affective product is this speaker's sense of suspended agency. As is the case in such other tracks as "Don't Look and It Won't Hurt" (*The Fitzgerald*) and "I Can't Black It Out if I Wake Up and Remember" (*You Can't Go Back*), the speaker is compelled to look, to wake up and stare inward as well as outward. He is compelled to return and remember and—in the process, recoil from—a traumatic history of loss and abandonment, of irredeemable violence.

In "The Kid from Belmont Street," Vlautin's wistful dragging of the monosyllabic word *you*—a word repeated six times in the song, across half of each individual line's time pattern—poignantly underscores the song's wishes and fears. It is a prescient expression of a looming desire to repair distances both external (between persons and the world) and internal (between one's past and present; between action and reflection). However, counterpointing this plaintive vocalization of desire is the song's strategic musical arrangement: the singular, spare notes of a piano underscoring the spoken word "haunt"; the tremulous crescendo of pedal steel; the closing, pensive trumpet solo, whose haunting lines circle around the bassline, chasing after and then surpassing the song's elusive, foreboding dark surface. This overall arrangement both reinforces the speaker's liminal status—the anomie accruing from his dilemma of ambivalence—and produces an affect comparable to what Dave Hickey has described as the function of Bob Wills's Texas Playboys' twin fiddle sound: to install an "unrequited sadness into country music" (Hickey 1997: 74). But the crucial point here is this: what gets communicated by a song like "The Kid from Belmont Street" is not just a portrait of a human consciousness under the sway of, say, morbid anxiety or an abiding sadness, but rather an articulation of the lineaments of that signal anxiety known as *dread*.

Like the pursuit-capture-escape sonic drama enacted by the trumpet and bass interplay that concludes "The Kid from Belmont Street," the speaker's desiring gaze falters, fails to be reciprocated in its transit between observer and observed, never reaches its destination. The resulting felt alienation and sense of abandonment signaled by the gaze's misfire gets condensed in other Richmond Fontaine tracks into repetitious images of sleeplessness, nightmares, and hallucinatory visions, as well as by Vlautin's penchant for deploying the word *disappear* variously as a motif and theme and, indeed, a minimalist aesthetic. In still other Richmond Fontaine tracks, the panicky dread and sense of suspended agency verging on catatonia, a result of the misfire of the gaze of recognition in "The Kid from Belmont Street," centers on the disappearing traces of written signifiers adorning letters and postcards. Sometimes these letters and postcards do get composed but, in the end, they are never mailed. Sometimes, such written correspondence is sent and delivered to an addressee—but over time the interpersonal communication enacts a narrative of verbal entropy: written signifiers evolve into dashed-off, cryptic drawings, only to then disappear altogether, leaving in place the spectral emptiness of the blank white page or the reverse side of a postcard (see "Northline": "her letters turned to postcards and then/never appeared"; "Willamette": "My brother left home one night.../No calls or letters were sent"). Hence, the *specular* gaze and the *speculative* laying bare or opening to that other person or thing that calls us out inevitably intersects with the *spectral*, configured in Vlautin's songwriting either as haunted memory traces or as unhomely architectures of abandonment and ruin, such as Belmont

Street. Such as, in "Don't Look and It Won't Hurt," a "foreign room with foreign noise/in a foreign bed, in a foreign town," to which a female victim of domestic abuse retreats in order to relieve her "immobile panic."

For starters, then, what we might call the DNA of Richmond Fontaine's soundtracks articulates four strands of an overall "poetics of exposure," to draw on Eric Santner's elaboration of this concept in relation to such writers as Rilke, Benjamin, and Sebald (Santner 2006: 46–47; 52). As we see exemplified by the example of the lyric speaker in "The Kid from Belmont Street" and that of "I Can't Black It Out If I Can Wake Up and Remember," the sensoria of Vlautin's characters and narrators are like photographic plates, sensitively exposing the imprint of past lives and the traces of lost possibilities. His characters and narrators are relentlessly exposed to the disruptive shocks of urban and natural world environments, a condition typified by the recurrent motif of gambling at casinos and racetracks. His characters and narrators are revealed, for better or worse, as always already enmeshed in a matrix of relationality, an opening to an Other condensed for us by various song titles like "Whitey and Me," "Two Broken Hearts," "Ruby and Lou," "Two Alone," "Three Brothers Roll into Town," and "Two Friends Lost at Sea." And in Vlautin's overall poetics of exposure, human lives are *exposed* to the world's fundamental opacity, its unknowability and at times harrowing inscrutability. Exposure to this existential condition transpires when there is a sighting of human or animal death (e.g., the traumatizing sight of a dead boy found near abandoned mine shafts in "Incident at Conklin Creek") or by various protagonists in the songs feeling pursued by revenants or contemplating the gradual erasures of their corporeal presence (e.g., "A Ghost I Became"). Vlautin's lyrical and musical poetics of exposure are especially exemplified by his characters' and narrators' stories of physical (and sometimes mental) vagabondage through the *phantasmagoria* of contemporary everyday life in the post-regional U.S. West. Effectively and affectively translating both illuminated fantasies or dreams and the darker realities signaled by signifiers of transit and transience, of loss and abandonment, this phantasmagoria is epitomized by the recurring architecture of transit sheds (motels and rooming houses;

restaurants; bus stations; bars; prisons and county jails; hospitals; casinos and racetracks; parking garages).

As Anthony Vidler reminds us in an essay on "vagabond architecture," *vagabondage* represents a social and legal construction in modern bourgeois society. This construction centers on a person without any estate or fixed abode—a homeless wanderer, so to speak, whose lack of a proper stake in society is endowed with the attributes of criminality. This social and legal construction thus discloses the word's etymological lineage, wherein the Latin *vagari*, principally meaning "wandering about," morphs into the French *vagabond*, "whatever strays," and its cognate *vagrant*, which specifically came to connote the danger or threat posed by unruly or disordered persons, things, and imaginations. Because of this etymological evolution, vagabondage (or nomadism) assumed another possible alternative connotation apart from that of dangerous or subversive criminality. That is, a vagrant person or imagination operating at the margins or in the interstices of the disciplinary, bounded spaces established and regulated by institutions of power in bourgeois society could be regarded "a preferred role of the bohemian, the outcast artist, the rebellious poet" (Vidler 1992: 204).

Such a poetics of exposure in Richmond Fontaine's work centers, at bottom, on the necessity of one's bearing witness for those marginalized and exploited as a result of the traumatic kernel of violence that accompanies the structural dislocations attendant upon capitalist modernity's emergence and domination. It is this historical context that constitutes the "plain fact" Greil Marcus, for one, hears informing the barely concealed panic detected in Stan Ridgway's (and as I have been suggesting, in Vlautin's) deadpan or plain vocal style. In the tradition of Walter Benjamin's *flaneur*, Vlautin creates for his characters a compelling pose of vagabondage at once literal and imaginary, "a sensibility that actively reads a city," where the contingent, accidental intersections of subjects and objects function to diagnose as well as implicitly critique late modern fantasies of technological and economic progress (ibid.: 210). As we shall explore further, Richmond Fontaine's soundtracks of vagabondage display a poetics of exposure that solicit not only our shared recognition of the singularity of another's suffering but also, through their rhetorical and musical staging of "empathic unsettlement," a dramatization of the necessity for a compensatory extension of the self toward the world in all its melancholy, dark beauty, and often-disastrous complexity (LaCapra 2001: 699).

> *"I write about the true things that hurt me or I can't figure out,*
> *the things that scarred me up or put a dent in me, things that wake*
> *you up in the middle of the night worrying."*
>
> —WILLY VLAUTIN

RIFF 2

In Vlautin's composition "Exit 194B," from *The Fitzgerald*, the lyric speaker reflects on his family's history. Focused within a house located along the frontage road of this interstate freeway exit, it's a house that "looks like any other house I suppose/but it haunts me still and won't let me go," as a result of the looming, absent presence of his dead youngest brother. Taken together, the song's spatial opposition of mobility with immobility, its narrative slippage or category confusion between past and present, and its conflation of the specular and the spectral produce a sense of suspended agency or paralysis that here, as well as in numerous other Richmond Fontaine tracks, indexes the emergent post-urban U.S. West, "where suburb, strip, and urban center have merged indistinguishably into a series of states of mind and which is marked by no systematic map that might be carried in the memory" (Vidler 1992: 184–5). In "I Fell into Painting Houses in Phoenix, Arizona" (*Thirteen Cities*), the narrator discloses, "The suburbs in that town are a sprawl/We never knew where we were at all." Literally and metaphorically, Vlautin's nomads are "Lost in This World," to cite the title of another track on this album, an epistemological and ontological predicament condensed for us in "Western Skyline" (*Winnemucca*) by the imagery of blindness and inclement weather and an interrogative mood: "The sky was cloudy, it was near dark/and you said, 'I can't see. Can you tell me where are we?'"

The catalogue of motel names that comprises the bulk of the lyrics to "Westward Ho" (*Thirteen Cities*) concludes with the lines "Motel life ain't much of a life, and a motel ain't much of a home/But I found out

years ago that a house ain't either." And too: "Is this all there is?/Is this
what life is," asks the middle-aged speaker in "A Night in the City" (*You
Can't Go Back*) who doesn't go home after work, adding, "A woman who
sleeps right next to you/But she ain't yours at all."

Through the journeys of the vagrant mind and body, Vlautin's characters, like Edgar Allan Poe's nightwalker in "The Man of the Crowd,"
endure the essential *unhomeliness* of experience: hence the repetitive
images of bleeding and scars and broken glass and hence the trauma-
tized bodies reeling from beatings, incoherent and "immobile from
panic," seeking haven by being on the move, only to arrive in a basement room or in a "foreign room with foreign noise,/in a foreign bed,
in a foreign town" ("Don't Look and It Won't Hurt"). In Vlautin's lyrical and sonic landscape, then, the settings and imagery of vignettes
of vagabondage across architectural thresholds (hallways; doors and
windows) or temporary inhabitation in transit sheds (motels; restaurants; casinos; bars and clubs; parking lots and garages; warehouses;
boarding houses and rental rooms) operate as physical and psychical
metaphors. The overall contemporary erosion of the bourgeois psychical, bodily, and social well-being is portrayed (ibid.: 167)—a recurrent
Richmond Fontaine theme often underlined musically by the discordant chord progressions that mirror the speakers' "continuous vertiginous sliding between affective states of terror, amusement, and sheer
banality" (ibid.: 186).

Songs such as "Exit 194B," "Santiam" (*Winnemucca*), and "I Can't
Black It Out If I Wake Up and Remember" (*You Can't Go Back*) are
grounded in a character's primary memory of a particular dwelling
place—a transient recollection that, as it unfolds, moves incrementally
toward recessed, enclave interior spaces such as kitchens or bath-
rooms or basements. But as we discover in other songs, such as "The
Janitor" and "Welhorn Yards" (*The Fitzgerald*), the retrospective recon-
struction of past traumatic events more accurately discloses the work
of post-memory, which transpires when "the peculiarities of the memory of events that hover between personal memory and impersonal
history, events that one has not lived through oneself but that...
through exposure to the stories of those who did experience them,
have nonetheless entered into the fabric of the self" (Santner 2006:
158). The narrator in "Welhorn Yards," for instance, listens to a tale of

dispossession and abandonment by a man named Harry, whose blood-stained shirt and cut face get transformed later, during this narrator's "worst nightmares of sleeps," into the image of a madman with hair on fire and bleeding eyes, threatening to kill him. In such instances of post-memory, in short, the primary memory's externalization of events into recessed, enclave external spaces gets exchanged for the archiving of recollections in the crypt-like recesses of the unconscious. There, the "deposits of an unredeemed suffering" (ibid.: 114), preserved like archaic dream traces, motivate, paradoxically, the lyric speakers' petrified unrest, a condition that oscillates between an exhausting, obsessive puzzling over the matter of things and the hallucinogenic intensity associated with manic agitation.

Thus, the "vertiginous sliding" between affective states in Richmond Fontaine's lyrical and musical poetics of exposure is attached not only to the vagabondage of bodies and minds but also paralleled by Vlautin's signature *montage* construction: the phantasmagoria that devolves from a matrix of illusory optical effects thwarting the lyric speakers' ability to make experiences cohere; the resulting swift shifts in thought and spatial or temporal registers; the predominance of vivid images or objects that loom up before the lyric speakers' eyes, such as scarred white legs and bloodshot blue eyes, the blue glare of a TV screen across a face, or a worn-out sock on a corpse found in an abandoned mining camp. Like the commodity form's fusion of concrete materiality and spectral exchange value, a casino's neon lights blaze into the night—but their optical illumination gets introjected by Vlautin's cast of pedestrian vagabonds instead as a felt darkness ("Casino Lights"). Conversely, the ghostlike, flickering apparition created by the glare of streetlamps, seen on the white curtain of snow on a city street, weirdly transforms "the night time into light." It conjures up an emergent paranoiac space, which a young couple is seeking asylum from by entering the narrow confines of a public telephone booth, where their gaze can center on each other's presence rather than the disruption of the car wreck in the near distance ("Somewhere Near").

The illusory and seemingly unnatural exchange of properties between night and day in these examples suggests how the phantasmagoria spawned by Richmond Fontaine's poetics of exposure—to the elements; to the opacity of the Other; to the structural dislocations of late capital—articulates the uncanny return of the repressed violence of past personal, regional, and transnational history through suddenly disruptive apparitional presences that transform everyday domestic life into unhomely psychic and exterior architectural spaces. Here we can consider as a representative example "The Boyfriends" (*We Used to Think*), a song whose initial, straightforward, somewhat melodic account of a 4 a.m. love tryst suddenly swerves into a full-blown musical and vocal panic attack. When a child suddenly appears in his mother's apartment bedroom as she engages in casual sex with the lyric's narrator-character, it triggers a primal scene of uncanny remembrance and signal anxiety on the part of the lyric speaker: himself as a child walking in on his mother during various moments of casual sex during her short-term relationships with serial boyfriends. Whether one's consciousness becomes preoccupied with the work of primary memory or post-memory, it seems that in Richmond Fontaine's world the relationship to the truth of reality desired by direct recall or attested to by material evidence (such as photographs, written correspondence, or newspapers) inevitably is corrected. Vlautin's narrator-characters attend to that which ruptures or stains the smooth surfaces of reality of the post-urban and post-regional U.S. West, their bodies and minds drifting through and across "the dust of inscriptions no longer decipherable because lacking so many words, whether carved in stone or shaped in neon...cross[ing] nothing to go nowhere" (Vidler 1992: 185).

> "That sense of place has been the most important thing to me, because when you put the record on suddenly you're dreaming, and you're far away."
>
> —WILLY VLAUTIN, *Portland Monthly*

RIFF 3

The mise en scène in "We Used to Think the Freeway Sounded Like a River" consists of two houses adjacent to a "freeway overpass where endless miles of cars would pass." The lyric speaker lives in one of the houses with his female companion. The other house, however, is abandoned and in ruins, its backyard swimming pool now a concrete dumpster "full of shopping carts, a mattress, and old car parts." In this setting, the lyric speaker describes a few of the everyday rituals that transpired in and around these two properties: playing around the pool; listening "to the crooners croon" on a radio or record player; making drinks "with a blender that your mom gave to me and you"; watching the sun set over the nearby freeway overpass. However, one night, the couple arrives at their house discovering its front door wide open, and upon going inside see all their "things gone or broken," their clothes strewn around, and their "pictures wrecked." Thus, the speaker's initial iterative mode depicting the ritual repetitions comprising a semi-idyllic urban pastoral shifts abruptly to a singular perception of a pivotal event that divided their lives into a time "before" and a time "after." Once, the sound of traffic moving across a concrete or asphalt surface was regarded as aligning with the melody composed by nature (a river) and sung by crooners. In the aftermath of the home invasion, the broken pool, with its detritus and the strewn "wreckage" of their possessions, assumes a new prominence in the overall narrative of declension—material evidence allegorizing the entrance of the Lacanian Real on the scene, rupturing the urban pastoral imaginary in progress.

On one level, the abandoned house's squalor and the freeway's noise and collection of industrial pollutants index "the production of poverty and misery, people not only out of work but without a place to live, bag people, waste and industrial pollution, squalor, garbage, and obsolescent machinery." On another level, that the wreckage of the abandoned house has seemingly spread like a viral contagion and infected the couple's dwelling place exposes a "contentious internal liminality" in the urban New West, occasioned by the invasion of those on the margins into the city's center and its citizens' gazes and psyches (Jameson 1991: 127-28). It is a "contentious internal liminality," evident in the very dynamic of perception, with its inherent perceptual gap between observer and observed, subject and object; it is liminal betwixt and between space, evident as well in the spatial assemblage of the two houses juxtaposed with the freeway and in the temporal break between the recollected plenitude of the recent past and the fallen present moment, anticipated by the images of waste and abandonment. As a result, such things or objects enumerated by the speaker's gaze interestingly do not reveal themselves as, say, *things* existing in and of themselves. What overlays their sheer material presence, rather, are the speaker's projected investments in them, their transformations via his gaze into the status of quasi-objects that are quasi-subjects configuring relationality itself as a melancholia "that is felt by the [human] subject and *for* the [human] subject" (Schwenger 2006: 2).

From this perspective, in the inherent gap or internal liminality in the dynamic of perception, it is us, or some projected version of ourselves, who are to be lamented. Less important is the loss of the things or objects themselves, which will always remain mute and unmoved as well as removed, at a distance, even as their presence serves to modify the speaker's intentions and affect. In the dramatic monologue titled "St. Ides, Parked Cars, and Other People's Homes" (*Thirteen Cities*), for example, the speaker finds himself alone at night, reflecting on the contrast between his youthful utopian dream of suburban success and the present moment of his narrative utterance: "Drinking St. Ides, looking at parked cars and homes/Looking at parked cars and lawns and other people's homes." We should note how the focus in this narrative of personal accounting is not exactly on how certain vanished or inaccessible objects of desire become fetishized so as to render them eligible for mourning. Rather, this pensive personal account exposes how, in the dynamic of perception, desired objects or things—a stable marriage and a job with vacation time; auto and home ownership—are "*simultaneously* apprehended and lost" (ibid.: 2—emphasis added). "To be so unsure of life you forever sink/Wasn't that supposed to fade after a while?" this song's speaker asks. On the one hand, both the speaker's gaze and his embodied corporeality *incline* toward the material signifiers of upward class mobility rather than his lingering anxiety over proletarianization—cars, lawns, and the homes in the near distance. But his apprehension of these things—the cars, the manicured lawns, the homes—makes him apprehensive. His voyeuristic gaze of possession is contended against tonally (due to the visceral pull of Vlautin's plaintive voice and the incremental silences that hover between the acoustic guitar's notes) and is also enmeshed with his implicit recognition that his once-vibrant dream can seemingly never be fulfilled, realized if at all only by means of the encrypted and cryptic archival space of memory.

The dynamic of perception that engenders such melancholic responses thus must be seen as always in transit across not only external distances but also across unsettled, at times agitated, *interior* distances—hence the aptness of the phrase stressed above on a "contentious internal liminality." With this point in mind, Vlautin's particular rendering of melancholy establishes a "psychic equivalent" of his songs' portrayal of the vagabondage of people, memories, and material objects, in and through the recalcitrant opacity of the social world (ibid.: 8). "A Ghost I Became" (*Thirteen Cities*) evocatively illustrates this restless transit across the deserts of both interior and exterior distances, as well as Vlautin's recurrent grafting together of specular gazes with a haunting spectrality. This song's narrative centers on its lyric speaker's serial moments of self-presence before a mirror. Foregrounding the alienating perceptual gap between the subject and his mirror reflection, the speaker eventually struggles to recognize his own face, experiencing a revelatory moment of misrecognition. As this highly compressed, self-reflexive narrative unfolds, he begins having desert dreams "so real they haunted me." The speaker's harrowing transformation over time into a dematerialized specter ("ghost") is underscored by the emergent, proleptic desire for his subjectivity to become realized in and through sheer motion. In what transpires as an inversion of the desert pilgrimage or vision quest paradigm, this latter-day Huckleberry Finn imagines himself "heading farther, heading farther now/I'm heading farther out and away," across the blank page of the desert toward the vanishing point of the horizon. This landscape is an analogue for the desert of the real his self has become.

"Heading farther out and away": As this and numerous other examples in Richmond Fontaine's soundtracks of vagabondage disclose, the various speakers' melancholy, petrified unrest and contentious internal liminality proceed through plots of *disappearance*. Indeed, "disappearance" constitutes arguably the key word in Vlautin's lexicon (along with related words "disappear" and "disappearing"). Characters are seen to "disappear for a while" or "disappear down the road" or "disappear into heartbreak" ("Winner's Casino"; "Welhorn Yards"; "Disappeared"); songs bear such titles as "Disappeared" or "The Disappearance of Ray Norton." Whether missed or missing persons and objects, memories, and opportunities, these are effectively dramatized as being lost not once, but twice: first, in the dynamic of perception itself; second, in the act of representation. So we hear the speaker in "I Got Off the Bus" (*You Can't Go Back*) realizing, "I know what you abandon dies/What you leave leaves you too/I know you can't go back/If there's nothing to go back to."

In this instance, Vlautin's diction concisely conveys the unsettling epistemological and ontological status emerging when abandonment and disappearance (dying and leaving) overdetermine both lived experience in the present and remembrance of the past. The speaker's rhetorical shift, from narrating the various stops on his ultimately failed return home to this final stanza's summary judgment, strategically deploys words that are neither literal nor aspire to the figural. The "what" and "nothing"; the ambiguity inherent in the second-person pronoun "you"; the enjambment of "leave" and "leaves"—this rhetoric exemplifies how "the state of homeless drifting would correspond to an uprooted condition of language" (Miller 1995: 11). As in the figure of speech called *catachresis*, where "language moves from word to word in a perpetual drifting," Vlautin's lyric speaker drifts into a liminal position betwixt and between, of certainty and uncertainty, signaled by the subjunctive mood (the final line's "If" clause). The palpable truth of something and some things always remain leavened by its potential erasure into the "nothing" of silence or of the distance on the look of/at death.

In its rhetorical compression and its misnaming or use of mixed metaphors, catachresis represents a figure of disorder or category confusion—of "drift" and "disappearance," to use key Vlautin words. It is thus a figure of speech homologous with the phantasmagoria effect produced through Vlautin's visual (and aural) montage technique. And in its unsettling obfuscation of the true ground of meaning's location, catachresis effectively conveys Vlautin's post-urban sensibility "of the fragmentary, the chance, and the marginal" (Vidler 1992: 185). In contrast with the end result of successful mourning, Richmond Fontaine's melancholy soundtracks of vagabondage, sketched here, predominantly center on a clear-sighted recognition of the precariousness of existence and the subsequent refusal to come to terms with the particular histories of traumatic loss and abandonment, displacement and dispossession. Even while affectively reeling from a desired object or person's loss or disappearance, Vlautin's lyric speakers typically cling to any vestiges that remain of an actual imagined prior apprehension.

Such memory fragments or material residue of prior possession become encrypted in the interior archive space created by primary recall or post-memory, whose architectural analogues are the secreted, enclave spaces that exist within the various narratives or transit shed structures they temporarily inhabit. Thus, the narrative in the lyrics present in these soundtracks typically is structurally "doubled" by compressed, embedded narrative flashbacks and fragmented dream sequences that rupture the surface narrative's sequential drive toward closure. The uncanny effect created by such doubling is coupled not only with repetitive rhetorical uses of catachresis, but also—as briefly noted above with reference to the songs "The Kid from Belmont Street," "A Ghost I Became," and "Four Walls"—with a leitmotif of the protagonist's gaze at mirrors or through the windows of hotel and motel rooms; cars and buses and trucks; public telephone booths; and restaurants.

Consider the lyric narrative in "Five Degrees Below Zero" (*Winnemucca*), which focuses on an unnamed man sitting in the claustrophobic interior of a Greyhound bus, on his way to his uncle's house in Las Vegas after having lost his money at gambling and having pawned all of his possessions. Vlautin focalizes the narrative through this character's thoughts, as his gaze initially focuses on his traveling companions: a guy sitting behind him, probably high on speed; an obese woman sitting next to him with metal braces on her legs; two guys directly in front of him, drinking off a liquor bottle; and a girl across from him giving herself an ink-pen tattoo and ignoring her crying child. His gaze then shifts in an effort to look out the bus window, but "snow covers everything" on the ground and makes the "sea of stars unseen." His gaze into the distance thwarted by the snowstorm in progress, he cannot as a result avoid seeing his own reflection in the bus window staring back at him. "Swimming in a sea of rage," he demands the bus driver drop him off, leaves his coat and other belongings on the bus, and begins walking into the desert. Spying city lights in one direction, he walks in the opposite direction for hours, so it seems, and gets lost, unable to find the snow-covered highway, exposed to the elements in the five-degrees-below-zero weather.

In this optical network of glances and reflections, then, the threshold space of the bus window situates this character's field of anxiety through the uncanny figure of the double: the reflection of his face and upper body in the bus window's glass creates a doubling of the present moment, with his morbid, retrospective reflections on his life of loss and suffering. As is the case in other songs that feature various modes of transit (cars, trucks, vans), the bus ride and the song's overall mise en scène articulate an unhomely world. On the one hand, the snow-covered desert blankness outside the window's threshold mirrors his feeling of inner desolation and emptiness; on the other, the phantasmagoric panorama of the bus's interior apparently triggers a signal anxiety over something (e.g., "the pull" of alcohol or drugs) he has already experienced, and perhaps will not be able to resist, as he witnesses the repressed desires embodied in and enacted by his fellow travelers. Thus, the estranging, uncanny effect created by the repetition of the double motif accrues precisely because the double does not, in point of fact, double a presence, but rather supplements it, driving home the felt reality of absence—of difference, distance, and separation. So, in this optical network of observer and observed, all are seemingly trapped in a voyeuristic space of glances and reflections. This entrapment provokes an unsettling dread—what has been reframed in this riff as a sort of petrified unrest—and an agitated departure into the blank nothingness of space, a journey that anticipates the one later envisioned by the speaker as moving at velocity "out and far away," disappearing into the deserts of Utah and New Mexico in the form of "A Ghost I Became."

"I like to think I'm a melancholic without being depressing."

—WILLY VLAUTIN

RIFF 4

In "Polaroid" (*Post to Wire*), an unnamed couple leaves a frozen parking lot and enters a bar, "where everyone inside was half ruined and almost gone." Dialogue uttered by the woman to the bar's clientele reveals another, prior narrative nesting inside that regarding their presence in the bar. For it turns out the couple has been searching in the cold darkness for her father, who has been reported as missing from his work and whose current home address is a mystery. The bar crowd cannot provide any helpful information, but the bartender buys the couple some drinks and eventually takes a Polaroid snapshot of them, hanging it on the bar mirror amidst other photographs of the bar's regulars. So, for a while at least, it seems to the beleaguered couple *as if* "The whole world was alright like / No one was beaten or forsaken or had given up / When they'd just seen light."

So it is that, just as there are in moments of celebration the lineaments of melancholy, so too amidst a world of loss and abandonment there just might erupt surprising moments of reprieve. Signified here by the double figure emerging out of the blank white page in the form of a developed Polaroid photograph, leaving its ghostly imprint on all the gathered faces reflected in the bar's mirror, this recognizable rendition of the family portrait genre holds at bay, "for a little while" at least, the potentially more tragic narrative underway outside its warm, well-lit space.

To be sure, as the speaker says with crystalline precision and immediacy in "Northline," "isolation is my biggest fear" and likely fate (*Winnemucca*). To be sure, it is imperative that we strive to recognize and understand exactly what the diction in "You Can't Go Back," of "what" and "nothing," connotes with regard to the social and economic dislocations and dispossessions spawned by an accelerated capitalist modernity, one keyed to disposability and instantaneity. Nevertheless, there remains the evidence of the bartender's generous response to the couple's plight, where a literal poetics of exposure (the photograph) functions to compose a collective gathering. And, to return to the beginning of these gathered riffs, there nevertheless exists the wistful, final line uttered by the lyric speaker in "The Kid from Belmont Street": "But I will help you out of this."

In the end, a crucial point to make about Richmond Fontaine's melancholy soundtracks of vagabondage is the abiding desire to deploy both words and music, "not to pretend to give us access, [but] *to awaken our longing* toward what must always remain inaccessible, in the world and in us," due to the inherent inequities in power relations (Schwenger 2006: 14—emphasis added).

Thus, alongside the rhetorical predominance of catachresis in his lyrics, we must account for Vlautin's countervailing propensity: to conjure up the subjunctive mood of alternative futures through the various embedded lyrics or nested narratives, prompted by primary recall or post-memory, that braid into the sadness of the lyrical present a tone of hope, however faint. As if in compensatory reaction, there exist in these songs recurrent microspaces that counterpoint the disorienting phantasmagoria and serial macronarratives of loss and abandonment. In "Four Walls" (*Thirteen Cities*), for example, a motel room's four walls, which surely "lock us in," nevertheless also contain a window through which the character gazes with clear glass. As a result, and in contrast to the bus window through which the character gazes in "Five Degrees Below Zero," such a window, the lyric speaker imagines, could allow for moonlight to penetrate the room's secluded space and intermingle with its interior "colored light." In still another instance of "doubling," this intermingling of light in the motel room— reminiscent of Hawthorne's imagery in "The Custom House," describing the transformation of brute reality by the romance mode—could make "our hearts sing like Mariachis."

Indeed, not answering such a call whenever it erupts into the familiar contours of our everyday, precarious life can be dangerous: "Watch out or your heart will be nothing but scars" ("Watch Out," from *We Used to Think*). As is also the case in, say, novels such as Cormac McCarthy's *The Crossing* and James Welch's *Winter in the Blood*, in Richmond Fontaine's poetics of literal and metaphorical exposure there emerges the necessity of bearing witness. Not a standing-in for those relentlessly marginalized by capitalist modernity and its custodians of power, but rather a shared recognition of "the sheer singularity of the Other's suffering." Such a shared recognition, or what Dominick LaCapra terms "empathic unsettlement," it must be stressed, "does not assimilate the other into ourselves," but rather promotes "an unsettlement that…manifests empathy (but not full identification) with the victim" (LaCapra 2001: 41). Empathic unsettlement thus resists harmonizing narratives and attendant mythologies that attempt to provide closure, and hence promotes reassurance by smoothing over or eliding traumatic histories or by promoting an individual's spiritual uplift or overcoming of obstacles and achievement of success. As Greil Marcus has written with regard to the art and the implicit politics of the musical group the Clash, real politics are not about litmus tests of "concern" but about the everyday life one endures and ultimately shares with others. It is a politics that can be realized onstage where, as in certain magical performances, "the limits and contradictions of one's life could be tensed, revealed, and broken through," producing the kind of self-discovery that could, just could, be a means to solidarity (Marcus 1999: 29).

With all this in mind, then, what we can learn from Richmond Fontaine's poetics of exposure—and by extension Willy Vlautin's novels, the seeds of whose characters and plots can be found in the fragments of various songs—is an extended witness bearing that, as if illustrating an uncanny form of repetition compulsion, hones in on the affective state of dread: that paradoxical mixture of numbness and excitation, of anticipation and foreboding, whose persistence speaks to the deep structural stresses antagonizing the social body at the geographical scale of the local and regional. Richmond Fontaine's poetics of exposure dramatizes our fundamental vulnerability to the matter of things and to things that matter. But this abiding poetics of exposure to the recalcitrance and opacity of the world at large also, in its production of empathic unsettlement, centers on our vulnerability to the call of Others—on the ethics and politics of *relationality*. So, the recurrent image of blood on faces and torn shirts just might also be transformed into the image of glass shards used by two lovers to draw blood from their arms to, in a ritual of communion, seal their fidelity to each other ("Two Broken Hearts" from *Post to Wire*). Or the city lights in the distance that the character walks away from in "5 Degrees Below Zero" just might morph, as we witness in the final stanza of "Western Skyline," into the lyric speaker's utopian vision of himself and the wounded friend he holds in his arms, in the future as it once was in their shared past: walking arm in arm, down a street of neon-colored lights, a vagabondage under a "Western Skyline," "where you will be and you'll be set free" (*Winnemucca*).

The dark, melancholy beauty of Richmond Fontaine's West of nomadism solicits not only our mutual recognition of the sheer singularity of the Other's suffering but also our compensatory self-extension into the world in all its dark beauty and often-disastrous complexity. So it is that Vlautin's soundtracks of vagabondage expose both "the saturnine gaze and the awakening to the answerability to the neighbor, to acts of neighbor-love" (Santner 2006: 91). In the end, this inextinguishable "longing" in the heart of Richmond Fontaine's melancholy soundtracks of vagabondage is precisely why Vlautin's self-assessment of himself, as being melancholic without at the same time being depressing, is exactly right. It is an assessment that captures an elemental truth about how and why his artistry, in both music and words, goes to the very heart of one's being.

Works Cited

Elliott, Gwendolyn. 2016. "Room to Wander: Willy Vlautin's Persistent Portrait of the Western Drifter." *No Depression*, Spring: 26–29.

Fluff & Gravy Records. 2016. "Today We Celebrate Richmond Fontaine." Fluff & Gravy Records website, March 18. http://www.fluffandgravy.com/news/. Accessed April 16, 2016.

Hickey, Dave. 1997. *Air Guitar: Essays on Art and Democracy.* Los Angeles: Art Issues Press.

Jameson, Fredric. 1991. *Postmodernism, or the Cultural Logic of Late Capitalism.* Durham: Duke University Press.

Jarman, Casey. 2016. "Interview: Willy Vlautin on Richmond Fontaine's Farewell and the Price of Living Hard." *Portland Monthly*, April 15. https://www.pdxmonthly .com/articles/2016/4/15/willy-vlautin-on-richmond-fontaine-s-farewell-and-the -price-of-living-hard. Accessed October 15, 2016.

LaCapra, Dominick. 2001. *Writing History, Writing Trauma.* Baltimore: Johns Hopkins University Press.

Marcus, Greil. 1999. *In the Fascist Bathroom: Punk in Pop Music, 1977–92.* Cambridge, MA: Harvard University Press.

McCarthy, Cormac. 1994. *The Crossing*. New York: Knopf.

Miller, J. Hillis. 1995. *Topographies*. Stanford: Stanford University Press.

O'Hagan, Sean. 2016. "The New Review Q and A." *The Guardian*, April 24. https://www
.theguardian.com/music/2016/apr/24/willy-vlautin-richmond-fontaine
-interview-delines. Accessed October 15, 2016.

Santner, Eric L. 2006. *On Creaturely Life: Rilke, Benjamin, Sebald*. Chicago: University of
Chicago Press.

Schwenger, Peter. 2006. *The Tears of Things: Melancholy and Physical Objects*. Minneapolis: University of Minnesota Press.

Vidler, Anthony. 1992. *The Architectural Uncanny: Essays on the Modern Unhomely*. Cambridge: The MIT Press.

Vlautin, Willy. 2006. *The Motel Life*. New York: Harper Perennial.

———. 2008. *Northline*. New York: Harper Perennial.

———. 2010. *Lean on Pete*. New York: Harper Perennial.

———. 2014. *The Free*. New York: Harper Perennial.

Walsh, Ben. 2016. "Interview with Richmond Fontaine: 'We're Ending the Band While
We All Still Like Each Other.'" *Independent*, October 19. http://www.independent
.co.uk/arts-entertainment/music/features/richmond-fontaine-willy-vlautin-post
-to-wire-you-cant-go-back-if-theres-nothing-to-go-back-to-a7369296.html.
Accessed November 1, 2016.

CHAPTER 3

ON THE THREAD OF A TUNE

Northline's Music

by NEIL CAMPBELL

*A child in the dark, gripped with fear, comforts himself by
singing under his breath. He walks and halts to his song.
Lost, he takes shelter, or orients himself with his little song as
best he can. The song is like a rough sketch of a calming and
stabilizing, calm and stable, center in the heart of chaos...
it jumps from chaos to the beginnings of order in chaos and is
in danger of breaking apart at any moment. There is always
sonority in Ariadne's thread. Or the song of Orpheus.*

—DELEUZE AND GUATTARI, *A Thousand Plateaus*

THE NOON-TIME OF EXPERIENCE

As the quotation above suggests, music guides, comforts, shelters,
challenges, and unsettles us, offering patterns and rhythms whose
presence can stabilize and calm the world, while simultaneously retaining the "danger of breaking apart at any moment." There is an edge
implied here where chaos and order interchange and overlap, where
music defends us against anxieties and fears but can never alleviate
them completely. Through embracing this "edge" and opening up an
apparently closed and safe territory, music performs another function,
a "launching-forth," a *becoming*:

> Finally, one opens the circle a crack, opens it all the way, lets
> something in...launches forth. One opens the circle...in another
> region...created by the circle itself. As though the circle tended

on its own to open onto a future, as a function of the working forces it shelters. This time it is in order to join with the forces of the future.... One launches forth, hazards an improvisation. But to improvise is to join with the World, or meld with it. One ventures from home on the thread of a tune. (ibid.)

Willy Vlautin's music and use of music in his fiction works across these tensions: from territorial reassurance and human comfort to an edge that transforms such a territory, *launching forth* from habit to the possibility of difference and hope. Like the critical regionality discussed in the introduction, music enables an opening of the containing circle into "another region," transforming from *within* musical styles like punk, country, and folk; deterritorializing until the closed and known open outward to the world like "the great refrain in the little refrains" (ibid.: 350). Iain Chambers argues that music places us "on the threshold of an elsewhere that opens my world to the disturbing presence of something that I recognize but which flees my desire for comprehension" (2001: 118). Such provocative spatial metaphors conjure a musical experience expressing the multiple affects music has on the listener-as-participant, suggesting music's capacity to transport us, move us (in every sense), and so take us outside our frames of reference, self, and locale to some tantalizing "elsewhere". However, like Deleuze, Chambers goes further, articulating "disturbance" as a result of the moment when the familiar ("something that I recognize") shifts beyond any capacity to "comprehend" it fully, with music stretching us away from repetition and familiarity. Music veers from the expected and the known outward to thresholds and an "elsewhere," challenging these expectations melodically, lyrically, and culturally, becoming "an event that evades the closure of my understanding" (ibid.). Thus, music's potentiality *opens* us to worlds of experience, emotions, places, people, memories, pasts, presents, futures, a whole swirling affective territory through jarring patterns of repetition and difference.

In Chambers's words, as if describing Vlautin's writing, "music establishes a potential site that summons a response: a re-membering that directs us elsewhere," opening up time, memory, and meaning in such a powerful way that we "temporarily exit from the narratives that frame us in order to re-negotiate our 'home' in them" (ibid.: 119, 120). As this book shows in many different ways, the idea of *home* is central to Vlautin's writing, focusing on the difficulties associated with maintaining or regaining any sense of home in a time of fragmentation and isolation. Although "our [musical] memories reach out to protect us from oblivion," offering solace and reassurance in times of difficulty, as we shall discuss with regard to *Northline*, below, they can concurrently "trace in its echo other dreams, further futures" (ibid.: 120), as though the same songs carry new, emergent meanings, traveling beyond their original incarnations and across multiple performances. Chambers expresses it perfectly: music "has no single location, it continues to continue without an immediate reason. It is everywhere and nowhere: the hole in time, the slash in space, the noon-time of experience" (ibid.). So despite music having "locations" or familiar genres (punk, country, rock, Americana, folk), it continually escapes these, as in the hands of Richmond Fontaine, for example, where fugitive traces and lines of flight consistently blend and blur such definitional territories. As we engage with the multiple possibilities of music and its rhizomatic potential to move us in many directions at once, as we shall see in *Northline*, it is as if we are carried on "transversal journeys sideways into the expansion of the present" (Chambers 2001: 122). Once again, Chambers explains this potential of music perfectly:

> Sounds and voices that arrive from the edges of my life, the frontiers of my experience, manage to impose an interval in my understanding. Here music casts me elsewhere, opening a breach in the institutions and habits of the quotidian. Suspending the prescriptive, music permits a possible inscription in a gap in which one takes leave from the predictable in order to recite, and thereby resite, a language, a history, elsewhere. (ibid.: 123)

As the epigraph to this chapter suggests, musical refrains are territorializing, like animals marking their patch, "prescriptive" in forming a predictable territory, "autonomous, self-sufficient, and closed in upon themselves" (Deleuze and Guattari 1996: 349). However, Deleuze and Guattari also argue for a "second type" of refrain that is capable of working with and transforming the first type "from within," "us[ing] it as a springboard" (ibid.) for deterritorialization, reaching out from familiar generic refrains to modes of difference and alterity which, according to Jeremy Gilbert, is "precisely what constitutes musicality" (Buchanan and Swiboda 2004: 132). Such creativity is a "passage" or exchange of forces, an "opening of the assemblage [of prescriptive, familiar refrains] onto a cosmic force," from the local and immediate to wider horizons (Deleuze and Guattari 1996: 350). "Yet," they insist, vitally, that "one was already present in the other; the cosmic force was already present in the material, the great refrain in the little refrains" (ibid.). In what follows, I will examine how Willy Vlautin uses music *within* his fiction to supplement the narratives, opening them out to "a possible inscription in a gap in which one takes leave from the predictable," launching forth into the wider horizons of his work.

WHAT HURTS YOU AND HAUNTS YOU

Other chapters in this collection comment more on the music of Richmond Fontaine; here I will chiefly discuss the use of music in Vlautin's fiction, primarily focusing on *Northline*. As Vlautin explains, "My older brother, who was a folk songwriter, bought me a guitar and said 'Write about what hurts you and haunts you.' That's pretty much what I've done ever since" (O'Hagan, 2016). However, the songs do not stand apart from the novels, but rather, as Vlautin has described them, they are "married" to each other. They create a whole existential territory fashioned of places, people, memories, and affects that accumulate within his layered landscapes like elaborate refrains of repetitions and differences, lines and trajectories that are interwoven across the fabric of the work (see Vlautin 2008: 10). This territory consists of the raw geography of western streets, bars, racetracks, and motels—Reno's 4th Street, the Yukon Lounge, Turf Paradise, Harolds Club, Sante Fe Restaurant, and the Sutro—or Felony Flats in "A Girl in a House in Felony Flats," from *Lost Son*, reappearing in "Three Brothers Roll into Town," or recurring characters like Lonnie Dixon, Wilson Dunlap, Wes, Ray, and Annie.

Like his literary and musical "saints," Vlautin loves to build a world through repetition—whole, intimate blue-collar, everyday landscapes like John Steinbeck's Cannery Row, William Kennedy's Albany, Bruce

Springsteen's Jersey shore, or Tom Waits's beat-up downtown—and yet these apparently local spaces consistently reach beyond themselves through intense human dramas: "the great refrain in the little refrains."

Importantly, the songs and the novels inform one another tonally, thematically, and specifically, moving backward and forward in time with Vlautin constantly working through and circling back to obsessive motifs, doubts, and apprehensions. One example is the song "Allison Johnson" from *Post to Wire* (2003), written before the novel *Northline* (2008, discussed below), wherein Vlautin creates a vignette of uncertainty where the narrator claims, "I won't let you down," painting a picture of a relationship with a house, kids, and "the cottonwood trees" that "sway to the music that we play." However, the voice intones, "Allison Johnson don't fade on me," as if not all is well in this partnership and something, just out of sight, threatens them. Typical of the way Vlautin's songs relate to his fiction, there is an ambiguity here, as though the song *could* be a coda to the novel, and suggesting Allison's life to come with Dan Mahony, based precariously on a tentative love mixed with fear and uncertainty, as the end of *Northline* makes clear. Thus the song, as Chambers put it earlier, "is everywhere and nowhere: the hole in time, the slash in space, the noon-time of experience," provoking us as we read the novel, providing an unsettling ambiguity across time, but always echoing back to Vlautin's persistent theme: "I hoped. Because it's better than having nothing at all" (Vlautin 2006: 206). Similarly, his songs ignite ideas that fold into novels, like "43" on *We Used to Think the Freeway Sounded Like a River*, with its strong echoes of Freddie McCall's life in *The Free*: divorced, in debt, and growing marijuana in his basement. Or *The Fitzgerald*'s "Laramie, Wyoming," with its clear relationship to *Lean on Pete* ("He ran away towards his aunt's house in Laramie, Wyoming"). Or "Westward Ho," on *Thirteen Cities*, echoing back to *The Motel Life*: "Motel life ain't much of a life, and a motel ain't much of a home/But I found out years ago that a house ain't either." Above all, there is an atmosphere swirling through the world of Vlautin's postwestern ballads best summed up in a few key phrases: "I'm sorry for all the things I haven't done" ("Lost in the World"); "Broken, blown, lost and blue" ("The Warehouse Life"); and

"To be so unsure of life you forever sink/Wasn't that supposed to fade after a while?" ("St. Ides, Parked Cars, and Other People's Houses").

In Vlautin's first novel, *The Motel Life*, music operates in the first sense of the refrain discussed above, becoming primarily a "calm and stable center in the heart of chaos." It blocks out the world and takes minds somewhere else, often marking out the spatial territory of the novel, as the Flannigan brothers move from motel to diner to store to highway: "He turned the stereo back up"; "I put the radio on low to a country station we all used to listen to"; "A radio was playing in the background" (Vlautin 2006: 13, 57, 70). Territorially, music marks places and experiences, such as when Frank walks past the Fitzgerald in Reno and hears "a lounge band inside playing the song 'Boy Named Sue' by Johnny Cash. The song was a favorite of mine and I decided to go in" (ibid.: 142). The exception is Willie Nelson, whose music accompanies the Flannigan brothers as they try to escape Reno, becoming a touchstone for their journey: "Put on that Willie Nelson tape, will you?...I got that song "Railroad Lady" stuck in my head again" (ibid.: 15). Of course, it is no accident that the song's refrain fits their mood perfectly, with its call of "trying to get home again" matching their quest for some impossible "home" throughout the novel.[1] Nelson, too, becomes embedded in one of Frank's elaborate stories told to his sick brother: "Willie Nelson found me in the street with a bottle of whiskey crying in the rain. That's how he wrote that damn song 'Blue Eyes Crying in the Rain' cause my eyes were crying in the rain" (ibid.: 169).[2] Nelson's unconventional persona as the "Red Headed Stranger" draws him into Frank's fantasy of escape, becoming one of their imagined group of "desperadoes" riding the high country back to a fictional ranch where they "work the cattle and grow the alfalfa," and in the winter go "on the road with Willie Nelson" (ibid.: 169). In Frank's mind, their adventures and camaraderie inspire his future songs, since "Old Willie, he wasn't famous yet, but he was getting there" (ibid.: 170). And so, like Paul Newman in *Northline*, Nelson becomes life-affirming, a sign of the possibility of "getting there" from where you are now. Nelson *will* achieve, *will* express the everyday through his songs, and *will* connect to a wider world, and so his imagined affiliation with the Flannigans provides a source of hope in this dark book. Later, when Jerry

Lee encourages Frank to express himself more and to open up rather than "hold things in," he cites Nelson as an inspirational source: "If you read the Willie Nelson book, you'd know that. He always says that" (ibid.: 196).[3] Music provides a space for imaginative appropriation of experience beyond the here and now, like Chambers's "re-siting," with the tentative hope of getting out and "getting there" like Willie Nelson, as if temporarily negotiating a way through their limiting existence.

Although less significant in *The Motel Life* than in *Northline*, as we shall see, music nonetheless offers this possibility of alteration, expression, and sustenance, an idea that is particularly marked towards the end of the novel, when Frank goes out to buy a cassette deck, commenting, "I'm gonna walk the dog and go get us some music and some food" (ibid.: 192). Thus Frank asserts *music* and *food* as inextricably linked within life, as both sustenance and sustaining, capable of nourishing, enhancing, and even saving life. Vlautin himself has often referred to music in similar ways, telling how Patti Page's song "'You Belong to Me'...has saved me for years" (Vlautin and Campbell, 2013), while allowing even the character of Jimmy Bodie in *Northline* to echo these sentiments: "Music's saved my ass so many times" (Vlautin 2008: 30). It is this complex relationship of music to life, as a form of sustaining power and aid to "flourishing," that I will go on to examine more closely in this chapter through a detailed consideration of *Northline* (see Hesmondhalgh, 2013).

NORTHLINE

On the Thread of a Tune

Well, I love *Northline* because it feels like a sad ballad to me. There's a bit of Raymond Carver and a bit of Tom Waits in there. It wasn't until I read Carver's stories that I realised you could write about the lives of beat-up, working-class Americans like the ones I saw around me in Reno (O'Hagan, 2016).

The "sad ballad" of *Northline* is—unsurprisingly, given its mix of Carver and Waits—a narrative full of music, forming a subtle, layered context through which its events unfurl and informing characterization, atmosphere, geography, and thematic development. The references to music and musicians provide a moody, atmospheric backdrop to the shifting lives of the novel's characters and the overlapping worlds they inhabit. Justin St. Clair asks, "What business does music have in a book in the first place?" (St. Clair 2011: 93), and, using theoretical discussions of film soundtracks, argues for three distinct forms of cinematic usage: music that issues from within the narrative (diegetic), a film's musical score superimposed onto the film's story (non-diegetic), and finally music imagined by a character within the film but not accessible to others (metadiegetic). St. Clair applies these categories to *Northline* to understand the in-text references to music, the soundtrack that accompanies the book, and the sounds found only in the minds of characters, uncovering mostly examples of the first type of music but few of the others. I propose a different approach, viewing the musical elements as interlinked and woven into the experiential layers of *Northline*, emanating *directly* from the text as well as *indirectly* through our "use" (or not) of the accompanying soundtrack. Music operates, therefore, dialogically: enhancing, contrasting, and troubling the narrative in a number of complex and fascinating ways that this section of the chapter will explore.[4]

Northline begins in Circus Circus Las Vegas with "a small band" that "played lifelessly in the corner, in near darkness" (Vlautin 2008: 1), reminding us of the ubiquity of music in the geographies of our lives: in elevators and supermarkets, via car radios and ambient sound, in hotels and casinos. In the gothic underworld of Circus Circus, music is no longer the "sustenance" discussed above, but rather another form of consumption aligned with the whole landscape of unquestioned leisure in which it resides. Such "lifeless" (that is, non-sustaining) music offers no solace or escape, no challenge or stimulus, and so, unsurprisingly, it becomes the internal "soundtrack" for the novel's opening scene, depicting the brutal sexual exploitation and control of Allison Johnson at the hands of Jimmy Bodie. Later, it finds perverse echoes in the skinhead music at the desert festival, which is played "fast," with its tattooed singer "screaming as hard as he could" (ibid.: 39), simply to provoke the audience and feed its desire for violent, unquestioning behavior.

In fact, as the novel unfolds, Allison is drawn to a very different type of music by choice: Patti Page and Brenda Lee. These female singers from the 1950s allow Vlautin to throw light on Allison's character and desires as she wrestles with her own feelings of self-worth and troubled relationships. It owes something to the role of music in Vlautin's favorite novel, William Kennedy's *Ironweed*, where Helen Archer, a once-accomplished singer and now a down-and-out, thinks of the songs she loves as "directly, simply, about the currency of the heart and soul," and that singing them becomes "a living explosion of unbearable memory and indomitable joy" (Kennedy 1986: 54, 55). Through music, Helen, like Allison, "mastered the trick of escaping into music and the pleasures of memory" (ibid.: 120). In two of the scenes in which Allison contemplates suicide, she is or has been playing her only tapes of Page and Lee, as if to equate her own struggles with those of women who had expressed in their music deep, emotional concerns and yet had succeeded and lived long, rewarding lives.

As Vlautin told me,

> Patti Page is like a 40s movie. She's pure escape. "Tennessee Waltz," "Old Cape Cod," and most of all "You Belong to Me." That song has saved me for years. You work a dead-end job at a warehouse or in Allison's case a restaurant, and you put on headphones after your shift and suddenly you're a million miles away. You're in love and you're traveling all over the world, and you're free, at least for the 3 minutes of the song. I don't think her music taste dreams for an ideal past, she just dreams of escape, of movie escape. (Vlautin and Campbell, 2013)

Page permits Allison to move beyond the terrible limits of Bodie's world of racism, violence, and Western masculinity, providing, as Willie Nelson does for the Flannigans, a means to imagine a different life, "like a 40s movie" in which romance, escape, love, and empowerment are all possible. Thus, music performs the role defined earlier by Chambers. It provides a temporary "exit from the narratives that frame us in order to re-negotiate our 'home' in them," so that rather than dwell in the traumatic "now" with all its pain and depravation, Allison's musical choices remove her temporarily into what St. Clair calls "idealized replacement 'pasts'" (St. Clair 2011: 98), functioning as alternative "homes" within which she shelters. So while listening to Page's "Tennessee Waltz," which Vlautin has described as "loaded with comfort and ease" (Garner, 2008), Allison moves out of her framing, her Bodie-defined world, to imagine some "elsewhere." Of course, Patti Page also achieved success in a man's world, becoming the best-selling female artist of the 1950s. Her songs often convey, even in their titles, something of Allison's journey: "Confess," "With My Eyes Wide Open, I'm Dreaming," "Would I Love You (Love You, Love You)," "Why Don't You Believe Me," and "Let Me Go Lover." One song, "Conquest," in which "The hunted became the huntress," explores the reversal of role, as a woman takes control. It becomes almost a rallying cry for women like Allison, who are put upon by men like Bodie, to find their own source of power and to "re-negotiate" their own sense of home in the world. As Jack White of the White Stripes put it, explaining why he rerecorded the song, "The lyrical message in 'Conquest' is exactly what you root for in life with people you know. You hope they'll have the sense to switch a situation around if they're in peril. I love how bold the song is, and simple at the same time. It's kind of irresistible" (White, 2008).[5]

This desire "to switch a situation around" explains more precisely the way in which Page's work provides an intertextual supplement to Vlautin's "dreams of escape, of movie escape," and shows how, despite the consensus ideologies of postwar America and the idealized women that Betty Friedan examined in *The Feminine Mystique* and that Patti Page invoked, her work proved there were nonetheless powerful, resonant struggles inherent within even the most anodyne songs. This also comes through in Allison's liking for Brenda Lee's music which, as Vlautin explains, has both personal and thematic connections to the novel:

> There was an old bar in Reno I used to go to called The Last Dollar Bar. It was my daytime stop. I'd go in there and play the jukebox and drink beer. The jukebox stopped at 1970, all 45s, mostly country.... I didn't know who a lot of the artists were. I eventually found a song called "We Three, My Echo, My Shadow, and Me,"

by Brenda Lee. The flipside was "I'm Sorry," and both seemed like they were written specifically for Allison Johnson. Romantic and lonely and self-doubting. They are very cinematic and grand but also intimate. Like a movie. When you hear a song that transports you, that takes you out of your daily life, that makes you disappear into it, that's luck. There's a handful of Brenda Lee songs that seem tailor-made for Allison Johnson. I listened to a record called *The Brenda Lee Story* hundreds of times while working on the book. She has a lot of spotty records but that one is a classic. (Vlautin and Campbell, 2013)

Once again, Vlautin's intertextual association of Lee with Allison deepens and extends the novel's minimalism, refracting Allison's struggle through the prism of Lee's "cinematic" style, which is *both* "grand" and "intimate." The gutsy texture of Lee's song "We Three, My Echo, My Shadow, and Me" speaks directly to Allison's identity crisis: "We three we're all alone living in a memory my echo, my shadow, and me" and "I walk with my shadow I talk with my echo but where is the one I love." It articulates Allison's divided subjectivity, her struggle with her different selves, always defined by others throughout the novel. Similarly, in Lee's "All Alone Am I" ("All alone with just a beat of my heart/People all around but I don't hear a sound/Just the lonely beating of my heart"), the lyrics emphasize Allison's experience outside the actual narrative, providing an extratextual dimension to the novel, like a hidden soundtrack. Exactly as Vlautin commented, these short songs explore emotional landscapes that are strangely cinematic. There are many such examples in Richmond Fontaine songs, conjuring up fragments of lives being lived as "romantic and lonely and self-doubting" against the backdrop of the mythic West's supposed land of opportunity. As noted in the introduction, Vlautin admired the "worlds" created by Springsteen or Waits, and music functions within his fiction similarly, with "worlds" erupting from within Lee's songs as intense, affective tones through which memories become unbearable, drawing one back to painfully haunted places. In "Emotions," for example:

Emotions you get me upset why make me remember what I
    wanna forget
I've been so lonely, lonely too long, emotions please leave
    me alone
You worry my days yes you torture my nights
Never a dream knows those dreams never turn out right.

The melodrama of these songs, as with Patti Page's too, performs vital cultural work, permitting expressions of powerful feelings in ways often discouraged or repressed in patriarchal cultural forms. Allison Anders, a filmmaker greatly admired by Vlautin, whose name is echoed in that of Allison Johnson, has spoken of melodrama as "a genre...that tells the story *from the inside out*," charting the "interior journey of a character," so that "their actions happen as a result of what's going on inside of them. In most films you have the action going the other way. The action happens and affects the character...I think it's all heightened by people's need to address their spiritual yearning" (Mercurio 1996: 26). Melodrama's commitment to intense emotion, and to the "heightened" yearning Anders speaks of here, confirms Jackie Byars's argument that it "operated...as a site for struggles over deeply disturbing materials and fundamental values," giving voice to such complex forces and exploiting "excessive uses of representational conventions to express that which cannot (yet) be said, that which language alone is incapable of expressing" (Byars 1991: 11, 13).

When Allison is alone with nowhere to go and no one to communicate with, she turns to the pop culture worlds of Paul Newman, Patti Page, or Brenda Lee. In the music of the latter two, in particular, she finds an intensely expressive, emotive, feminine world that both resonates with her own feelings and simultaneously offers, however subliminally, some hope for "re-negotiating" change and empowerment. Whereas Allison writes letters and notes to herself throughout the novel, trying to articulate her inner torments and fears only to destroy them, music has the innate capacity to persist and talk back to her (like the *imagined* Newman does too), offering her guidance, solace, and sustenance. Music functions as a form of intimate exchange for Allison, a mutual gift like those she shares throughout the novel with other characters, "her friends, her allies, her confidantes" (Vlautin and Campbell 2013), helping her relearn how to trust and care about the world. As Vlautin puts it, just as she is drawn to Newman, Lee, and Page, "she's attracted to kindness. A serious break for her. I think so many live on the fence between hope and kindness and then bitterness and disillusionment" (ibid.).

These intimate exchanges initially materialize through her flight away from Bodie with the truck driver T. J. Watson, who "gave her twenty dollars and his home address" in return for "a list of television shows [Allison] thought he might like" (Vlautin 2008: 51). They continue while she works at her job as a waitress at the Cal Neva, through her contact with others who, like her, seem vulnerable, and whose lives are equally precarious, and they culminate in her various "exchanges" with Dan Mahony. As Judith Butler has written, "Precariousness implies living socially, that is, the fact that *one's life is always in some sense in the hands of the other.* It implies exposure, both to those we know and to those we do not know; a dependency on people we know, or barely know, or know not at all" (Butler 2010: 14—emphasis added). Of course, Allison is weak, vulnerable, and afraid, but she gradually adjusts by "exposing" herself and trusting others, which, although risky, reopens life for her in ways that are more positive. As Vlautin has said of Allison, "In her heart lives romance and goodness, it comes to light in her dream life with Paul Newman. One of her greatest attributes is that she gravitates towards kindness given to her.... When someone is nice to her, she accepts it. She knows what type of people she wants. That's her saving grace" (Vlautin and Campbell 2013). As I have suggested, music is an initial stage in this "accepting" process, allowing Allison access to others' lives, engaging her, through such dialogues and exchanges, to learn to live again: to live "socially" among others who are open to tentative "exchange" ("kindness given") without violence or abuse, and thereby *placing one's life in the hands of the other.* Later, in her friendship with Penny Pearson, Allison discovers she has a similar relationship with Neil Diamond, her "favorite man," whose music speaks to her and should, she feels, connect to "every good woman" (Vlautin 2008: 132–33).

In contrast with Allison's melodramatic songs, with their intimate invitation to such opportunities for exchange and learning from others, Jimmy Bodie's favored music, and his appropriation of it, functions rather to confirm and reinforce his own identity as Western, a white man "married to the past":

> He likes Johnny Cash and Merle Haggard. He likes rockabilly and early rock and roll. Again he's longing for a time that doesn't exist. He really believes that the past was better, and again he gets great comfort from the music of the past. It makes him feel less alone and it gives him strength and identity. Both Allison and Jimmy's music is music of white America, of a past and gone America. But Allison dreams of disappearing into a movie where Jimmy dreams of an America where he's still king. (Vlautin and Campbell 2013)

In Bodie's imagination, he is king of a West defined by the music he listens to and the lifestyle he leads. It's a point underscored by the basement room in which he lives: "an American flag hanging by the door, and a lamp made from the fender of a 1946 Ford coupé," with books on "guns and self defense...tattoos...immigration, US history...a framed picture of his mom and dad," and records by "Hank Williams, Johnny Cash, David Alan [sic] Coe, Buck Owens, Chet Atkins. Hundreds of country and rockabilly records" (Vlautin 2008: 8). It is here in this philosophically closed world where, having abused Allison in Circus Circus, he leaves her naked and handcuffed to the bed for ten hours. Further asserting his patriarchal power, marking her body with tattoos and bruises, Bodie defines his macho signature and his perverse attachment to an interpreted outlaw "westness," identified with an essentially narrow and uncompromising version of masculinist regionalism.

The genealogy indicated by the records in Bodie's room suggests a type of "hard country" (Ching 2001), or "outlaw" music tradition, built on Hank Williams's honky-tonk sound and colorful lifestyle, but which, as writer Bill C. Malone puts it, "capitalized on the undying appeal of the cowboy (although in the guise of the desperado or badman) and of the rambler" (Malone 1987: 398). Ching similarly claims "the Outlaws titillated the public with an aura of the Wild West," best epitomized by the western "Wanted" poster adorning the cover of the 1976 Waylon Jennings/Willie Nelson/Jessi Colter/Tompall Glaser collaboration *Wanted! The Outlaws*, which included the track "My Heroes Have Always Been Cowboys." On "The Last Cowboy Song," the Highwaymen, a supergroup with Willie Nelson, Johnny Cash, Waylon Jennings, and Kris Kristofferson, sing of the mythic cowboy, invented by and represented in the works of Frederic Remington and Louis L'Amour, an image preserved and then actively distorted in Bodie's dream of the West.[6] Bodie's records such as those by David Allan Coe, betray a narrative that chimes with his political positions more directly. Coe boasted of a prison record for murder and released *Longhaired Redneck* in 1975, and in his other songs, like "Take This Job and Shove It" and "If That Ain't Country," in which he sang of his father's redneck violence and hard drinking, he claimed that "if that ain't country I'll kick your ass."

Of course, in reality, many of these outlaw artists challenged the Nashville studio system and its "bloated business strategies" with a more "progressive" or "liberal vision," emphasizing through the "performative guise" of the cowboy a style drawing on "anti-authoritarianism" alongside a "discourse of authenticity, and libidinal charge" (Mellard 2013: 117, 118). But this air of independence is twisted in Bodie's hands to emphasize a form of harsh inwardness, built on whiteness, colonial privilege, and rugged masculinity and symbolized by his idea of the "Northline." He *appropriates* their image as outliers for his own ends, turning their maverick status toward his own right-wing, racist ideology based on distortions of patriotism, regionalism, and blue-collar experience. His musical tastes, although caught in a moment of time, also function like Allison's in that they validate his existence and bolster his flagging self-esteem. On hearing a Merle Haggard song, for example, he comments to Allison, "Music's saved my ass so many times" (Vlautin 2008: 30). Unlike Allison's emotional engagement with Page and Lee, Bodie's outlaw and rockabilly music "saves" him by creating a space in which his unchanging view of the past is validated as a West locked into Malone's cowboy-rambler dream. Ultimately, this feeds his fantasy of escape, which is, according to Kenneth Bindas, "the most prevailing image" in country music (in Aquila 1996: 226), linking it to an alternative West in the North: "Bodie lives in the dream of the West. When his life begins to unravel he dreams of heading north, of drawing a line North, a Northline, and picking a new spot to live, a new life where he's different, the area's different. There's nothing there that will scare him. The world won't be changing. All he'll do is work hard and be the man he wants to be. It's his dream" (Vlautin and Campbell 2013).

Whereas Allison moves slowly toward personal adjustment and seeing through others' eyes, in contrast, "Bodie, at his root, is scared of change…he's just failing to adapt and to embrace the change of his world. He stops growing and the dark side of his nature comes out" (ibid.). So his musical taste is fixed, like his attitudes, in a particular fantasy orbit aligned closely with a narrow point of view, his "Northline," even if, in truth, the actual music he collects is much more nuanced and far-reaching. Ironically, it has been argued recently that outlaw country "used the style to explore shifting and contradictory expectations of masculinity in the age of women's liberation" (Pecknold and McCusker 2016: 2), yet it is clear that Bodie is blind to the radical potential of this music. As Vlautin himself has argued, if Bodie could fully understand the subtleties and resonance of the music he listens to, there might be some "hope," since "a guy that likes decent music can't be all bad" (Garner 2008).

The contrast with Allison is stark and it reinforces Bodie's efforts to control her. For although she wears "Johnny Cash Live at San Quentin" T-shirts, goes to his concerts, and discusses Faith Hill, her taste, as we have seen, goes back to "a past and gone America" of strong feminine singers, sensitive, "gentle and non-threatening" (Vlautin and Campbell 2013), and to actors like Paul Newman. Or to a type of musical space that Vlautin associates with the 1959 hit "Mr. Blue" by the Fleetwoods, which he finds "hauntingly beautiful," with melancholic lyrics and a mood that reflects Allison's loneliness, loss, isolation, and heartbreak: "Then turn around headin' for the lights of town/Hurtin' me through and through/Call me Mr. Blue" (see Garner 2008). Greil Marcus has written similarly of how "the Fleetwoods were an uncanny oasis on the radio, a locus of exquisite longing and delicate suspension, a floating sound that, for the two or three minutes each play lasted, made everything around it seem to count for nothing" (Marcus 2014). While Allison struggles to express herself and move beyond her own anxieties and doubts, she is soothed by the "uncanny oasis" such music can provide, speaking for her and providing a melodramatic mirror of emotion and human exchange through which she slowly finds the strength to "move back into the world" (Vlautin 2008: 166). This strength comes through, too, in the possibility of a new life with Dan Mahony, himself timid and uncertain, equally scarred by violence, but offering no threat to Allison. For, as she puts it, he "couldn't take control of her...he could barely take control of himself," and so with him "she felt all right" (ibid.: 178). Dan is unthreatened by the future, and so the antithesis of Bodie, highlighted when Paul Newman tells Allison, significantly, "He reminds me a lot of myself" (ibid.: 182), coalescing the "new man" in her life with the 'Newman' she relates to and confides in throughout her painful journey.

When Dan takes her out into the Nevada desert, away from the claustrophobic anxiety of Reno, as in the famous scene in *The Misfits*, musical references are replaced with different sounds, those of "trains [that] roll by," "the sound of...cooking breakfast," and "just listening to the fire" (ibid.: 186, 187, 188). With Dan, Allison occupies a space with less anxiety and fear, a space closer to the worlds of Page and Lee, where women hold their own in a man's world and recognize "there ain't no place where you can escape to." Because, ultimately, you will always "run into yourself" (ibid.: 185) and, as a consequence, true strength comes only when you can deal with that reality, however tough that might seem. As Newman tells Allison, "the past is the past" (ibid.: 183), and it is only when she finds Dan that she begins to leave behind her reliance on Page and Lee, letting herself create her own memories away from Bodie. In the final scene, as the sirens wail, marking the demolition of old Reno, Allison comes through her anxiety, repeating, "Please don't let him find me" again and again like the refrain of a comforting song. But as she "opened her eyes to see" Dan, it is as if she has, in these moments of trepidation, created her own song—in Deleuze and Guattari's beautiful words, found a "thread of a tune," full of "fear and hope and uncertainty"—that still might guide her back into a world with "a spirit and a heart and beauty". (Vlautin and Campbell 2013).

NORTHLINE'S SOUNDTRACK
Darkness Awakening

The final source of music in *Northline* is Willy Vlautin and Paul Brain-ard's soundtrack, which functions dialogically with the words on the page, moving the reader through place (the Western inflections are uppermost), while challenging expectations (soft music in violent scenes) and creating an "atmospheric attunement" (Stewart 2011) or "space of affect" (Ingold 2015: 73) within which the novel operates. Vlautin told me, "I hoped the book would have a cinematic feel, and so it made sense to me to write a soundtrack.... The soundtrack itself is put in chronological order, not the exact same as the book" (Vlautin and Campbell 2013). The soundtrack, therefore, serves multiple func-tions when listened to while reading the novel. Central is its stated cin-ematic quality, influenced, as Vlautin explains, by his love of certain instrumental and other film music such as that used in Bob Dylan's *Pat Garrett and Billy the Kid*, Ennio Morricone's *Once Upon a Time in the West* (where he singles out "Jill's America" as "the greatest music I'd ever heard" (Garner 2008)), and Ry Cooder's *Paris, Texas*, which had a very distinct influence on the novel:

> That's all I was trying to do with *Northline*...to have the same feel that *Paris, Texas* has as a soundtrack. When I listen to the *Paris, Texas* soundtrack, I just can't help but think about Harry Dean Stanton—regardless of the spoken word part in it, which I think is amazing. But if you take that out of the soundtrack, it still makes me always think of...Stanton and his jealousy, and his wife and his boy. And I haven't seen that movie in 15 years. (Goodman, 2008)[7]

Equally important is Calexico's "Sonic Wind," "a big inspiration" be-cause it "felt like the novel," with Jacob Valenzuela's "heartbreaking" trumpet solo "creating a mood...so [you] have the feeling of place," ideal for *Northline*'s narrative arc (Garner 2008; Goodman 2008).[8] The "cinematic" aspects of the soundtrack relate clearly to how music *car-ries* memories and *provokes* recollection, while also conveying the place and situation. In *Northline*, "the whole novel [is] dipped in melancholy, the melancholy you feel after hearing a heartbreaking song" (Vlautin and Campbell 2013).

Yet the soundtrack operates in different ways in relation to the novel. Often "purposefully mimetic" (St. Clair 2011: 102), its score emphasizes the episodes within the novel. An example is "Main Theme," with its western folk qualities that build through guitar, drum, piano, and finally pedal steel, conveying a sense of journeys, horizons, and dreamlike yearning. The West's traditional, mythic optimism is present, as in the novel, but is forever being twisted by Bodie's encroaching extreme politics and racism and by the harsh economics and sexism of Allison's everyday life. The "horizons" of optimism flicker through the soundtrack as upbeat moments, heard most in the tracks "Paul Newman Saves the Night" and "Dan Mahony Walks Allison Johnson to Work"; but they are always intercut, countered by darker, more sinister rhythms, often falling away to discord, as in "The Busboys from the Horseshoe" and its companion piece, "The Night That Never Goes Away." There is a deliberately disjunctive quality to the soundtrack, seemingly often at odds with the novel, such as in "The Busboys from the Horseshoe," a chapter in which Allison recalls her rape, existing in tension with track 2 on the CD. St. Clair calls this "an unsettling musical counterpoint" (2011: 101), and Vlautin explained that his

> idea was not to write music for the rape, but for when she is alone on the pavement staring at the sky just after the attack. Almost surreal, sad, horrified, hopeless, shock and relief that's it's over. The aftermath. The music of that song has a coldness to it, like the air and the pavement. At the end of the song I always pictured her getting up and walking to her car. The whole time she's in a haze, in shock…completely alone. Did that just really happen? That aftermath feeling I hoped the music reflected. Dazed and slow and melancholy and with darkness underneath, darkness awakening. (Vlautin and Campbell, 2013)

The soundtrack's slow guitar notes pick over a swirling, dreamy background, which maintains an undercurrent of something sinister and dark, even as the bright sounds dance across the aural landscape, ending in a deep, discordant finale disappearing into silence. To consider the chapter and track together intensifies the horror of the scene, because we enter Allison's mind in its "aftermath," the terrible gap between brutality and survival, the space she so often occupies in the novel itself. As the dreamy soundtrack plays, as if inside her head, in the novel the impacts of the rape entwine as sensations: "She couldn't breathe" but *feels* her legs on the "frost-covered street," *hears* "a car drive by," and *sees* the "beeping lights of an airplane overhead," until "her breath released...disappeared into the sky, and she could breathe again" (Vlautin 2008: 84). Almost like a jolting rebirth, Allison feels her way back into the world again with the characteristic resilience she learns and enacts throughout the novel, and the musical score captures and emphasizes this with its qualified dreaminess. As Vlautin puts it in the quote above, ultimately it is "darkness awakening."

Characteristically in Vlautin's work, there is always hope, even in the bleakest of narratives. Here, the soundtrack seems to hold on, like Allison does in the novel, to the thread of a tune to lead her, like Ariadne, through the darkness: "It's the idea that if you persevere, if you can overcome anxiety and fear, and you run towards kindness and decency and not bitterness and hate, that maybe, just maybe you'll be alright" (Vlautin and Campbell 2013). Specifically, in relation to Allison, Vlautin said this: "I know she'll be all right because she doesn't quit. She fucks up, but she still gets up and tries to make better decisions than she did the time before....She's smart enough to not keep making the same bad decisions" (Bernheimer 2008). This point is underscored by two contrasting sections of the soundtrack, "Doc Holidays" and "Paul Newman Saves the Night." The former, with its slow, wailing pedal steel, suggests crying and breath-like repetitions, and refers to another scene in the novel where Allison is sexually violated by two men. The latter is a track with jaunty guitar and harmonica and a strong backbeat, like a heartbeat, rising up, as if rallying, with the effect of talking back to the previous track's worrisome slowness. Just as the novel itself ends with "fear and hope and uncertainty," as Allison and Dan embrace among the ruined casinos of old Reno, so the soundtrack's final song, "A New Life," presents the echoing pedal steel. Once again, with the flicker of the horizon in a high-pitched, tuneful stretching out toward something unspecified, some countrified percussive, shimmering moment, reminiscent of Dan's comment to Allison out in the Nevada desert: "I had this place to daydream in" (Vlautin 2008: 188). After all, pitch, as Tim Ingold argues, also means "to throw, to cast into the world" (Ingold 2015: 108), and here, as the musical pitch sharpens, it casts us outward, into the possibility, however uncertain, of "A New Life" for these two scarred characters. As the soundtrack concludes, it loops back to the main theme, with its reassuring, plaintive, and simple tune, but without closure. For it remains "fugitive," with its musical lines refusing to connect or flow as a "straight line from source to recipient" (like the Northline), since what we experience, throughout the novel's soundtrack, is rather a "swirl in the in-between" (ibid.: 111).

When discussing the possible function of the soundtrack, Vlautin hoped that listening to it "would keep the novel alive a bit longer," and in many ways it enables this, as I have suggested, by emphasizing and extending the novel's concerns, its "liveliness" (Vlautin and Campbell 2013). The soundtrack, working both with and against the novel (like a "swirl in the in-between"), reminds me of Deleuze and Guattari's comment on minor literature: with "its cramped space," which "forces each individual intrigue to connect immediately to politics," they wrote, "the individual concern... becomes all the more necessary, indispensable, magnified, because *a whole other story is vibrating within it*" (Deleuze and Guattari 2003: 17—emphasis added).

Hence, in the "cramped spaces" of the soundtrack and the related chapters of the novel, Allison's individual concerns—nervous anxiety, exploitation, sexual violence, and fear—become "magnified" through the intersections of music and words, so that it is as if "a whole other story is vibrating within it," within the smallest and seemingly most "minor" moments, feelings, and events. This shapes, in Kathleen Stewart's words, "an attention to matterings, the complex emergent worlds, happening in everyday life. The rhythms of living that are addictive or shifting.... The enigmas and oblique events and background noises that might be barely sensed and yet are compelling" (Stewart 2011: 445). Consequently, in the spaces of the soundtrack, the novel lives on "a bit longer" in "knots of sound and feeling" (Ingold 2015: 20), "a space opening out of the charged rhythms of an ordinary," producing "little worlds of all kinds" that form and collapse, and have "a capacity to affect and to be affected" (Stewart 2011: 446, 452).

Thus music functions in this fugitive way in the novel, following different "lines," some reassuring, some challenging, never providing any easy or definite closure, but always *swirling between* so as to complement *and* supplement the narrative and deepen our response to its characters, places, and themes. However, ultimately, as Allison and Dan stand amid the ruins of old Reno, they have together, perhaps, created their own tentative "song." As Ian Buchanan has written, referring back to the quotations at the beginning of this chapter, "The song is our future, a future of our own dreaming. To put it differently, we need not venture into the dark, chaotic world of the unhomely again so long as we have a song" (Buchanan 1997). As Vlautin puts it, Allison and Dan "can get by, even flourish, but even so the scar is there. It might wear down and the color might eventually return towards the natural skin color but it'll always be there just as it's always there in their heart" (Vlautin and Campbell 2013).

But as David Hesmondhalgh reminds us, music engenders relationships outside ourselves, contributing to such moments of flourishing where "flourishing is not the same as happiness or pleasure," because it contains more complex relations of "loyalty, tenacity, sacrifice, courage, and even love" (Hesmondhalgh 2013: 17–18, citing Martha Nussbaum). It is toward this possibility of flourishing and a future of our own dreaming that *Northline* directs us, venturing outward, with Allison Johnson, from her unhomely home on the thread of a tune to a potential new life, "with different loops, knots, speeds, movements, gestures, and sonorities" (Deleuze and Guattari 1996: 312).

NOTES

1. Vlautin describes his own relationship to Willie Nelson in many interviews: "Willie Nelson was like my saint. I would think of him as my protector. When I listen to his music, he made me think that perhaps my mom wasn't so hardcore right wing and such a hater of the arts, because she liked Willie Nelson. So, he gave me hope for my mom and my relationship with her." John Freeman. "Escape To The Country: Willy Vlautin Of Richmond Fontaine's Favourite LPs," *The Quietus*, April 6, 2016, http://thequietus.com/articles/19996-willy-vlautin-richmond-fontaine-favourite-albums-interview.

2. Of course, Nelson did not write the song "Blue Eyes Crying in the Rain," for it was written in 1947 by Fred Rose. Originally performed by Roy Acuff, it was later recorded by Willie Nelson as part of his 1975 album *Red Headed Stranger*.

3. Most likely drawn from *I Didn't Come Here and I Ain't Leaving: The Autobiography of Willie Nelson*, published June 22, 1989, given that *The Motel Life* is set in 1996 (the year of the Tyson/Holyfield fight on November 9.

4. Vlautin's new novel, with the working title *Don't Skip Out on Me*, will also have an instrumental soundtrack.

5. Covered by the White Stripes on their 2007 album *Icky Thump*.

6. The Highwaymen are referred to on Richmond Fontaine's *Winnemucca* (2002) — see introduction—and on their final album *You Can't Go Back If There's Nothing to Go Back To*.

7. George Pelecanos has referred to Richmond Fontaine's music as "cinematic Americana"; see "George Pelecanos' Week in Culture," 2012, http://www.vulture.com /2012/06/george-pelecanos-week-in-culture.html.

8. Valenzuela plays on Richmond Fontaine's album *Thirteen Cities*.

WORKS CITED

Aquila, Richard (ed.). 1996. *Wanted Dead or Alive: The American West in Popular Culture*. Urbana: University of Illinois Press.

Bernheimer, Kate. 2008. "Hard Time Tales of Willy Vlautin." http://www.powells .com/post/original-essays/hardtime-tales-of-willy-vlautin

Bindas, Kenneth J. 1996. Cool Water, Rye Whiskey, and Cowboys: Images of the West in Country Music. In *Wanted Dead or Alive: The American West in Popular Culture*, edited by Richard Aquila (Urbana: University of Illinois Press).

Buchanan, Ian. 1997. "Deleuze and Pop Music." *Australian Humanities Review*. http:// www.australianhumanitiesreview.org/archive/Issue-August-1997/buchanan .html. Accessed September 28, 2017.

Buchanan, Ian, and Marcel Swiboda (eds.). 2004. *Deleuze and Music*. Edinburgh: Edinburgh University Press.

Butler, Judith. 2010. *Frames of War: When Is Life Grievable?* London: Verso.

Byars, Jackie. 1991. *All That Hollywood Allows: Re-Reading Gender in 1950s Melodrama*. London: Routledge.

Chambers, Iain. 2001. *Culture After Humanism*. London: Routledge.

Ching, Barbara. 2001. *Wrong's What I Do Best: Hard Country Music and Contemporary Culture*. New York: Oxford University Press.

Deleuze, Gilles, and Felix Guattari. 1996. *A Thousand Plateaus*. London: The Athlone Press.

———. 2003. *Kafka: Towards A Minor Literature*. London: The Athlone Press.

Garner, Dwight. 2008. "Living With Music: A Playlist by Willy Vlautin." *New York Times*, April 30. http://artsbeat.blogs.nytimes.com/2008/04/30/living-with-music -a-playlist-by-willy-vlautin/?_r=0. Accessed November 21, 2016.

Gilbert, Jeremy. 2004. "Becoming-Music: The Rhizomatic Moment of Improvisation."

In *Deleuze and Music,* edited by Ian Buchanan and Marcel Swiboda. Edinburgh: Edinburgh University Press.

Goodman, Frank. 2008. "A Conversation with Willy Vlautin." *Puremusic.* http://www .puremusic.com/pdf/88wv.pdf. Accessed November 21, 2016.

Hesmondhalgh, David. 2013. *Why Music Matters.* London: Wiley Blackwell.

Hulse, Brian and Nick Nesbitt (eds.). 2010. *Sounding the Virtual: Gilles Deleuze and the Theory and Philosophy of Music.* Farnham: Ashgate.

Jack White. "Jack White, Patti Page share a 'Conquest'—and a vision." 2008. *USA Today,* January 2. http://usatoday30.usatoday.com/life/music/news/2008-01-01 -page-white_N.htm. Accessed September 28, 2017.

Ingold, Tim. 2015. *The Life of Lines.* London: Routledge.

Kennedy, William. 1986. *Ironweed.* Harmondsworth: Penguin.

Malone, Bill C. 1987. *Country Music, USA.* Wellingborough: Equation.

Marcus, Greil. 2014. "The Fleetwoods." *Greilmarcus.net.* http://greilmarcus.net/2014 /09/17/days-between-stations-two-groups-from-different-decades-1193/. Accessed March 2016.

Mellard, Jason. 2013. *Progressive Country: How the 1970s Transformed the Texan in Popular Culture.* Austin: University of Texas Press.

Mercurio, James P. 1996. Contemporary Melodrama: Interview with Allison Anders. *Creative Screenwriting* 3, 4: 25–28.

O'Hagan, Sean. 2016. "Willy Vlautin: 'I had a picture of Steinbeck and a picture of the Jam.'" *The Guardian,* April 24. https://www.theguardian.com/music/2016/apr/24 /willy-vlautin-richmond-fontaine-interview-delines. Accessed April 2016.

Pecknold, Diane, and Kristine McCusker (eds.). 2016. *Country Boys and Redneck Women: New Essays in Gender and Country Music.* Jackson: University of Mississippi Press.

St. Clair, Justin. 2011. "Soundtracking the Novel: Willy Vlautin's *Northline* as Filmic Audiobook." In Rubery, Matthew (ed.), *Audiobooks, Literature, and Sound Studies,* edited by Matthew Rubery. London: Routledge.

Stewart, Kathleen. 2011. "Atmospheric attunements." *Environment and Planning D: Society and Space* 20: 445–453.

Vlautin, Willy. 2006. *The Motel Life.* London: Faber and Faber.

———. 2008. *Northline.* London: Faber and Faber.

———. 2014. "Riding With Lowell George: Music to Help You Try and Get Through." In *Hang the DJ: An Alternative Book of Music Lists,* edited by Angus Cargill. London: Faber and Faber.

Vlautin, Willy, and Neil Campbell. 2013. Unpublished email interview, February.

CHAPTER 4

"ONE OF THE
ONLY CERTAIN TRUTHS"

Willy Vlautin and the Landscape of Nowhere

by Jeffrey Chisum

From a certain point of view, Willy Vlautin's novel *The Motel Life* begins twice, and both of these beginnings are anchored, ironically, in endings that take the form of death. In the book's opening passage, the narrator, Frank Flannigan, drunkenly witnesses the apparent suicide of "some sorta duck," which crashes through his motel room window and which, he says, "would have scared me to death if I hadn't been so drunk" (Vlautin 2006: 1). The other beginning—the inciting incident that sets the book's plot in motion—involves the vehicular manslaughter of an unnamed "kid" by Frank's brother, Jerry Lee: "It was like that, Frank, I swear it was. Just like that, out of the blue. Out of nowhere" (ibid.: 23). Both beginnings are underscored by absurdity: Frank reacts to the duck by noting that "all I could do was get up, turn on the light, and throw it back out the window" (ibid.: 1). Jerry Lee insists that his killing of the "kid" wasn't genuinely his fault: "If Polly Flynn hadn't burned my pants, I probably would have stayed the night with her.... Can you imagine that? Just her burning those pants killed a kid" (ibid.: 23). In both cases, there is an overriding sense of rootlessness, of purposelessness, and of malign happenstance. These aren't characters who *do* things; rather, they are characters to whom things are *done*. Frank and Jerry Lee Flannigan react and act in ways that might be described as self-preservation (as, indeed, do most of the characters in Vlautin's fiction), but one gets the sense that other factors are molding their fates. And as the two beginnings in *The Motel Life* suggest, the source of the forces impacting the Flannigan brothers' lives is unseen, frightening, absurd, intimately tied to questions of mortality and death, and perhaps most importantly, springing from some vast and unseen source—from "nowhere" in particular. Though Vlautin's novels take place in fictionalized versions of very real places, his depictions of the Western desert landscapes, and of the characters' passages through them, emphasize a fundamental anomie and the largeness and emptiness—both real and symbolic—of the place. It is this quality—this "landscape of nowhere"—that shapes the characters' lives in Vlautin's work, and that lends the novels their unmistakably melancholy power.

If Vlautin's fiction is sad, it is also, in its way, hopeful. But it needs to be said that these are very much stories borne of the desert—out of the Great Basin—and though only two of them are set entirely in Nevada, all four of the books are recognizable as products of what might be called a "Silver State" aesthetic. This is the same state that gives us legal gambling and prostitution; the Nevada Test Site; the 40-Mile Desert; Burning Man; Pyramid Lake; the Loneliest Highway in America; Area 51; and a physical landscape which, according to William Fox, is "the most mountainous place on earth except for Afghanistan" (*Living in the Big Empty* 2008). It has given us writers like Walter Van Tilburg Clark, Robert Laxalt, Joanne de Longchamps, and Claire Vaye Watkins, and visual artists such as Robert Caples and Craig Sheppard. The commonality here is a connection to the wide-open spaces that characterize the West more generally, but which achieve a special and dramatic focus in Nevada—Vlautin's home state.

There is perhaps no other place in the United States that is more often described by both admirers and detractors as "the middle of nowhere" than Nevada. In the mid-1800s, a Mormon pioneer named John Steel, sent to colonize the area near Las Vegas, lamented in a letter that "the country around here looks as though the Lord had forgotten it" (qtd. in Bowers 2002: 7). The sense of the place is encapsulated in the title of Bernard Schopen's detective novel *The Big Silence* (1989), set both in Reno and in the surrounding rural desert areas. In her essay "Literary Place-Bashing: Test Site Nevada" (2001,) Cheryll Glotfelty thoroughly documents the various ways in which commentators have reacted negatively to Nevada's wide-open spaces. The conceptualization of the place as a nowhere place or a nothing place helps to explain why "sinful" activities like prizefighting, gambling, and prostitution were allowed to take root: If you are going to engage in "dirty" activities, isn't it best to partake in a place that's blighted already? The notion of nowhere conjures up the idea of a void—a place where sin, garbage, waste, and negativity can be dumped or deposited. Think, here, of the Yucca Mountain nuclear waste repository, or of the tiresome Las Vegas slogan—"Everything that happens in Vegas stays in Vegas." Because this place is a nowhere place, you don't have to treat it with the same respect that you would if it was *somewhere*.

But emptiness can also suggest something unspoiled—an opportunity for escape, a place to clear one's head. The literature of the desert is, on the one hand, a literature of privation and struggle (Twain's *Roughing It* and Michael Ondaatje's *The English Patient* are perhaps two good examples), but it's also a literature of reflection and spiritual growth (think of the work of the Desert Fathers, of Frank Bergon's *The Temptations of St. Ed and Brother S*, or, generally speaking, Edward Abbey's *Desert Solitaire*). In this sense, the desert is something like a distillation of the Western frontier more generally. Just as the Old West held out the (often fictitious) promise of bonanza, El Dorado, or a water passage to the Pacific Ocean, the desert offers a reprieve from the busyness and chaotic stresses of city life, overpopulation, and political restrictions—the messiness of human interaction. It helps to crystalize feelings of isolation and individualism, connection with nature, and lonesomeness. Nowhere, in other words, isn't necessarily an undesirable place to be.

The phrase "middle of nowhere," and words and phrases relating to emptiness and rootlessness, occur again and again in Vlautin's fiction: on the first page of *The Motel Life*: "The streets were empty, frozen with ice" (ibid.: 1); about the kid whom Jerry Lee hits: "He just came out of nowhere" (ibid.: 4); on what to do with the incriminating car: "We could take the car out in the middle of nowhere, in the woods" (ibid.: 10); on contemplating a nonstop road trip: "You wouldn't have to live anywhere at all" (ibid.: 25); on gazing out the window: "besides the occasional ranch, there was nothing but sagebrush and barren hills around us" (ibid.: 26). Or as Frank watches Jerry Lee take the Dodge:

"I stood there and watched until the tail lights just flickered into noth-ing" (ibid.: 35). As Frank sits at the counter of a diner and looks out the window: "Each time I looked back there was nothing" (ibid.: 36). When Frank catches up at last with Jerry Lee in the hospital, Jerry Lee reports that, after leaving, he kept driving until "finally by sunrise I was in the middle of nowhere" (ibid.: 51). Later, when Earl Hurley, the hard-drinking proprietor of Hurley's Used Auto Hamlet, gives Frank advice, he suggests a kind of escapism: "Think about the life you want.... Make it a place where you want to be...It doesn't matter what it is" (ibid.: 80–81), only to later contradict himself when he (Earl) says, "There's a world out there. If you don't open your eyes, you ain't ever gonna see it" (ibid.: 156).

Early in *Northline*, Jimmy takes Allison to a party some distance away from Las Vegas: "They were in the desert now with nothing around them" Allison has suicidal thoughts as she pictures "[herself and Jimmy] driving on a mountain road, in the middle of nowhere" (Vlautin 2008: 36). Meanwhile, Jimmy observes that "'there sure ain't nothing out here'" (ibid.: 38). Meeting up with her friend Nan Endrick at the party, Allison reinforces the point: "It's hard to believe we're out in the middle of nowhere" (ibid.: 40). After she hitches a ride to a far-flung Flying J truck stop, she arranges a ride back to Vegas with a line cook named Justin Hardgrove, and as they are driving she starts to panic: "The man was sitting next to her and they were in the middle of nowhere" (ibid.: 57). Much later in the novel, with her life achieving something resembling stability, Allison goes on a camping trip in the Black Rock Desert with Dan Mahony, her love interest, who recalls a prior trip out into the desert that he took with his uncle: "By the end of the trip I was a hell of a lot better than I was when I first got in his truck on the way out here. Everything makes better sense when you're in the middle of nowhere" (ibid.: 188).

In *Lean on Pete*, the young protagonist Charley Thompson is left to his own devices for long stretches, without any adult supervision. At one point in the novel he is home alone and watches a movie on TV "about a guy who becomes a mountain man and lives by himself for a long time in the middle of nowhere" (Vlautin 2010: 54–55). The movie has a tragic dimension, though, and Charley notes, "It was a horribly sad movie," and that he "thought about it for a long time before [he] went to sleep" (ibid.: 55). Later, after his father is attacked and hospitalized, Charley talks to the horse, Lean on Pete, about what happened, and he tells the horse, "I wished he and I could just disappear. We could live in a place where there was no one else around" (ibid.: 63-64). After he absconds with Pete, Charley "drove for a long time without seeing anyone. [He] was out in the middle of a desert" (ibid.: 149). He ditches the truck eventually and sets out on foot, Pete in tow: "In front of us was nothing but desert...I could see nothing. No main road or trees or anything" (ibid.: 154).

"Nowhere" in Vlautin's fiction is not usually nowhere, then: It's a real, specific, physical place—usually the desert—but its meaning is multifaceted. For the Flannigan brothers, it often represents escape and a hiding place; for Allison Johnson, it is at one point a tomb—a final resting place—and then later, when she's with Dan Mahony, it is redemptive and restorative—an arid Lourdes. And for Charley Thompson and Lean on Pete, nowhere is an obstacle to be traversed—a place that is harrowing in its realness. Metaphor and concrete physicality intersect and nowhere begins to seem like a reflection of the characters' souls, of their hopes and despair.

This is fitting, and Vlautin's novels fall in line with a long tradition—as in thousands of years—of desert literature. From the Bible through the writings of the Desert Fathers, on through works like Percy Shelley's "Ozymandias" and Yeats's "The Second Coming," and up to Edward Abbey's *Desert Solitaire* and Cormac McCarthy's Western works, the literature of the desert fuses the symbolic and the real, absence and presence, belief and doubt, and life and death in the most atavistic way. As the theologian and literary critic David Jasper writes in *The Sacred Desert*, "the literature of the desert—of saints and travelers, or poets and even, perhaps especially, of charlatans—remains as it has always been: a place of romance. Physically the harshest places on earth, deserts also defy our sense of reality, its proportions and the boundaries we set on our lives and experience" (Jasper 2004: 71). This echoes William Fox's observations in his book-length study of the Great Basin, *The Void, the Grid, and the Sign* (2000), in which he argues that the vast and mountainous spaces of that desert—which spans most of Nevada and Utah and (depending on which map one consults; perhaps fittingly, this is a landform that does not have defined or agreed-upon borders) into parts of Oregon and Idaho—cause a state of cognitive dissonance in people. As Fox writes in the preface, "we think of the desert as undifferentiated land, an area without landmarks, hence not a landscape. Land is a state of matter, landscape a state of mind, and the desert is notoriously resistant to colonization" (Fox 2000: ix).

Indeed, there is an acceptance of this dissonance in Vlautin's fiction, which perhaps serves to mark him as a distinctly Nevadan writer. One finds this acceptance in the work of other Nevada writers, like Walter Van Tilburg Clark, Joanne de Longchamps, Claire Vaye Watkins, and Shaun T. Griffin, for instance. And it is perhaps instructive to compare Vlautin's depictions of the Nevadan nowhere and his characters' attitudes toward it with the depictions one finds in nonnatives' work. Mark Twain, for instance, in *Roughing It*, writes:

> [N]ow we were to cross a desert in *daylight*. This was fine—novel—romantic—dramatically adventurous—*this*, indeed, was worth living for, worth traveling for! We would write home all about it.... The poetry was all in the anticipation—there is none in the reality. Imagine a vast, waveless ocean stricken dead and turned to ashes; imagine this solemn waste tufted with ash-dusted sagebushes; imagine the lifeless silence and solitude that belong to such a place;...imagine ash-drifts roosting above mustaches and eyebrows like snow accumulations on boughs and branches. That is the reality of it. (Twain 1872: 123)

Whereas Twain depicts a landscape that is malign and death-tinged, Vlautin's desert nowhere is instead far more subdued—a place of quietude at times, even. The characters don't seem to despise it in the way that Twain does; instead, they seem often to not quite see it—it is a void that's defined primarily by its emptiness, by its physical embodiment of nothingness.

For millennia, that has been one of the main draws of the desert—its ability to purify and strip away the appurtenances of civilization. Discussing the Desert Fathers, David Jasper writes:

[I]n this impossible place, whose immensity could be embraced only by the imagination and of which, seemingly, there was no end, the world is defined anew. It was no longer the "world" of farms, villages, and towns ordered under human government and shaped by human hand. Rather, it stood over against the fragility of human endeavor, and yet in the sterile sands the ascetic realized what it is to be most truly human. (2004: 36)

Edward Abbey puts it another way in *Desert Solitaire*: "The finest quality of this stone, these plants and animals, this desert landscape is the indifference manifest to our presence, or absence, our coming, our staying or our going. Whether we live or die is a matter of absolutely no concern whatsoever to the desert" (Abbey 1994: 267). The appeal in part is the leveling effect—the removal of human grandiosity, aspirations, and history—and, all too often in Vlautin's work, it is the past that the characters seek to escape.

Surely that is another reason why deserts are referred to as nowhere: they render history on an epochal scale that is difficult to reckon—"cognitive dissonance," in Fox's terms. The idea is well captured in Shelley's poem "Ozymandias," which lays waste to the title king's aspirations to glory; the final lines describe the remains of a broken monument: "Round the decay/Of that colossal wreck, boundless and bare/The lone and level sands stretch far away." The poem describes a paradox in the form of memories—or historical landmarks—that have endured (the remains of the statue; Ozymandias's reputation; the poem itself), and a willful forgetfulness that is epitomized by the desert itself—the "lone and level sands" that flow in undulating waves toward the horizon. It is, once again, a contradiction held in equipoise—the "cognitive dissonance" described by Fox. He elaborates on the human reaction to this in *The Void, the Grid, and the Sign*:

[W]e have three common responses to such overwhelming dissonance. We can leave it behind us, which is what most people have done in the Great Basin, crossing it as quickly as possible with eyes averted as we seek the green solace of California or the

Midwest. Or, we can break it down into pieces small enough to analyze. We isolate one peak at a time in the distance and imagine ourselves climbing up its steep alluvial fans; we ruminate on the nearest sagebrush, obtaining comfort from the small sliver of the spectrum it delivers to our color-starved eyes. Or, we can assign it a symbolic value in order to file it safely away where we can ignore it: we define it as the Big Empty, as a wilderness—or as the nearest synonym to that word in the dictionary, a wasteland. (Fox 2000: 13)

Fox's choice of words is significant: We "file it *safely* away where we can *ignore* it." The safety is connected to the ignoring, the disappearance, the fading away, the slipping away from the constraints of history, the dissolution of the identity and the self. This describes Vlautin's characters, too—their motivations and their actions, and also their attitudes toward the desert, toward nowhere. For the Flannigan brothers, or Allison Johnson, for instance, this desert nowhere is a solace in that it represents escape from their painful pasts—it is "safety"—but it is also ignorance, a vanishing, a self-abnegation. A kind of death. (And, as David Jasper notes in his chapter on the Desert Fathers, "quite deliberately, monks' cells were constructed after the manner of tombs" (Jasper 2004: 36)). For the Flannigans, Allison Johnson, Charley Thompson, and other Vlautin characters, what would normally be thought of as a civilized home space is so corrupt and malign that the tomblike and spiritually purified alternative of the void, of the wasteland, starts to seem desirable.

Nowhere, then, is a liminal space: somewhere in between nature and civilization, between guilt and innocence; perhaps, even, between living and dying. Indeed, in Nevada, the desert landscape is inseparable from the notion of liminal existence between life and death, which is to say: ghosts. The Great Basin landscape, so often devoid of green or other signs of plant and animal life, can seem like a dead place. Twain, it's worth noting, calls it a "waveless ocean stricken dead and turned to ashes"; Sherman Alexie, in his short story "This is What It Means to Say Phoenix, Arizona," describes two characters' passage through the Nevada desert, and the scene is telling:

Thomas Builds-the-Fire slid behind the wheel and started off down the road. All through Nevada, Thomas and Victor had been amazed at the lack of animal life, at the absence of water, of movement.

"Where is everything?" Victor had asked more than once.

Now when Thomas was finally driving they saw the first animal, maybe the only animal in Nevada. It was a long-eared jackrabbit.

"Look," Victor yelled. "It's alive."

Thomas and Victor were busy congratulating themselves on their discovery when the jackrabbit darted out into the road and under the wheels of the pickup.

"Stop the goddamn car," Victor yelled, and Thomas did stop, backed the pickup to the dead jackrabbit.

"Oh, man, he's dead," Victor said as he looked at the squashed animal.

"Really dead."

"The only thing alive in this whole state and we just killed it."

"I don't know," Thomas said. "I think it was suicide."

Victor looked around the desert, sniffed the air, felt the emptiness and loneliness, and nodded his head.

"Yeah," Victor said. "It had to be suicide." (Alexie 1994: 71–72)

Alexie's passage is interesting for several reasons. They observe, at the outset, an "absence...of movement," though of course both of them are indeed moving through the desert in their pickup. Victor remarks on the seeming emptiness—"Where is *everything*?"—and is disturbed enough by what they aren't seeing to ask the question "more than once." The repeated question itself seems like a rebuke of the discomfort that they feel. The lone relief comes in the form of a jackrabbit, which they proceed to run over and kill—a death via vehicular slaughter, not unlike the inciting incident in *The Motel Life*—and their interpretation of this death is to view it as a suicide. There is nothing alive in this desert-nowhere, supposedly, and the lone thing that *does* happen to be alive doesn't want to be—it has a death wish. The living, actual nowhere of the Nevada desert is so intolerable to existence that life looks for ways of escape. Meanwhile, the entire scene is suffused with "emptiness and loneliness." The scene concludes with Victor and Thomas climbing back into the truck and driving away with no further mention of the incident. But its presence within the larger story—involving the death of Victor's father, and his (Victor's) and Thomas's journey to settle the father's affairs—seems meant to communicate a point about death and memory, and the ways in which the desert landscape provides a physical canvas for these ideas.

Perhaps the reason why the desert nowhere described in these texts is such a place of unease has to do with the way it challenges our sense of memory. As Fox, John McPhee, Wilbur Shepperson, and others have written, the desert landscape can seem as if it is a place with no memories—a place that erodes and wipes away history and civilization—or perhaps more accurately (and to reference Fox again), a place whose historical scale is so vast that it escapes human understanding. In his book *East of Eden, West of Zion*, Shepperson argues that Nevada—due in no small measure to its desert nowhere physicality—"has not been one of these special visionary places like the 'old sod' of Ireland, the Green Mountains of Vermont, or the Shenandoah Valley of Virginia that are dear to people who have never visited them...[m]emory and imagination require being stabilized and implanted in a way not yet experienced in Nevada" (Shepperson 1989: 9). Elsewhere, Shepperson provides further explanation for this state of affairs: "The phenomenon of building and collapse, start and failure, caused a dearth of ideas and a sameness; stability would have permitted the evolution of social uniqueness. The older things grow, the more different they become" (ibid.: 3). The "building and collapse" Shepperson refers to concerns the roughly five hundred ghost towns that dot Nevada's landscape—Shepperson describes them, aptly, as "miniature black holes" (ibid.: 3). Of course, it's not as if the ghost towns have been forgotten: one need only visit Rhyolite or Bodie, high in the Sierra Nevada, to see that this isn't the case; Shepperson instead seems to be referring to a cultural stability that would capture these places—the memory of them—in a different light. Ghost towns are "dead," largely uninhabited places, but we nonetheless uneasily remember them, which is to say that they exist in a kind of historical nowhere. They are a reminder that even seemingly dead spaces can still be haunted and populated with signs of the passage of time, and with ghosts.

In that regard, it makes a certain amount of narrative and symbolic sense that Allison Johnson, in *Northline*, so often finds solace in the form of her conversations with an apparition-like version of Paul Newman, who appears to her during times of stress and who "haunts" the narrative like a ministering angel. He's first mentioned in an early scene, as Allison returns to her mother's house after a harrowing stretch of time spent handcuffed to her abusive boyfriend's bed (and one wonders whether the surname of this boyfriend—*Bodie*—is significant). "Anyway, it's Paul Newman, all night and all day," her mother tells her. "Your dream man's on a TNT marathon. Paul Newman for twenty-four hours" (Vlautin 2008: 12). Allison's life in *Northline* seems often to be defined by a kind of sadness-tinged anomie: for most of the book she is adrift, barely connected to the people she is closest to, and her relationships are repeatedly severed. Perhaps the deepest human connection she feels, then, is to Paul Newman—a "dream man" who exists in disembodied, nonstop ("all night and all day"), televised form. He is thus similar to other kinds of ghosts insofar as he doesn't obey the rules of the normal temporal order. In the novel, he is simultaneously everywhere and nowhere; omnipresent and perpetually absent.

Later, as she is being driven back into Las Vegas by Justin Hardgrove—the man from the Flying J truck stop—Allison starts to panic and summons up the specter of Newman as a means of dealing with the stressful situation: "But she kept her eyes closed and concentrated, and then suddenly he was there. She was Paul Newman's nurse, rolling him around in a wheelchair, talking to him. He was young, not old, and it was warm out, sunny, and trees surrounded them. She was dressed in a white uniform" (ibid.: 57). The landscape, it's worth noticing, is quite different in this imagining than the desert surrounding Las Vegas. Newman, in this fantasy, tells Allison about a retreat—an escape from her downtrodden life: "About twenty miles from here there's a big old house. It's near a lake. There's a pier that you can sit on. You can jump off it and go swimming. I bought that place 'cause of you. I know that's the sorta place you'd like to live in. I want us to live there together" (ibid.: 58). This apparition then proceeds to give Allison

advice about her current situation, and he urges her to get herself together and, ultimately, to leave: "My recommendation is to start new.
Get the hell out of Dodge, as they say" (ibid.: 60). The layers of location,
of movement, of direction in this scene are revealing. Where is Allison, exactly? Where is she going? On one level, she's sitting panicked
in the car of an unfamiliar male (he drinks from a bottle of red wine
as he drives and is "halfway through the bottle when she [begins] to
hyperventilate" [ibid.: 56]) as they drive toward North Las Vegas: she is
in motion. On another level, she has retreated to a fantasy-space in her
head, where she acts as a nurse to a wheelchair-bound Paul Newman.
As Newman speaks to her in this dreamworld, she is prompted by him
to envision his country retreat "near a lake" and, in the end, she's ad-
vised to "get the hell out of Dodge." Where to? Newman doesn't say.

Allison nonetheless heeds his advice and makes her way to Reno,
where she struggles to regain her footing. She drifts from place to place
until she winds up in a rather ramshackle apartment in downtown
Reno. She is at home taking a bath when she again starts to panic (she
has been sexually assaulted by a coworker and then raped), and Newman appears once again: "This place ain't much, but I think you'll do
all right," he says (ibid.: 86). They chat about his movies, and she tells
him, "I just wish we could disappear together." "We do all the time,"
he replies (ibid.: 87). The fantasy scene concludes with Newman ad-
vising her to "buy a TV, you think too much" (ibid.: 89). The final time
Newman appears in the novel is as Allison struggles to calm her frayed
nerves after hearing two men have a fistfight in the parking lot of her
apartment building. Once again, Paul Newman offers soothing advice
to her: "Save your dough and move to a nicer place." He also delivers
an ironic commentary on escape: "Remember, kid, there ain't no place
where you can escape to. There's no place where there aren't weirdos
and death and violence and change and new people. You head up to
Montana or Wyoming and you'll run into the same things as you do in
Vegas or New Orleans. You'll run into yourself" (ibid.: 185). Newman's
phrasing is significant: "there ain't no place"; "there's no place where."
Allison, in the novel, is forever occupying a shifting location—a nowhere—and Newman's final line, "You'll run into yourself," links this
to her identity.

The final two chapters of the book elaborate on these ideas. In the penultimate section, titled "Camping," Allison and her kind, scarred love interest, Dan Mahony, retreat to the Black Rock Desert for a recuperative excursion, and in the last chapter, "The Strip," Allison and Dan huddle together and watch as a pair of buildings in downtown Reno are demolished. Allison thinks she sees Jimmy Bodie among the crowd of onlookers and starts to panic and, in the final lines, place and time (which is to say, history) converge as she grabs Dan Mahony's hand for reassurance and kisses him: "And in weakness she gave everything to him right then and there among the people and the fallen, ruined old casino buildings" (ibid.: 192). As with the scene where Allison rides in the car with Justin, the man she doesn't know, the layering speaks to the complex, melancholy way that death, temporality, and place are interwoven to produce the power of the scene. Jimmy Bodie is a phantom in the crowd—it's not actually him. Meanwhile, the pair of buildings is reduced to rubble "in less than a minute": only the ghostly memory of them remains. Allison gives "everything" to Dan Mahony, "right then and there among the people," beside buildings that are "fallen, ruined [and] old." Nowhere, in Vlautin's work, is actually a multifaceted juxtaposition of place (whether real or imagined), time—or the passage of time—and the attendant emotions of the characters. The mood Vlautin creates at the end of *Northline*, and indeed, arguably, in all of his work, is one that is simultaneously sad and desperate yet hopeful. Nowhere offers the hope of escape and a new start, but it lacks a clear anchor to either time or place, and that sense of disconnectedness is—just as Sherman Alexie noted—one of "emptiness and loneliness."

The antidote to these feelings in Vlautin's work would seem to be language and narrative. Allison is at last awoken from her spell of anxiety via speech—both her own and Dan Mahony's: "'Please don't let him find me. Please, please, please, please.' She repeated it again and again until Dan spoke to her and she opened her eyes to see him" (ibid.: 192). And storytelling is perhaps the core coping strategy at the center of *The Motel Life*, as Frank Flannigan makes up narratives to take the edge off the unpleasant situations that he and Jerry Lee find themselves in. During a reminiscence early in the novel, Frank remembers spending time with Annie James, who, it turns out, has a series of curling iron burns on the inside of her arm—an injury that was likely inflicted on her by her abusive mother. Frank offers to take her in, and suggests that they get breakfast, but she makes a counter-request: "You could tell me a story like the ones you tell Jerry Lee" (Vlautin 2006: 41). The story he tells her involves the two of them getting abducted and taken aboard "a big yacht. A boat for rich people" where, though they are permitted to be together, they live a life of indentured servitude— Frank assists the cook, and Annie helps with the cleaning (ibid.: 42–43). Eventually, the ship is struck by lightning, killing the evil, James Bond–inspired villain (he has "a metal eye, and his hands were just hooks") and freeing a speedboat, which they use to escape. As day breaks, they steer into "this beautiful bay" and find a deserted mansion. "No one is inside, just us," Frank says. "We sit on this huge deck and they have a telescope and we try to find our crew, but no one's in sight" (ibid.: 44–45). The remedy for their painful lives is, interestingly enough, an escape from slavery to an isolated but nonetheless lonely paradise. And once again, the layering of time, place, imagination, and storytelling emphasizes the mood and feeling: Frank is actually sitting alone in a diner in an unnamed small town, remembering being with Annie James and Jerry Lee at their room at the Mizpah Motel, and in turn recalling a story that he made up about a deserted mansion on a beach. The humorousness and absurdity of the story help to undercut what could otherwise be a thick and unbearable sense of loneliness. The act of speaking, and the storytelling itself, and the remembrance of it, seem like gestures of hope in the face of the despair that the characters face.

Later in the novel, Frank pens a story for Jerry Lee, who is in the hospital with a self-inflicted gunshot wound, to "help pass the time and give him a break from the TV" (ibid.: 62). Like the story he tells to Annie, this narrative is a meandering and absurd tale involving tennis-playing prostitutes, a man named Lyndon Johnson (not the president) getting abducted and probed by aliens, a pilgrimage to Los Angeles followed by a move to Alaska, and, finally, a stint in "the state mental ward" (ibid.: 63–67). Perhaps the defining feature of this story is its sense of rootlessness: the narrator, a character named Dickie Junior, can't seem to stay in one place, and yet, after his move to Alaska, he determines that the frontier—"The last place in America for freedom, for individuality, for honor, for peace"—isn't perhaps as inviting as he assumed. He writes, "After reading *White Fang* I knew the wilderness was no place to live. Have you read that fucking book? You'd have to be nuts to live like that." He leaves Alaska but, upon returning home, he winds up getting "committed...to a private mental hospital for evaluation." Storytelling in *The Motel Life* takes place in Frank's mental space, and within that space, notions of frontier, wilderness, and nowhere are linked to mental instability. "But I didn't give a shit," the narrator of the story explains. "Why should I? It's better than working." Of his time in the state mental wards, he says, "It took me three months to get out of there, but it wasn't as bad as you'd think." The story, in other words, ends on a hopeful note, with the absurdity serving to fend off the pain lurking beneath the fecklessness of the story.

Much like Allison and Paul Newman in *Northline*, these imaginative excursions into narrative places—fictional nowheres—serve a palliative purpose. When Frank tells a story to his mother's friend, Claire Martin, she responds by laughing. This story is about his apparently fictional cousin Harvey, a huge, hulking person ("He was the ape of the family") whose family struggles to transform him into somebody who is "mean," so that he'll be a great football player. But they fail, and he retaliates by publicly accusing his mother—Frank's Aunt Carol—of forcing him into a sexual relationship. The story concludes with Aunt Carol in a state of ruination: "All she does is drink. She lost her job and ended up waiting tables at the Sizzler. The End" (ibid.: 90–92). Claire Martin asks Frank if he made the story up: "Some of it's true, but most of it's not." "It put me in a good mood, Frank," Claire says, and he replies, "It always does. It's a sad story, but for some reason it always puts people in a good mood" (ibid.: 92). Bad things, ruined lives, are recast as cheerful comedy within the dislocated frame of Frank's storytelling. The nowhere space of the narrative, along with the sunny absurdity of the plot, cast the tragic elements in a more tolerable light. (One wonders which elements of the story, per Frank, are "true.") Compared to the lives they actually leave, a "sad story" like this offers a hopeful escape into a different kind of nowhere.

Perhaps the most haunted, trapped character in all of Vlautin's fiction is the wounded and bedridden Iraq War veteran, Leroy Kervin, in the ironically titled novel, *The Free*. Like Allison Johnson and Frank Flannigan, Kervin relies on the dislocated power of imagination and storytelling as a means of trying to escape the pain of his situation, though these imaginings (or hallucinations?) often wind up serving as a means for Leroy to relive his botched suicide attempt. In other words, they function both as escape (from his mute, bedridden state) and reminder (of how trapped he is, how much pain he is in, both physically and emotionally). In these imaginings, Leroy travels—or flees or seeks refuge—just like the main characters in all of Vlautin's other novels, and the descriptions of the fantasy destination mirror the ones in *Northline* and *The Motel Life*. In one of these passages, roughly halfway through the novel, Leroy's love interest, Jeanette, describes "a friend whose parents had a cabin a hundred miles north of Vancouver." She continues: "You can't believe how beautiful it is there. It seemed like the most beautiful place ever made, like the most beautiful place that ever existed" (Vlautin 2014: 138). As with the paradisiacal retreats envisioned by Annie/Frank and Allison/Paul Newman, this cabin, as a place, is fantastical: "You can't believe how beautiful it is." The real and the imagined—the beautiful and the painful—converge in this scene, and in the character of Leroy Kervin.

At heart, Willy Vlautin's novels revisit themes of place, and find characters who are forever on the move, always in search of home, but who are seemingly comfortable nowhere. They seek alternative lives in physical landscapes, and also in the imaginary places of their visions, hopes, and dreams, and to no small extent these imaginings emerge as a powerful form of alternative and hopeful reality: "Why would I know all these things that aren't real?" Leroy asks at one point. "Why would I be dreaming about things like this if they weren't true?" (Vlautin 2014: 210) Trapped as the characters so often appear, their fates nonetheless seem untethered to the bleak, usually desert landscapes, and the end implication seems to be that the only real escape is death. This idea is summed up in the character of Jerry Lee Flannigan, who dies at the conclusion of *The Motel Life*; in the image of the destroyed buildings at the end of *Northline*; in the horse's ruined body, abandoned in the Western hinterlands, in *Lean on Pete*; and, of course, in the character of Leroy Kervin in *The Free*. Even though his imaginings provide a means of escaping his hospital bed, he nonetheless relives his traumatic suicide attempt (he flung himself onto a sharp wooden post, which pierced his chest) over and over again in these dreams. Interestingly, Leroy's death (echoing the opening of *The Motel Life*) happens twice—he dies physically, in the hospital, and also within his dreamworld, and Jeanette, pleading to him, frames this in terms of place: "But please don't leave me, Leroy" (Vlautin 2014: 278). Leave her he does, though, to the nowhere that awaits us all. Part of the sadness of the scene is the result of forces in contradiction with each other ("cognitive dissonance"): the inevitability of Leroy's death is in conflict with Jeanette's pleas—with her attempt to control what happens, and to forestall time. It's sad, in a sense, because it seems so unfortunate—so unlucky.

It therefore follows a certain dramatic logic when, in *The Motel Life*, Frank observes that it's "bad luck," which is "one of the only certain truths": "It falls on people every day.... It's always on deck, it's always just waiting. The worst thing, the thing that scares me the most is that you never know who or when it's going to hit" (Vlautin 2006: 9). Landscape and place in Vlautin's fiction become metaphors for fate and luck, and these seemingly material and physical things turn out instead to be unstable: unsuitable as home spaces, places from which one runs away. Or they are transformed into disembodied fantasy realms—stories, hallucinations, and dreamlike states of mind. These are characters dwelling in "the middle of nowhere," which turns out to be a richly complicated and emotionally dense place after all. And as bleak and sad as they are, Vlautin's novels also always seem to offer a glimmer of hope. Each of the characters ultimately does have some means of getting away—of fleeing. Though they occupy a shifting and mercurial nowhere, the characters themselves serve as a form of resistance to the emptiness that the place embodies. They carry on, like Allison Johnson and Dan Mahony at the conclusion of *Northline*, still standing, amidst the rubble and the dust, breathing and alive.

Works Cited

Abbey, Edward. 1994. *Desert Solitaire*. New York: Ballantine Books.

Alexie, Sherman. 2005. "This is What It Means to Say Phoenix, Arizona." In *The Lone Ranger and Tonto Fistfight in Heaven*. New York: Grove Press.

Bowers, Michael W. 2002. *The Sagebrush State*. Reno: University of Nevada Press.

Fox, William L. 2000. *The Void, the Grid, and the Sign*. Salt Lake City: University of Utah Press.

Glotfelty, Cheryll. 2001. "Literary Place-Bashing: Test Site Nevada."In *Beyond Nature Writing*, edited by Karla Armbruster and Kathleen R. Wallace, 233–247. Charlottesville: University Press of Virginia.

Jasper, David. 2004. *The Sacred Desert*. Malden, MA: Blackwell Publishing.

Living in the Big Empty. 2008. KNPB Public Television film, executive producer Dave Santina.

Schopen, Bernard. 1989. *The Big Silence*. Reno: University of Nevada Press.

Shepperson, Wilbur S. 1989. *East of Eden, West of Zion*. Reno: University of Nevada Press.

Twain, Mark. 1872 [1995]. *Roughing It*. Berkeley: University of California Press.

Vlautin, Willy. 2006. *The Motel Life*. New York: Harper Perennial.

———. 2008. *Northline*. New York: Harper Perennial.

———. 2010. *Lean on Pete*. New York: Harper Perennial.

———. 2014. *The Free*. New York: Harper Perennial.

CHAPTER 5

"THE ONGOING TEXTURE OF THE DRIFT"

Illustrating Willy Vlautin and Richmond Fontaine

by NEIL CAMPBELL, GREG ALLEN,
NATE BEATY, AND WILLY VLAUTIN

If the music and the fiction are inextricably bound up together, as this book argues, then there is yet another dimension to Willy Vlautin's work, and that is the illustrations that have so often accompanied both the novels and the CDs. The artists who have defined this style are Nate Beaty and Greg Allen, whose various drawings and paintings chart the regionality of Richmond Fontaine and of Vlautin's fiction. Their work differs in many ways, and yet coheres uncannily to map a distinct space of "the ordinary stuff—the ongoing texture of the drift," as Dave Hickey puts it (1997: 10). There is always something local at work in their art that chimes with Richmond Fontaine's and Willy Vlautin's immediate sense of place, and to follow Hickey, their collective focus on "everyday life" is never a deficiency but always a resource. As if "beguiled by the tininess of it" (ibid.), we are drawn in by the local details, whether in pen and ink drawings or hyperrealist paintings, and the worlds spinning out from the ordinary stuff. From the dive motel signs on 4th Street, Reno, to the dying mustang by the edge of a desert highway, Beaty and Allen provide visual soundtracks to Vlautin's work, full of doubt, yearning, vulnerability, and hope. Like all good soundtracks, they are suggestive, elusive, and provocative, in that they both illustrate the mood and supplement it, turning the audience from "passive voyeurs," as Jacques Rancière puts it, into "active participants," as if composing with the "elements of the poem before them" (2009: 4, 13). As we view these artworks, we translate them, appropriating their stories not simply in order to repeat them but to make from their elements our own texts. The "elements" of artwork in Beaty and Allen challenge us to "see, feel, and understand" for ourselves (ibid.: 13) and, in so doing, to relate to the wider concerns of place and people, to some dynamic sense of community. For, as Rancière insists, "An emancipated community is a community of narrators and translators" (ibid.: 22), thinking and feeling for themselves.

NATE BEATY

Into the Mood

WILLY VLAUTIN: "I had written *The Motel Life* for myself. I hadn't really even thought of publishing it, but I knew it needed illustrations at the top of every chapter. I had a friend who ran a comic book company and asked him if he knew any illustrators and he said he just got off the phone with the perfect guy as he'd just been laid off and was looking for work.

"I called him up and we met in a coffee shop a couple days later. I came with a stack of photos and ideas and while we were talking he drew one of the pictures that ended up in *The Motel Life*. He was so damn cool and good. I couldn't believe my luck. He must have done ten or fifteen that week. I was so nervous that he wouldn't like the book and wouldn't finish the project that for a long time I wouldn't let him read it, thinking maybe if he did he'd quit. I can't say enough great things about Nate, and we've worked together ever since."

NATE BEATY ON WILLY: "Willy paid me out of pocket for chapter illustrations for his novel he was shopping around. We'd meet up at cafes in Portland in 2004, where he'd hand over well-weathered bills he'd scraped up while painting houses. I didn't think the book was going anywhere, having a plethora of artist and writer friends with fantastic work that often didn't go any further than 100 copies of a Xeroxed zine. I figured this was just another low-key illustration gig for a friend that only a handful of people would see.

"I'd put Richmond Fontaine on the headphones to get into the mood when drawing. The chapter illustration list for *The Motel Life* was originally just a handful of black and white photographs of Reno that Willy

Nate Beaty, "Reno sign." Used by permission of the artist.

had taken, but it slowly evolved into more and more complicated scenes. I ended up drawing some of them in the Oregon woods using the light of the campfire, a few while I was living in a greenhouse on Orcas Island, and others were drawn in a tiny Astoria house overlooking the Columbia. It felt appropriate to slather ink while surrounded by cold, rain-drenched firs to capture the heavy atmosphere of the brothers Flannigan" (Nate Beaty email: October 2016).

Nate Beaty's pen-and-ink drawings throughout Willy Vlautin's *The Motel Life* (2006) provide a witty, geographical tour, opening with the "Reno: The Biggest Little City in the World" sign in chapter 1, through motel signs (Morris, Sandman, Sutro, Rancho, Mizpah, The Fitzgerald, Rancho Sierra, Travelers Inn, Stockman's Casino), bars (Halfway Club, Reno Turf Club, Elbow Room), significant landmarks (The Gun Rack, Hurley's Used Auto Hamlet, St. Mary's Hospital, highway markers to Elko), and moving further outward to cars, windshields, and the Western road trip itself. Each image forms the landscape through which the novel's characters move, circling around, dreaming, observing, as if weaving an intense local geography that both contains their lives and points beyond them to their intersections with worlds of escape and fantasy, struggle and pain, disappointment and yearning, mythic context and everyday optimism. Within the novel, of course, Beaty's

Nate Beaty, "Sandman Motel." Used by permission of the artist.

work becomes Jerry Lee Flannigan's drawings, described in chapter 19. Vlautin describes the motel signs as "within a mile of downtown, and most aren't even motels anymore. Once they were new and held vacationers and honeymooners from all over the country, and now they barely survive as residentials. And the people that stay there, they're on the slide too. They got worse as the buildings do" (Vlautin 2006: 112). They are Jerry Lee's mode of communication, his language in a society that has no place for his voice or his feelings.

Later, Beaty caught the mood of Richmond Fontaine's *Thirteen Cities* perfectly with a cover image of a dusty desert street and a solitary dog wandering across the frame in search of shade, with the telephone wires stretching out to the distant horizon as if taunting us with the possibility of movement, of escape, of another city out there. Elsewhere a collapsed man sits by an abandoned adobe, and the desert mesas surround it all with a timeless, austere grandeur. These meld into the spaces sketched on Beaty's map that adorns the inside cover, marking the thirteen cities the album refers to, from Portland to Tucson, Las Cruces to Walla Walla. Beaty would return to mapping the

Nate Beaty, "Halfway Club." Used by permission of the artist.

West for *Lean on Pete*, penning Charley Thompson's sketch maps "for his friend Lean on Pete," showing their journey from the local sites of Portland ("My Dad's Work," "Our House," and "Movie Theater") to their cross-states trek from Oregon to Wyoming.

On the last Richmond Fontaine record, *You Can't Go Back If There's Nothing to Go Back To*, Beaty once again contributed a perfect image, of a hand grasping a Harolds Club whiskey glass on which is tattooed "I stole more than I ever gave." In these words and gestures, he captures the sense of loss, regret, and vulnerability running through so much of Vlautin's work, proving once again how well attuned the illustrations are to the writing and music.

Nate Beaty, "Hand and Glass." Used by permission of the artist.

Nate Beaty, "Hurleys." Used by permission of the artist.

GREG ALLEN'S "POST-PETROCHEMICAL WEST"

"He's been a good pal to me for almost thirty years," Willy Vlautin says. "We're the only two guys from when we were young who never quit making art. It's done us both about in but we were never quite savvy enough to figure anything else out. He and I have always just kept at it." Greg Allen's work is there on *Winnemucca, Post to Wire, The Fitzgerald*, and the last album, *You Can't Go Back If There's Nothing to Go Back To*. On *Post to Wire*, an abandoned trailer has, scrawled across its side, "This is the land of broken dreams," revealing Allen's interest, like that of Vlautin, in the optimistic past translated into the disappointment of the present, and in the West as a focal point for terrible contradictions. Inside the cover is a smaller image of the open road and a highway stretching out to the horizon, as if to remind us of the other side of abandonment and the persistence of beauty and resilience and hope.

Like that of the lonely, head-bowed figure who walks in the shadow of the Harolds Club casino on the cover of *The Fitzgerald*, the direction of Allen's images is far from clear. He may be turning away from the lure of the casino and heading home, regretting another night of losing money at blackjack. These are, of course, invitations to stories, wonderful fragments, like Vlautin's songs themselves, beckoning us with every shade of possibility and dread. Allen explains that his paintings "capture a sense of place and time; the American West and the Age of Oil. The roadside motels and diners, gas stations and vehicles that fuel my depictions are the iconic outposts of a previous century. In the spare landscape and small towns of the West, post–World War II architecture, signage and design are rendered as monoliths, deifying America at the height of its power" (see Virtual Gallery, n.d.).

Allen's work charts this post-petrochemical West with care and compassion, with the artist as much aware of the past as he is of the encroachment of the present and the possibilities of the future. According to Reno's newsreview.com's Kris Vagner, Allen is "a longstanding Reno legend" whose work "looks deep and longingly into our own back yard, rendering with lavish detail the unsung beauty of rough, rural Nevada and bright, urban facades from decades gone by. He paints a hyper-realistic combination of loneliness and celebration, with a sensibility that's somehow at once worldly and sheltered. He can paint a sunset over Peavine Mountain without being saccharine or a broken-down mobile home without being ironic or clichéd. He reveres mid-20th-century Nevada, highlighting its grit and glamor as if they were one and the same."

It is hardly surprising then, that this work should appeal to Vlautin, whose own writing is so often concerned with the "worldly and sheltered" as he touches deep themes through his attention to the local. Commenting on his own work, Allen comes down firmly on the side of realism: "You can't tell me there's a lot of pathos in Mark Rothko, Jackson Pollock," he said. "You can't tell me there's a lot about the human condition in splatter art and solid color canvasses. I like work that is reflective of the state of humanity" (Vagner, 2016). This intensity comes through dramatically in Allen's own account of his friendship with Willy Vlautin.

GREG ALLEN: "An artist acquaintance came over the other day to pick up my donation to help him with his trip to join the North Dakota Access Pipeline protest. I hadn't seen him in many years and we caught up, talking shop and telling stories of battles won and lost in the war to survive as a regional artist in the middle of almost nowhere. On his way out the door, he stopped briefly to look over the few dozen titles in my bookcase. 'Have you read Vlautin's *The Motel Life*?' After telling him I had, he asked me what I thought of it, and I replied by telling him, 'It was good, I've read all his books.' Then, as an afterthought, I added, 'Willy's one of my oldest, and I consider him one of my best friends, even though we hardly ever see each other anymore. I met him back in 1988, shortly after I moved here from L.A. If it wasn't for Willy, I wouldn't have started painting when I did.' His eyes grew large as he said rather breathlessly, 'Really?' I assured him it was true. More than anything I'd said during our visit, the fact that I know the most recent in a long line of favorite Nevada sons impressed him.

"I moved to Reno in 1988 and met Willy Vlautin shortly after that, when Cyril Beatty, a guy I worked with, invited me to see his band, Grey Mauser, perform at a dive bar. Grey Mauser's music wasn't something easily pigeonholed, but at the point of a gun I'd say they were a cowpunk band, consisting of Cyril on drums and Willy, who played guitar and sang. Rocking blues cover bands were the order of the day, so in spite of the fact they had really good songs and put on a great show, Reno's mullet-headed and acid-washed-denim crowd hated them. They regularly cleared whatever venue they played, usually before the end of the second song.

"In 1990, I ended up singing in a hardcore band. I can't sing, and never had the desire to play music. What I did have was a blue Mohawk and a lot of anger. We ended up calling ourselves the Baby Oil Hand Job. We played blistering hardcore punk, and we relied on much speed to maintain our tempo, with our longest song approaching an entire two minutes. Our band, along with Willy and Cyril's Grey Mauser and Reno's only other punk band, Short Fuse, constituted a perfect punk storm. Fights at our shows were an expected and regular occurrence. Subsequently, only one bar would book our bands and only on Tuesday nights. Tuesday was delegated for punk shows because, as far as nights to go out on the town in Reno, Tuesday was Siberia. Before long, only a handful of diehard fans came to see us.

"That changed in May of '92 when Willy somehow finagled a Friday-night show at one of Reno's better venues. The turnout was huge, 300-plus. It was going to be our biggest and best show ever. Grey Mauser opened and people liked them for once, with Short Fuse playing next. As my band was on stage setting up, my fiancée came up to me in tears, and informed me someone outside threatened to kill her. I ran outside, and got into a fight with a 6'2", 220-lb. skinhead. I never saw the knife nor felt it, but I got messed up. I was eviscerated and had other injuries requiring eighty stitches to close. Turns out the 15-year-old was upset because he couldn't get in the bar to see my band perform.

"No venue would book a punk show as a result of the stabbing, resulting in the collapse of all three bands. Grey Mauser split up, Cyril gave up music and settled down to start a family, and Willy Vlautin, unwilling to stop making music, headed for the more promising scene in Portland. As for myself, after six days in the hospital, I was flat on my back for two months, which had the effect of ending my employment and, as a result, I lost my apartment.

"While recuperating I decided to teach myself how to paint. I was a good artist during my school years; however, after dropping out of high school I'd lost interest in it, although somewhere in the back of my mind I always knew someday I'd be an artist, whenever and whatever that was. With nothing left to lose, now was the time. I went all-in, pursuing it with total commitment, and the results were immediate. Friends bought me supplies, asking nothing in return, and the Reno community bought my work, not for much, and not enough to survive, but it was a start. After four months, I went back to work and painted in the evenings. If Willy hadn't booked that show I wouldn't have been stabbed, and without that cataclysmic event I don't know when I would have started painting, if ever.

"In 2002, Willy made one of his occasional reappearances in my life and asked if he could use some of my artwork for his band's upcoming CD, *Winnemucca*. We hadn't seen a whole lot of one another since the night I got stabbed. I really liked his new band even more than Grey Mauser, and I never missed a chance to see Richmond Fontaine on the rare occasions they'd come through Reno. As busy as he was, he always made time for us to catch up, and I'd show him my recent paintings using a pocket-sized photo album I would carry wherever I went to try and generate sales. He told me it was a paying gig, though I shouldn't expect to get rich from it. 'Of course,' I told him, 'Anything you want.' I'd have been happy to let him use my work free of charge, and I think I may have offered, but it had been a lean year and I was grateful for the opportunity.

"My offerings were rejected one after another. Willy told me that he'd seen one image a few years back he really liked in particular, describing it as a couple of guys carrying another guy. I knew the painting, and I was shocked. Occasionally I do personal, conceptual works that can be sarcastic, or reflect my anti-imperialist, social democratic views, or they can be morbid. They are not meant for public consumption, and the painting Willy was talking about was one of these. I explained that the painting was a triple self-portrait, and the two guys were both me, dragging a third guy, me, that was dead.... It didn't matter. Willy's mind was set. So I ended up on the cover of *Winnemucca*.

"Later, Willy asked me to do the artwork for the next release of what would later be named *Post to Wire*. He would always send me a test pressing to listen to so I could get a feel for the album, and he ex-

Greg Allen, "Post to Wire." Used by permission of the artist.

plained over the phone that he wanted images that would look like a series of postcards. Always desperate for money, I immediately sent him twenty-five or so pictures of my artwork. The main image he selected was from a painting I'd made from a photograph I took one year while taking the long way around from L.A. to Reno. Halfway between Baker, California, and Death Valley Junction, I passed an abandoned trailer and turned around to investigate… The trailer appeared to be post–World War II by design, which was apropos as it appeared to have been hit by a bomb, with the roof falling in and walls missing. Who could have lived here? Graffiti on the outside of the trailer informed visitors that this was 'The Land of Broken Dreams,' and indeed it was.

"Inside the CD, Willy used a painting I'd done of an elderly, grandfatherly figure holding a smoking pistol and demanding that a school-boy wave the large American flag he's holding more vigorously, commanding him to 'Whup it.' The painting was a statement regarding indoctrination and nationalism, and again Willy surprised me with his choice of work. The image on the back cover is of a thirty-foot-tall cement showgirl that once graced the Primadonna Casino on the main drag in downtown Reno. After the casino closed in 1978 and the building was demolished to make way for the purpose-built Fitzgerald's casino, the girl was relocated to the roof of the Virginia Street Book-store and Arcade.

"Willy hit me up to do their next release as well, and I have to say that after Richmond Fontaine's first three punk recordings, *The Fitzgerald* is by far my very favorite. Willy asked me to paint an image of the Fitzgerald casino, something I was happy to do, except for the fact that I thought the Fitzgerald was incredibly ugly. The facade looked like a strip mall movie theater circa 1982. I don't like to make ugly paintings, and I wasted weeks trying to suck it up and spit it out, to create beauty from a beast. My effort was futile; the damn thing was coming up ugly beyond repair, and my heart just wasn't in it. I decided my only option was to use an image I'd taken in front of the Fitzgerald, but facing the other way. Across the street stood the magnificent Harolds Club. Unfortunately, I had about four days left to do the job, and oil paint takes four days or more to dry. I had to minimize the detail and make the image monochromatic, which is to say one color, like black on white, or in this case brown on white.

"In spite of the fact I'd blown it bad [by missing deadlines], my friend came through for me again and again, providing a vital income stream during some very desperate times. It was a kindness that exacerbated my self-loathing, at least initially, until I finally realized the poor-me routine was getting old and it was time to get over myself.

"The next time I saw Willy was in 2008 when my then-girlfriend Kristine got tickets to see Richmond Fontaine open for John Doe's post-X project. Again, Willy had indirectly been the agent responsible for bringing something good into my life, given I went out to a local bar wearing a Richmond Fontaine shirt Willy sent me. Kristine liked the band and commented on my shirt, with the result being a two-hour

Greg Allen, *The Fitzgerald* cover. Used by permission of the artist.

gabfest outside the bar while her girlfriends periodically emerged to cajole her into rejoining their group.

"I'd abandoned hope of ever seeing my work represent Richmond Fontaine again, and I didn't see much of my friend during the intervening years, though we'd talk by phone from time to time. Last year, though, to my ever-lovin' surprise, Willy contacted me about doing another cover. The band had run its course, he explained, and he wanted my work on the cover as a way of coming full circle. He said he had a photograph he wanted me to paint, and was I up to doing the job? I replied by telling him whatever he wanted I would gladly do. I was about beside myself with gratitude to be given a chance to clean up the mess I'd made a decade earlier on *The Fitzgerald*. Throughout the intervening years, I'd made a fair amount of money from commission work for fans of Richmond Fontaine, and I was indebted to Willy in a big way, though he didn't see it that way. From where I was sitting, he'd provided a vital lifeline during a very difficult period of my life, but for Willy I think he saw it simply as part and parcel of being pals.

"The next time he was in Reno he came by my place and we talked for a while. He told me a story about driving down Highway 95, which runs from Reno to Vegas. Twenty miles outside of Tonopah, Nevada, he saw a horse just a little ways from the highway and he pulled over to check it out. He got out of the car and approached to within a short distance. At a point one would expect the horse to run off, it didn't. Stopping about thirty feet away, from that close vantage point Willy could tell the horse was old, very, very old. It was a dark-brown stallion, covered in scars from battles for supremacy to earn the right mate, and it was clear that it had been defeated by a younger horse and exiled from the herd. How long it had been alone was anybody's guess, but the horse had clearly given up. Now blind in both eyes, which were seeping and badly infected, it was obviously suffering. The horse was coyote bait, and slowly walked in circles awaiting its fate. Willy called the Bureau of Land Management (BLM), and they came out and put it down.

"I painted the image quick as I could and sent him a JPEG, as well as the original painting as soon as it was dry. There was no way I was going to lag getting the job done. Although he'd wanted to pay me for my work, I wouldn't accept it. It was the least I could do. Not long after completing the job, I became dissatisfied with the quality of the finish. I talked to Willy and, fortunately, he hadn't turned it in. I asked him not to submit it yet as I was painting it again, plus I had a painting to use for the back, which was almost resolved, and with a month before the deadline he agreed to hold off.

"I repainted it, this time monochromatic and with the horse larger in the image. I also finished the painting I thought would work for the back artwork. It was from a photo I'd taken at night of hopper and oil tank cars on railroad siding down in Mojave, California, many years ago. I thought both turned out great, my best work yet for Richmond Fontaine. Apropos, since it was the last work I'd do for my friend Willy Vlautin's band. It felt good to finish a project on a high note that I'd started almost fifteen years earlier."

Greg Allen, "Horse." Used by permission of the artist.

And finally...

Although very different artists, Nate Beaty and Greg Allen coincided brilliantly on the final Richmond Fontaine album, *You Can't Go Back If There's Nothing to Go Back To*, which looked back a good deal down well-traveled roads, capturing perfectly the coexisting forces of resilience and ruin. In sepia tones, Allen's painting captures a broken-down mustang by the side of a Nevadan highway, who turns to look at the artist with a terrible determination to live on, despite the almost inevitable darkness it faces in the desert around it. Inside the cover,

Greg Allen, "Desolate Drifter." Used by permission of the artist.

Allen's tattooed "Desolate Drifter" connects to Beaty's drawing of a left
hand holding a Harolds Club glass with a tattoo that reads "I stole more
than I ever gave," referring to the song "Whitey and Me." The tattoo
speaks of failure and limits, of disappointment and regret, and yet
it also functions as a constant, visible reminder of Vlautin's greatest
theme, the need to give to others in life: kindness, help, love, even a
song. In nature as in human culture, whoever is there, wherever you
are, and whatever hand life has dealt you, there is always resilience,
some glimmer of hope, a possible way beyond that moment. As the
very final words of the last album put it, "Do you think someday that
could happen for me? Do you think an easy run will find me?"

Thanks to Greg Allen (http://www.gregallenpainter.com) and Nate Beaty (https://
natebeaty.com) for their support in writing this chapter and their generous permission to use their wonderful images. Thanks again to Willy Vlautin for his comments
on their personal and creative relationships.

Works Cited

Berhorst, Kim. 2002. "Interview: Country-Rockers Talk Gambling, New Album and More." *In Music We Trust.* http://www.inmusicwetrust.com/articles/48h06.html. Accessed October 15, 2016.

Hickey, Dave. 1997. *Air Guitar: Essays on Art & Democracy.* Los Angeles: Art Issues Press.

Rancière, Jacques. 2009. *The Emancipated Spectator.* London: Verso.

Vagner, Kris. 2016. "Stranger than fact: Greg Allen." *newsreview.com*, July 21. https://www.newsreview.com/reno/stranger-than-fact/content?oid=21524178. Accessed September 28, 2017.

Virtual Gallery—Greg Allen. https://www.virtualgallery.com/galleries/greg_allen_a812229.

Vlautin, Willy. 2008. *Northline.* New York: Harper Perennial.

CHAPTER 6

QUIET VIOLENCE IN
WILLY VLAUTIN'S NOVELS

by Lars Erik Larson

It's always too soon to be cold for comfort
To belong to someone inside a locked room
But that always happens
when nobody's looking (nobody's looking).

—"Pauline Hawkins," Drive-By Truckers

Violence as a Failure of the Imagination

In her essay "The Longest War," Rebecca Solnit points out what by now should be obvious: "Violence doesn't have a race, a class, a religion, or a nationality, but it does have a gender" (Solnit 2014: 21). While violence is not exclusive to men, participation in violent crime runs at a male-to-female ratio of 9 to 1 (Eagleman 2011: 158). Alongside the unbearable maleness of violence is a salient misperception about its origins: while popular media amplifies the threat of riots, war, stranger danger, gun massacres, terrorism, and other forms of spectacular savagery, the vast majority of American violence has a very different source. For unlike these public forms of anonymous violence, most of America's brutal acts occur among acquaintances in private spaces often distant from the public eye. In the recent decade of 2005–2015, for example, terrorism in America took the lives of 71, while over 300,000 Americans died from gunshot wounds (Qiu 2015).[1] Almost two-thirds of these gun deaths were suicides, and of the homicides, most of the assailants knew their victims.

Why do we know about so many forms of relatively rare violence, while remaining under-informed about violence's most dominant domestic sources? Barry Glassner's study *The Culture of Fear: Why Americans are Afraid of the Wrong Things* explores the motivations for our misplaced fears. Glassner describes how Americans are awash in unjustified worries over such things as plane crashes, monster moms, black men, and illnesses spreading threats that are often merely metaphorical. He concludes that we fear these statistically un-fearsome things because "immense power and money await those who tap into our moral insecurities and supply us with symbolic substitutes" (Glassner 1999: xxviii). In America's commercial and media infrastructure, fear is easily monetized.

This chapter investigates a more just representation of violence by showing how Willy Vlautin's first decade of novels helps redirect our gaze to the nation's more common forms of brutality. Vlautin casts his eye on closed-door manipulations, beatings, rapes, and killings: private forms of damage that constitute what I refer to as "quiet violence." This pervasive form of American violence is quiet not only in how it gets silenced by the spaces of domestic privacy and media inattention, but also in how victims so often participate in the silence, choosing not to report out of fear, distrust in outside resources, or—most tragic of all—self-blame.[2] Vlautin's novels seek to amplify the sights and sounds of quiet violence, bringing greater awareness to an American epidemic.

The quartet of novels from *The Motel Life* to *The Free* focuses specifically on how this violence affects blue-collar lives in the hardscrabble landscapes of Nevada, Oregon, and Washington. In the deserts, urban backstreets, and small towns of Vlautin's sparsely populated works, brutality is continually muffled by private walls, the anonymity of transit, or the lack of bystanders. His characters navigate lives of lost jobs, insecure resources, unplanned pregnancies, incomplete educations, and ethical compromises, as well as the seductive intoxicants that both numb and exacerbate these problems. Lodged in these conditions, his protagonists are relentlessly vulnerable to quiet violence. Motivating this focus are Vlautin's own fears about what his characters endure. He describes his writing as prompted by what unsettles him: "...I try and look into things that eat at me or worry me and hopefully put some of them to rest" (Vlautin 2006a: 7). In particular, as Vlautin says in a 2002 interview, "I'm scared of violence, of seeing it, of being in it. It haunts me..." (qtd. in Vlautin 2008: 6-7).

From one point of view, the quiet violence in Vlautin's novels—as seen in such characters as Bodie in *Northline* and the various unstable men in *Lean on Pete*—might seem to spring from the problem of male rage. Realist Western narratives have often been constructed around the violence of a brute (for example *McTeague*, *The Big Rock Candy Mountain*, *Blood Meridian*). Such men are depicted as unable to regulate their emotions (especially anger) in socially constructive ways, unable to control their consumption of intoxicants (alcohol, opioids), unable to balance their peevish negativity or shame-driven paranoia with anything close to a concern for others. These characters often feel taunted by things they feel entitled to but find out of their reach (patriarchy, wealth, social stability, respect). And so they let themselves explode, at the expense of those closest to them—most often women and children. They inflict upon the more vulnerable a tattoo of bruises, toxic modes of verbal communication, and even homicidal rage. Avoiding domestic violence would therefore seem a simple matter of steering clear of these hearts of darkness.

Yet as Vlautin and other realist writers show, viewing domestic violence solely at the level of the individual is a mistake, for the systemic sources that generate male rage are central to the problem. As I will explore, Vlautin's novels, as they progress, gradually point to these larger sources (economic instability, limited employment options, housing insecurity, limited resources for coping with change), all of which helps to explain why there are few pure villains among his violent characters. Theirs is neither the mythically regenerative violence of classic Western narratives nor the winsome romances of control depicted in the daytime TV Westerns watched by so many of his characters. Their blind explosions instead express something more quietly desperate: a soul-crushing intensity that leaves victims and abusers saddled with thick layers of shame. Dislocated from American networks of opportunity, wealth, surplus, inheritance, and communal bonding, both the abusers and the survivors suffer alone and invisibly. Through these circumstances, Vlautin offers us a grammar of quiet violence.

The Oregon poet and conscientious objector William Stafford has defined violence as "a failure of the imagination."[3] Vlautin's novels reflect this definition in the attention they draw to the limited choices his characters believe they have, in contrast with the wider array they actually possess. They've been deprived of the chance to imagine more broadly, and this tethers them to the idea that violence is their only form of power—or in the case of victims, their deserved punishment. This narrowing of the imagination is what leads many of the abused to return to their victimizers: the sense that their abusers are all they have in the world (as we see in the case of Carol, the runaway teenager in *The Free*). The all-too-common return of the abused to their abusers shows how acquaintances can be a greater liability than the strangers we are taught to fear. Part of the characters' diminishment of imagination also comes from the isolated locales in which Vlautin situates his impoverished characters; isolation minimizes their networks of help. As William Lombardi points out, in spite of Vlautin's postwestern portrayal of a rhizomatic, networked West, characters' "institutionalized poverty" keeps them from joining this global imaginary: for Lombardi, Vlautin's characters may be "unselfconsciously aware of the world beyond their region but unable to conceive of global intersections in any meaningful way" (Lombardi 2013: 147). And so if redemption comes at all to Vlautin's characters, it is through newly formed habits of exercising their imaginations through such acts as drawing, storytelling, fantasizing, or connecting with the visionary strengths of others who can cultivate their trust.

By illustrating the quiet violence experienced by the working poor, Vlautin's novels form a counternarrative to the dominant media circulation of dramatic public violence. Of course, spectacular violence is indeed a clear and present danger: the violence of terrorism, war, and genocide disrupts nations across the planet, and scholarship wisely explores its effects and affects (see Butler 2010), as well as its language (see Cavarero 2009). Vlautin himself traces ligatures between the small towns of the American West and global wars, as with the veteran Leroy in *The Free*, whose mind had been shattered by a roadside bomb in Iraq—just as in a previous generation his suicidal uncle had been afflicted by the Vietnam War. However, in the current domestic context of the United States, Vlautin devotes far greater attention to the pressing problem of domestic violence—a category that includes physical, emotional, verbal, and sexual abuse by intimate partners.[4]

Sheer numbers can help justify why Vlautin prioritizes domestic violence over public violence. Rebecca Solnit insists that our ignorance of how often abuse happens keeps us from seeing how "quotidian assaults" add up to nothing less than a "pandemic of violence": "[w]e have far more than eighty-seven thousand rapes in this country every year, but each of them is invariably portrayed as an isolated incident" (Solnit 2013: 22, 23, 36). The National Coalition Against Domestic Violence sorts through the data on the ten million who suffer domestic violence annually in America (15 percent of all violent crime) to find that a woman is assaulted or beaten every nine seconds, domestic violence hotlines field nearly 21,000 calls daily, and only one-third of victims receive medical care for their injuries (NCADV 2016).[5] In an article for the *New Yorker*, Rachel Louise Snyder offers a comparison that suggests how domestic violence can be seen as a kind of war against Americans:

> One in every four women is a victim of domestic physical violence at some point in her life, and the Justice Department estimates that three women and one man are killed by their partners every day. (Roughly eighty-five per cent of the victims of domestic violence are women.) Between 2000 and 2006, thirty-two hundred American soldiers were killed; during that period, domestic homicide in the United States claimed ten thousand six hundred lives. (Snyder 2013)

As surprising as this 1:3 ratio between soldiers and citizens may be, Snyder believes the latter figure is an underestimate, as it includes only voluntary reporting. While many believe domestic violence is limited to a certain demographic, Snyder notes its presence across all classes and races. She cites the research of Jacquelyn Campbell, the field's leading expert, who located 20 predictors of domestic violence: "the sole demographic factor Campbell identified was chronic unemployment" (Snyder 2013).[6]

While all social classes may suffer from domestic violence, Vlautin's novels suggest how the underclass, those having the fewest resources and support systems and the most limited awareness of options for redress, suffer most. Today's resources for victims of quiet violence include restraining orders, police intervention, court prosecution, empowerment literature, domestic violence agencies, and shelters.[7] But Vlautin's characters remain at a distance from these, not knowing of—or feeling welcome to—them. Amid this want, Vlautin still provides hope. As Adriana Cavarero notes, a person's vulnerability has a positive side, for just as one is exposed to wounding, one is made equally "vulnerable" to acts of care ("wounding and caring...the singular body is irremediably open to both responses") (Cavarero 2009: 20). Correspondingly, Vlautin's victims receive a great many acts of care, almost always from strangers. Characters learn to rebuild their trust once they abandon their abusive familiars and embrace the intuitive kindness most strangers reliably offer. Such a narrative trajectory reverses the framework of stranger-suspicion arising from so much media attention to anonymous public violence; according to Vlautin's novels—as well as American statistics—it is our familiars we should be suspicious of, rather than people we do not know.

"...I GUESS THAT'S JUST THE WAY OF THINGS"
Frank's Wild Fears in *The Motel Life*

Vlautin's four novels all share this woven strand of domestic abuse. His first novel, *The Motel Life* (2006), is a winter's tale of abandoned brothers absorbing a series of bad choices they've made due to limited guidance and resources. Vlautin directs his readers to the quiet violence of parental manipulation and neglect that leaves the next generation unable to take care of itself.

The troubles of the young narrator, Frank, and his brother, Jerry Lee, arise from family instability during their elementary school years. Under the influence of Reno's culture of gambling, their father loses the family car and several thousand dollars. He tries to flee the debt by bringing his family to a Greyhound station, where his wife talks him into remaining in town: "Look, Jimmy, what kind of people are we if we just run?" (Vlautin 2006: 28). Despite their mother's triumph of conscience, that moment at the bus station sets up in the boys a long-standing reflex of fleeing social and economic responsibilities. Their father's continuing gambling debts eventually lead him to corruption, theft, imprisonment, and abandonment. As their mother explains, "He just couldn't adjust back to us. So he left" (Vlautin 2006: 55). She cautions them not to be angry over such neglect ("it doesn't work, it doesn't help"), so they fill the void with imagination: "...we just make up stories about him, about who we wished he was..." (Vlautin 2006: 56, 126). Their wise, steady, and employed mother might have kept them on track, but her death in their teenage years puts an end to their severely shallow kinship network. Their mother knows nothing of her in-laws, and domestic abuse in her own Montana family makes her prefer that her teenagers live alone rather than with them: "...I left Montana because of them. Because a lot of things happened there. So I'm not gonna send you there even if I could" (Vlautin 2006: 55). Her refusal to name the offenses that would lead to such a preference forms a dark picture of her past home life.

This family fragility leads the brothers to spend their teenage years living a floating life in a series of "on the slide" motels that cannot provide the spatial stability adolescents need. At this point, they have little guidance and oversight in making decisions (both drop out of school, eat fast food and frozen dinners exclusively, and are undiscriminating in choosing jobs). A chain of tragic misfortunes follows: Jerry Lee loses his leg hopping a train, absence of medical insurance depletes their mother's inheritance, and Jerry Lee accidentally runs over a teen. Following their father's impulse for flight, the brothers then enact a series of abandonments that compound their problems: Jerry Lee destroys his car, attempts suicide, and neglects his infections, while Frank's alcoholism leaves him paralyzed and sick. The brothers repeatedly blame their problems on the metaphysics of bad luck, but through the portrayal of family dynamics, Vlautin suggests a likelier source in failures of kinship.

Unfortunately, in *The Motel Life*, the Flannigans' case is not unique, for their Reno peers are left similarly vulnerable by unstable home lives. Frank's childhood friend Tommy Locowane has a mother who left and a father who beats him to the point that he leaves home at age seventeen. Frank connects Tommy's gambling addiction with his own father's, as Tommy has had to borrow thousands of dollars. Frank finds this weakness all too common in a city full of alcoholics gambling away their remaining resources: "[t]here's thousands of them" (Vlautin 2006: 138). Gamblers don't always lose, as Frank finds when he takes up Tommy's advice to wager the money from selling the only thing he inherits from his father (a handmade shotgun) on the Tyson/ Holyfield boxing match, and increases it sevenfold. But when Frank gives a portion to Tommy to pay off his debts, Tommy proves to be as hopeless as his father as he loses it all through further gambling and then disappears. Without home models of restraint, the characters seem helpless in controlling such forces as Tommy's gambling, Frank's whiskey drinking, or the abuse of Tommy's father.

Frank's only girlfriend, the studious Annie James, whose mother ranks high among the minority of abusive women in the novels, provides one further example of the cycle of quiet violence. Her mother's prostitution and methamphetamine use keep Annie's home life deeply unpredictable. As Frank says, "Her mom had an edge most of the time where you never knew what would happen or what she'd say" (Vlautin 2006: 39). This is why her teenaged daughter prefers to live at the orphaned brothers' motels rather than at home. We learn that the mother regularly beats Annie, burns her with a curling iron, steals money Annie had saved for a car, and, at one critical moment, forces her to collaborate in prostitution. Frank comes to shun Annie for the latter, refusing to respond to the weekly letters she writes him when her mother moves them down the freeway to Elko. Just as with Jerry Lee, Annie's experience of quiet violence leads to self-hatred and thoughts of suicide.

In the face of these conditions, and in particular the eventual death of his brother, Frank concludes the novel on a note of resignation: "...I guess that's just the way of things" (Vlautin 2006: 206). However, when it comes to domestic neglect and abuse, the novel shows how Frank's fatalism is misguided. For while Frank's parents fail him,

Vlautin points to other resources and ways of keeping these failures from becoming Frank's sole inheritance. Used car salesman Earl Hurley (whom Frank describes as "probably the greatest man I know") is one of the many father-substitutes populating Vlautin's novels (Vlautin 2006: 76). Despite Earl's own problems with drinking, gambling, and loss (he is a widower), he provides a model of how to stay committed to one's family while taking the time to support others. He gives the brothers vitamins to supplement their junk-food diet and offers sound advice on staying in school, quitting TV, and avoiding demeaning jobs. The fact that the brothers fall short of Earl's advice shows the need for long-term reinforcement that perhaps only a stable home life can provide. Yet the ideas stay with Frank, as does Earl's encouragement, which includes offering to help pay for college, praising Frank's work ethic and career potential ("You could have a future, kid"), and providing strategies for living ("Don't make decisions thinking that you're a low life, make decisions thinking you're a great man, at least a good man"; "Hope is the key") (Vlautin 2006: 151, 156, 81).

If Frank possesses his father's penchant for choosing addictions and flight when under pressure, Vlautin in turn has him cultivate his mother's and Earl's moral conscience for caretaking as a way of defeating the cycle of violence. Haunted by the death his brother inadvertently causes, Frank makes anonymous gifts to the family of the deceased, restores the health of an abused dog, and helps a runaway teen sleeping in the snow by buying him breakfast and a ticket to his Wyoming destination. The boy himself passes along the goodwill through tenderness to Frank's dog, murmuring, "You're a good goddamn dog" (Vlautin 2006: 187). Moreover, Frank is steadfast in taking care of his brother, while his brother talks him into forgiving Annie ("We're fuck-ups Frank, so we're gonna be with people that are fuck-ups.... But that doesn't make them bad people, does it?") (Vlautin 2006: 197). Meanwhile, Annie has avoided replicating her mother's abuse through holding a stable job, taking community college classes, and living independently from her mother in an Elko apartment ("I'm more than relieved she's gone") (Vlautin 2006: 178). If violence is a failure of imagination, Annie has imagined her way toward other options, just as Frank does with his penchant for storytelling and Jerry

Lee with his drawing. Frank's final note that he wrote this memoir (including three dozen of his brother's sketches) in a few weeks in an apartment—rather than a motel—suggests a restoration of domesticity, as well as a partnership of respect through the progress Frank and Annie have made. *The Motel Life* tenders Earl's fatherly advice that "[h]ope is the key" for a generation destabilized by family neglect.

"PLEASE DON'T LET HIM FIND ME"
Escaping from *Northline*

Vlautin's second novel, *Northline* (2008), traces an even more contagious strain of domestic violence. The novel's protagonist is Allison Johnson, a 22-year-old Las Vegas high school dropout, but for the first quarter of the novel, in a vicious echo of Allison's lack of self-possession, the narrator refers to her merely as "the girl." Abandoned by her father when young, taking up with her meth-addicted boyfriend Jimmy Bodie, and later fleeing to live alone in Reno, the alcoholic Allison spends most of the novel's forty-five episodes struggling to escape Jimmy's violent influence. Yet even with 400 miles' distance from her abuser, Allison perversely carries on Jimmy's contagion through her own self-hatred, self-harm, and suicide attempts. The fact that at the end of the novel—even after finding a partner she can trust—Allison is still mistaking strangers for Jimmy testifies to the indelible damage of abuse.

As Solnit notes, "Violence is first of all authoritarian. It begins with this premise: I have the right to control you" (Solnit 2013: 26). Jimmy Bodie feels entitled to such a right, and he has devoted the years of his relationship with Allison to gaining visible control of her body: his skinhead friends tattoo her with white-supremacist icons, and he brutalizes her for embarrassing him with her alcoholic blackouts, lectures her on his hatred of Latinos and African Americans, subjects her to physical imprisonments while he's high on speed, and makes empty promises while begging for forgiveness during his few moments of sobriety. Neil Campbell notes how Jimmy Bodie's abuse enacts a territorial fantasy: "Allison's body is marked by Bodie's world like a terrible cartography of masculine power and mythic fantasy, her skin a map of *his* dreadful preoccupations and obsessive controls over her choices and her movements" (Campbell 2016: 152). The novel's opening chapter has Jimmy subject the intoxicated Allison to a bloody concussion, a steel-toed kick, and a brutal rape, all within the tight silence and space of a casino bathroom. A second chapter, "The Basement," has Jimmy abandoning her naked and handcuffed to his bed for a day as punishment for her "violation" of blacking out—for her over-intoxicated body's lapses in following his control. "I don't feel like being around you today," he hisses, before leaving her to this gothic imprisonment in his cinder-block basement apartment (Vlautin 2008: 8). Once again, such privacy gives Jimmy the quiet and freedom to enact this authoritarian tableau upon his girlfriend of many years.

Jimmy Bodie's name connects him with the site of a famous abandoned gold-mining town 100 miles south of Reno: Bodie State Historic Park. As Patricia Nelson Limerick notes, ghost towns confront us with a "landscape of failure," valuable not for the usual feeding of tourist nostalgia but for learning from past mistakes (Limerick 1994: 27, 46). Not unlike this failed community of extractive labor, Vlautin's violent, white-supremacist character Bodie represents a socioeconomic dead end for the nation. Like his ghost town twin (now one of America's largest), Bodie continues to haunt Allison—and America—with his abortive dreams, antisocial threats, and attitude of isolation.

In spite of Jimmy Bodie's deplorable acts, Vlautin provides him with a sympathetic backstory. As Justin St. Clair observes of his fiction as a whole, "Vlautin has an uncanny knack...for humanizing even the most unlikable of his characters" (St. Clair 2011: 96). Abusive childhoods explain much of the present-day violence in Vlautin's novels, as when Allison discovers Jimmy outside a café chain-smoking away the memory of his father's physical violence, which he and his sister had endured regularly at home (Vlautin 2008: 33). Jimmy's one imagined way out of his violent discontent is his unfocused, feckless dream of escape to an imagined "Northline" of autonomy. Vlautin embeds this migratory dream with an irony: Jimmy feels anger at Latinos who have followed their own dreams to move north to Las Vegas. But Jimmy's resistance to demographic change in his hometown blinds him to this potential kinship, and he even goes so far as to torch a house near his mother's home to keep a Latino family out.

While Jimmy never acts on his Northline dream, a pregnant Allison manages to pursue one herself, fleeing north to Reno to put her baby up for adoption and escape Jimmy's unpredictable brutality. She is also trying to flee the painful memory of her rape by two busboys who had been drawn to her visible vulnerability—a trauma which she did not report because of self-shame (Vlautin 2008: 84). Just as physical violence was contagious, spread from Jimmy's father to Jimmy himself, the now-solitary Allison finds herself duplicating Jimmy's abuse through cutting, cigarette-burning her skin, and attempting suicide. At one point, excessive drinking in bars leads her to passive sex with strangers as a perverse form of self-punishment that culminates in her angry command to be hit (Vlautin 2008: 101–2). It is only through gradually achieving a sense of trust with a handful of Reno locals that she eventually escapes the powerful vortex of self-annihilation created by quiet violence.

Despite the miles now between them, Jimmy's abuse continues through the reach of vaguely threatening letters to coerce contact, in which he deploys shame, blame, jealousy, and, finally, control: "…I guess you know that I know you are in Reno. Now I know where" (Vlautin 2008: 179). A fistfight breaks out one night outside Allison's apartment between two men soon in need of an ambulance, followed by Allison's nightmare discovery of the baby boy she'd given up for adoption being neglected by his parents. Clearly, Jimmy is able to maintain power by keeping his girlfriend in a permanent state of fear and self-blame. In her penultimate moment in the novel, she is in the grip of panic from seeing a stranger who looks like him. She whispers to herself, during a siren's wail, "[p]lease don't let him find me. Please, please, please, please." Her final action is kissing Dan Mahony, the man she learns to trust: "[s]he kissed him with desperation. She kissed him with fear and hope and uncertainty" (Vlautin 2008: 192). Given the negativity of three out of four of those descriptive nouns, it is a melancholy end for a story about the psychological reach and spread of domestic violence.

And yet the "hope" included in this key line does offer a direction for victims; Allison benefits from the presence of influences that expand her imagination's range of options. This begins with her talks with an imagined, advice-giving Paul Newman, drawn from films Allison has watched ("he's probably the greatest thing that ever happened to me") (Vlautin 2008: 135). Neil Campbell reads him as "offering Allison some alternative vision of masculinity, a type of 'new man' in contrast to the brutal misogyny of Jimmy Bodie..." (Campbell 2016: 160). Instead of exploitation, this imagined Newman offers trust and support, including advice about abuse's generational cyclicality and the wisdom of her decision to leave:

> You think your dad was a son of a bitch? Jesus, Jimmy would rival his own, I bet. Imagine being stuck with him for the rest of your life. Imagine him yelling at you and changing the rules on you for forty years. (Vlautin 2008: 182–3)

Newman's increasingly influential presence in Allison's mind could be read as just another example of male mediation overpowering her life. Yet these thoughts are actually Allison's—not Newman's own. They are a projection of her own creative capacity for problem solving, as we see in the above example of her ability to imagine and compare alternate futures. Through this alter ego, we see Allison's growing awareness of a broader spectrum of options, including dodging a cycle that so many women are passively caught in while married to authoritarian men. In addition, these imagined exchanges with Newman lead to her socialization, for as Campbell notes, she "imagines a better life of contact, care, and communion which in other ways gradually emerges in her actual life as brief moments of exchange, gift giving, and reciprocity" (Campbell 2016: 162). Other figures provide Allison with such egalitarian moments, including the overweight Penny, who offers strategies for managing shame (despite her college education, she too confronts body shame and trouble finding a partner); a bartender couple who escorts her safely home after she passes out from intoxication (she reminds them of their runaway girl); the tattoo artist who gives her options for reclaiming her skin from Jimmy's racist icons (she chooses to turn them into black stars); and the customers she serves in her waitress job (each of whom models a functioning mix of strengths and vulnerabilities).

Most promising is her finding in her customer Dan Mahony a mate who seems a match for her vulnerable and "marked" condition. Having suffered one of the rare acts of random, public violence in Vlautin's novels (a severe beating by four strangers who objected to his long hair), Dan slowly returns to the social world through a brave system of routines. This includes a regular breakfast in Allison's casino, the Cal Neva—the name itself a merging of separate states. Like that of Paul Newman, Dan's gentle bearing offers Allison an alternative masculinity, including an interest in socializing with seniors; as Dan explains to her, "old people never bother you, they're generally a lot more decent to you than anyone else" (Vlautin 2008: 146). When an unnerving exchange at a liquor store leaves Dan hiding in bed for two weeks (a condition that parallels the three weeks Allison spent in isolation after her rape by the busboys), he earns this victim's trust: "Dan Mahony couldn't take control of her...he could barely take control of himself. So as she walked, she felt all right with him there" (Vlautin 2008: 178). As an alliance of victims, Dan and Allison exhibit a reciprocity that disrupts the brutality and self-doubt fostered by violence.

Northline's final chapter, "The Strip," ends with a moment of spectacular destruction: the 1999 demolition of the 64-year-old casino Harolds Club—a seven-story building with a highly illustrated façade representative of Reno's original casinos. Hundreds have gathered, craning their necks upward to watch, including Allison and Dan, who talk together in an attempt to make sense of the melancholy event. To a degree, the tableau mirrors the novel's opening scene, where circus aerialists lit by colored spotlights perform high above Jimmy Bodie and "the girl," who, by comparison to the practiced artists, feel small and unskilled (Vlautin 2008: 1). These vertical proxemics reflect the opening couple's underclass status in America: far from the spotlight, down in the darkness. Yet in the novel's end, after a great deal of practice, Allison has a name, power from reciprocation, a place in the sun, and a person she can trust to give "everything to him" without giving up herself (Vlautin 2008: 192).

The building's demolition is an example of spectacular public violence, a staged version of the kind of destruction that regularly draws great media and public attention. But while the demolition is over in "less than a minute," Vlautin emphasizes what endures: Allison's still-haunting memory of Jimmy, as well as the growing bond between Allison and Dan. Vlautin seals this bond through the drama of the couple's closing kiss: "She opened her eyes to see him. She grabbed his hand and kissed him. She kissed him with desperation. She kissed him with fear and hope and uncertainty" (Vlautin 2008: 192). By redirecting our gaze from the spectacle of public violence to the drama of two people recovering from lives of quiet violence, *Northline* achieves what Vlautin's novels collectively attempt: to bring greater attention to the nation's most pressing sources of private suffering.

"But You'll Come Back?"
Travels with Charley

Vlautin's third novel, *Lean on Pete* from 2010, tours America's epidemic of quiet violence through a hapless 15-year-old's exploration of houses along the roads between Portland and Laramie. As with Frank Flannigan, protagonist Charley Thompson suffers both paternal neglect and parental bereavement, and, like Allison, he must learn to escape the pull of those who would manipulate him. But this time Vlautin adds a centrifugal extension of his narrative to encompass a broader look at the domestic West. Charley is a novel-length version of the Wyoming-bound runaway boy in *The Motel Life*, helped by many acts of kindness (like Frank), but mostly having to help himself to survive. Between the opening page's Polaroid of his aunt Margy Thompson and the closing chapter's reunion with her in Wyoming, Charley spends a peripatetic summer witnessing not only his own family's dissolving but also the cruelties taking place in many other households.

The novel's only positive depiction of a home comes late in the book, when Charley is on the road in Denver and is invited to dinner at a fellow worker's home. Santiago is part of a two-parent family in a home filled with laughter, as well as pictures displayed on the walls—something Charley finds missing in most of the barren homes he sees. When Charley finds Santiago lighting a candle to honor his deceased mother and asks, "Was she nice?" he's told, "She was my mother. Of course she was nice," with a confidence that shows Charley how radically different Santiago's home life has been (Vlautin 2010: 255).

Charley's own mother left him as an infant, having felt done with his father after just a few years together. As Charley's father Ray tries to reassure him, one drunken night,

> She ain't called or sent a card but I know deep down she loves you. She really does. She's just fucked-up in the head and likes to party too much. I know it's hard to hear, but it's a good thing she's gone. I ain't shit but I like being here with you. (Vlautin 2010: 173)

Despite Ray's stated enjoyment of Charley's company, he treats his son more like a roommate than a dependent. After pulling up stakes and moving to Portland (one of a string of unexpected moves by the bridge-burning father), Ray doesn't come home for days, and leaves Charley little food and money on which to get by. While Charley's healthy habit of jogging appears to serve his football ambitions, we later learn how the exhaustion helps distance him from memories, including seeing his dad doing drugs and having sex, losing control from intoxication, and other brutalities: "I'd seen my dad hit my aunt in the face and call her names when all she did was tell him to come back when he wasn't so drunk and mean. I'd seen him wreck her car and then abandon it" (Vlautin 2010: 121). Charley notes how running helps him become "so tired I couldn't think about anything like that. It took a long time. It always takes a long time, but it always works" (Vlautin 2010: 121). Just as running helps Charley forget the quiet violence of his past, football provides an escape from the self-interested people that surround him, for in that activity "…you're part of a team. Everyone helps everyone else" (Vlautin 2010: 74).

But Charley spends most of the summer without such cooperation, confronting instead the violent death of his father at the hands of the jealous husband of a woman he had been dating. The man throws Ray through his house's picture window, leading to an injury that becomes fatal after a few days in the hospital. Before Ray succumbs, the symbolically gaping hole in their home frightens Charley into living at the nearby racetrack where he works. When he learns of his father's death, he responds in the same way he has dealt with most of the violence in his life: with self-consuming silence.

At the heart of *Lean on Pete* is the exploitation and abuse of horses in America's downsized racing culture, but Vlautin brings in the domestic theme through the "family" Charley tries to create through his connection to an abused horse. He sees how the owner of Lean on Pete, Del Montgomery, manipulates the horse's off-track races by using various drugs and traumatizing strategies, and mistreats him with too-frequent races and even beatings. Charley concludes that "[i]t seems like Pete's in prison," and so takes it upon himself to liberate him when he hears Del plans to have the horse killed (Vlautin 2010: 128). Stealing Del's truck and trailer, Charley escapes with Pete through eastern Oregon before breaking down. He finds himself using Pete as his only confidante, and among the many stories he tells the horse is about the time Ray left him with a distant friend for a week, a caretaker who—just like Ray—was neglectful and even left him alone for days. This anecdote leads Charley to swear he will care for Pete: "I just have to figure out how to make us money. I'll make sure you're alright so don't worry about that. We're a family now" (Vlautin 2010: 175). But this proves too immense a responsibility for a 15-year-old trying to be a better father than his father; while managing to keep them both fed and hydrated in the desert summer, he cannot fully comfort the long-traumatized horse, doesn't have the resources to keep the truck functioning, and ultimately watches the horse die when he bolts into traffic. In spite of his promise not to abandon Pete, he does this when the accident happens, and is thereafter plagued with nightmares and guilt for this duplication of his parents' caretaking failures.

While conditions are grim for both Charley's family and the community of low-end racehorses, domestic life is not tremendously better in the rest of the West either, as Charley sees from his travels. The manipulative horse owner Del lives in what Charley calls "the worst house I've ever been in"—a mess of neglect, hoarding, and decay (including the stench of a rotting dog) (Vlautin 2010: 102). On the road, Charley crawls into a great many people's homes to quench his thirst and find food, and notices (through this process of klepto-anthropology) how messy so many homes are, feeling particular sadness that so few have pictures on the walls. He meets two hard-drinking soldiers on leave from Iraq who inhabit a trailer and speak of mutual atrocities at the front. They have dinner at the house of a neighbor, Mr. Kendall, served by his obese granddaughter, Laurie, at which Kendall shames Laurie for her weight and Laurie shames him for drinking ("You get ugly when you drink beer") (Vlautin 2010: 167). She knows it will take him many days to recover from the night's hard drinking. When Charley wonders why she stays, cooking and cleaning for her abusive grandfather, her reasoning is, "I don't know where else to go" (Vlautin 2010: 168). In suburban Boise, Charley is sent to a group home for juveniles after being caught stealing. The home is run by an overweight couple who are as addicted to TV as they are to food. This tour shows the homeless Charley that even the housed suffer deep emotional vulnerabilities. Santiago's family remains the only exception.

A number of people along the way seem to be using their vehicles as precarious homes. A traveling Jehovah's Witness assaults the hitchhiking Charley with heavy-handed sermons. A hoarder in Boise has his car so stuffed with trash he can hardly bring himself to part with that he has to call for Charley's help when it jams him in his seat. A 16-year-old girl flees her home in Oregon out of aversion to her mom's boyfriend, and is living as if "adopted" by a couple on their way to Arizona. And a drunk man Charley meets in Denver lives in a camper truck that is unsafe for Charley, since he beats him several times, when awakened amid intoxicated delusions, and steals his earnings. This spectrum of sorrow convinces Charley that a homeless teen's goal should be not to establish oneself in any old home, but rather the *right* home.

Vlautin ends this domestic tour with what promises to be such a place, as he finds his newly divorced aunt in a small apartment in Laramie, Wyoming. Bloat and sadness keep her from matching her image in the old Polaroid, but she is genuinely happy to welcome her nephew into her life. She lives a steady and employed life as a librarian, and she lacks a TV and attraction to other such addictions. In the book's final line, when the cautious Charley asks if she'll return after her day at work ("But you'll come back?"), her reassurance reflects a too-rare commitment in the homes of the West. But it is a commitment that reflects Vlautin's faith, drawn from the novel's epigraph and taken from Steinbeck's *East of Eden*: "It is true that we are weak and sick and ugly and quarrelsome but if that is all we ever were, we would millenniums ago have disappeared from the face of the earth." While Vlautin's road book shows how our "weak and sick and ugly and quarrelsome" habits are manifest in the physical and emotional violence of homes (and stables), Charley's travels at least give a glimpse of the ethic of care that keeps us from disappearing altogether.

"I STARTED OPENING MY EYES TO THINGS"
The Free and the Home of the Brave

Just as *Lean on Pete* expands Vlautin's social canvas, from the case studies of *The Motel Life* and *Northline* to the narrative sprawl of characters across the region, his 2014 novel *The Free* continues the expansion. Vlautin presents a constellation of sympathetic protagonists grappling with quiet violence in a Washington town's failing neighborhoods—though the setting could stand in for any small town in recession-era America.

With this novel, Vlautin is less interested in representing individual abusers and abuse than he is in considering the larger motivators of domestic violence. Slavoj Žižek has called for such a strategy in his "sideways reflections" on violence, arguing that we too often focus on local events—violence committed by a "clearly identifiable agent"—when we should "perceive the contours of the background which generates such outbursts" (Žižek 2008: 1). Žižek explains that we need to probe the invisible origins of *systemic* violence before we can understand individual acts—which tend to monopolize our attention due to their visibility (Žižek 2008: 12). For example, zeroing in on a youth riot or a car bombing might sell news but tends to distract from the larger sources motivating the tension. Among the risks Žižek identifies in overlooking larger systems of violence: even those trying to reduce violence can end up unknowingly participating in it. In looking at systems of violence—as opposed to individual acts—Žižek finds that they are often state-founded, a pattern he shows throughout his study by exploring violence within capitalist and communist systems.

Given how *The Free* aims to explore such systemic origins, the novel ends up being Vlautin's most overtly political work. In contrast with characters in his previous narratives, the individuals in this novel are less likely to flee their mistakes or brutalizers, instead anchoring themselves to work toward a richer understanding of their situation. While they reflexively blame themselves for misfortunes, Vlautin parallels Žižek in bringing them toward awareness of broader culprits. They come to recognize their unequal participation in the military (the poor are most often manipulated into serving). They experience inadequate support for medical care (in these years before the Affordable Care Act). And they recognize how pay scales favor those with inherited wealth, making it necessary those without it to work multiple jobs. While "freedom" is usually regarded positively in the American context, Vlautin's novel of the overworked poor locates freedom's disadvantages and even its violence—particularly when one is "free" from networks of support and care.

The novel's ensemble of characters forms a circle of concern (both private and professional) around bomb-damaged Iraq veteran Leroy Kervin. In a book of awakenings, the opening chapter brings Leroy to consciousness and clarity for the first time since experiencing a brain-damaging explosion seven years earlier. Yet this promising awakening ("[w]as he finally free?") turns into a moment of panic at his fragility ("[w]as this all his life was?"), and seizes this "window" for suicide rather than redemption (Vlautin 2014: 1, 3). This he attempts by throwing himself on a picket fence gate—that boundary-drawing symbol of domestic Americana. Leroy's suicide attempt brings together the novel's narrative strands, involving his mother, Darla; his girlfriend, Jeanette; his nurse, Pauline Hawkins, and her various other patients; his group home's overworked night manager, Freddie McCall (who slept through the suicide attempt); and Leroy's own science-fiction-influenced nightmares.

Vlautin features these protagonists in a moment in their lives when most start making good decisions, responding with calm decency and generosity rather than outbursts of anger or violence. Mother Darla faithfully shows up to the hospital to read to her unconscious son the science fiction stories he loves; Pauline Hawkins not only takes care of the spectrum of her patients with equanimity but also her abusive, needy, mentally ill father; and Freddie patiently locates solutions for the many responsibilities of his overextended life. Critic Marisa Silver faults the book for the homogeneity of the characters' responses: "…Vlautin's refusal to let the characters react with anything but plain-spoken equanimity begins to feel like idealism, and it has the effect of flattening the narrative" (Silver 2014). However, in light of Vlautin's previous novels, readers might see this equanimity as a kind of evolution away from the blind, violent explosions of past narratives, toward the emotional control that leads to more constructive ends.

One exception to this set of people acting through the better angels of their natures is Pauline's patient Carol (or "Jo" as her abusers rename her), a deeply vulnerable teenage runaway who resembles Vlautin's earlier protagonists. Having been rejected by her born-again family, Carol takes up with a young group of homeless Seattle men who manipulate her into sex while neglecting her emotional and medical needs. Pauline identifies with how Carol felt at her age ("[a]lone and voiceless and unwanted and worthless"), and rescues her multiple times, but Carol returns to her abusers with the haunting justification that "[t]hey're the only people I know" (Vlautin 2014: 91, 132). Pauline reasons with her to cultivate independence as a way to avoid abuse: "Look, I know you're alone but you have to learn how to be alright alone. If you don't you'll end up in situations like you're in, and you don't deserve that" (Vlautin 2014: 155). But the girl's shame-driven paranoia keeps her from freeing herself from her own victimizers, and a distraught Pauline loses her in the crowd of thousands of people experiencing homelessness in Seattle. Through Pauline's patient and brave concern for Carol, Vlautin reveals that her abuse derives not from her choices but from hypocritical religion, opportunistic patriarchy, and a social network too thin to keep people like Carol from falling through.

Other characters similarly recognize the systemic origins of their troubles. Despite his multiple jobs, night manager Freddie cannot pay the medical bills for his uninsured daughter's condition, and has to sell the house that has been in his family for three generations. Freddie knows that his former boss at the paint store where he worked had planned to hand over the business to him as a reward for his work ethic, but the boss's wife convinced her husband to pass the business to his nonworking son instead (Vlautin 2014: 11). Through this, Freddie understands how American wealth is determined less by meritocracy than by the random forces of inheritance.[8] But it is only when his former wife finds she has to hand over their kids to his custody to keep them safe from the explosive anger of her new husband that he realizes he can be a good father without having enough money or space. As he comes to recognize, "I liked being a dad, more than anything else maybe" (Vlautin 2014: 186). After selling his house, Freddie has only his job, kids, and a broken-down car, and so for a time the family may have to live a motel life. But his skill at caretaking—a talent he has exercised for years—will keep him from perpetuating the cycle of American domestic abuse. Freddie credits taking care of Leroy with shifting his fascination with violence toward a more sober understanding of its implications. As he says to Leroy's mother, "I started opening my eyes to things" (Vlautin 2014: 186).

The same can be said for Pauline Hawkins, who achieves a healthier relationship with her dependent father, opens her emotional walls to a companion for the first time in years, and changes jobs to work with children as a school nurse to avoid the unhealthy compassion fatigue and night-shift hours of her years of hospital work. With her understanding of her father's mental illness, Pauline empathizes with her mother's decision to leave her and her father when she was five. Pauline resolves not to be angered by this domestic rejection and, in telling this to Carol, she hopes the runaway will find similar strength in doing the same (Vlautin 2014: 228).

Pauline's character would go on to inspire a musical tribute on the Drive-By Truckers' 2014 album *English Oceans*. The song ("Pauline Hawkins") echoes the invisibility of many such characters in Vlautin's novels: "It's always too soon to be cold for comfort/To belong to someone inside a locked room/But that always happens when nobody's looking (nobody's looking)." The fact that so many of Vlautin's socially unseen characters manage to escape the control of others inside "a locked room" speaks to Vlautin's trust in plural domestic possibilities—for them and for America. Ultimately, the small-town land of *The Free* is peopled by survivors who, in figuring out how to take care of others, learn at last to take care of themselves. Above all, they are aided by having their eyes opened to the systemic causes—as opposed to the merely personal and local causes—of the misfortunes and violence that beset their lives.

If Vlautin's novels rarely depict the spectacular acts of terrorism, shooting rampages, and other devastations most feared by the public, they don't deny that these events happen. But his works suggest that we invest our attention in sources of violence that are far more pervasive: recession-era America's environments of toxic stress, mean streets where the vulnerable are taken advantage of, domestic pockets where patriarchy is reinforced by physical threats, and communities where violence is passed down from generation to generation, leading to soul-shriveling shame. If violence involves a failure of imagination, then it makes sense for authors to enlist the novel form to help stretch our minds to grasp a broader range of choices. As America reels from the latest headline-hogging public devastations, Vlautin's works steadily report on how the most fearsome American tragedies are happening quietly in our unhomely private spaces.

Notes

1. As Margot Sanger-Katz reports, annual deaths from terrorism in the United States have only risen above fifty-two times since 1970 (because of 9/11 and the Oklahoma City bombing), and during most of the timespan the number has remained in the single digits. Moreover, globally, "deaths from terrorism appear to be declining, not rising" (Sanger-Katz 2016).

2. Taking rape as an example (a crime in which 85 percent of perpetrators are acquainted with their victims), Jon Krakauer notes how "[r]ape is the most underreported serious crime in the nation. Carefully conducted studies consistently indicate that at least 80 percent of rapes are never disclosed to law enforcement agencies" (Krakauer 2015: 129, 123). What compounds the tragedy of this underreporting is research suggesting that 90 percent of rapes are committed by serial offenders (Krakauer 2015: 136).

3. While the quotation "violence is a failure of the imagination" has been attributed to William Stafford, we can see him directing the idea specifically at the violence of war in the 2003 edited collection *Every War Has Two Losers*; see pp. 142 and 153.

4. While I seek here to distinguish terrorism from quiet violence, arguably domestic violence is itself a form of terrorism at a smaller scale; both categories involve an attempt to motivate through a power-based threat of bodily harm.

5. The Center for Disease Control and Prevention offers further statistics on what they categorize as "Intimate Partner Violence": http://www.cdc.gov/violence prevention/intimatepartnerviolence/datasources.html.

6. Jacqueline Campbell's research found that the risk of abuse turning into homicide has a timeline pattern, "spiking when a victim attempted to leave an abuser, after a couple split, dipped slightly for the next nine months, and dropped significantly after a year" (Snyder 2013).

7. Interestingly, concerning one resource that Vlautin's characters do not draw upon—the shelter—Snyder notes how the problem with this disruptive solution is "the burden of the change falls on the victim, not the perpetrator" (Snyder 2013). An alternative to this inadvertent punishing of the victim, Snyder reports, is the use of police GPS to keep domestic violence offenders from proximity with victims. Such a resource would reduce the constant dread felt by stalked women like Allison Johnson in *Northline*.

8. Coincidentally, Freddie's recognition that capitalism largely rewards those with inherited wealth rather than merit forms the central lesson in a monumental economic study published in the same year as Vlautin's novel: Thomas Piketty's *Capital in the Twenty-First Century*.

Works Cited

Butler, Judith. 2010. *Frames of War: When Is Life Grievable?* London: Verso.

Campbell, Neil. 2016. *Affective Critical Regionality*. London: Rowman & Littlefield.

Cavarero, Adriana. 2009. *Horrorism: Naming Contemporary Violence*, translated by William McCuaig. New York: Columbia University Press.

Eagleman, David. 2011. *Incognito: The Secret Lives of the Brain*. New York: Vintage.

Glassner, Barry. 1999. *The Culture of Fear: Why Americans Are Afraid of the Wrong Things*. New York: Basic.

Krakauer, Jon. 2015. *Missoula: Rape and the Justice System in a College Town*. New York: Penguin Random House.

Limerick, Patricia Nelson. 1994. "Haunted by Rhyolite: Learning from the Landscape of Failure." In *The Big Empty: Essays on Western Landscapes as Narrative*, edited by Leonard Engel, 27–47. Albuquerque: University of New Mexico Press.

Lombardi, William V. 2013. "It All Comes Together in…Reno? Confronting the Postwestern Geographic Imaginary in Willy Vlautin's *The Motel Life*." *Western American Literature* 48 (1 and 2) (Spring and Summer): 141–162.

National Coalition Against Domestic Violence (NCADV). 2016. "Statistics." http://ncadv.org/learn-more/statistics. Accessed December 2016.

Piketty, Thomas. 2014. *Capital in the Twenty-First Century*. Translated by Arthur Goldhammer. Cambridge, MA: Belknap Press.

Qiu, Linda. 2015. "Fact-checking a Comparison of Gun Deaths and Terrorism Deaths." *Politifact*, Oct. 5. http://www.politifact.com/truth-o-meter/statements/2015/oct/05/viral-image/fact-checking-comparison-gun-deaths-and-terrorism-/. Accessed November 2016.

Sanger-Katz, Margot. 2016. "Is Terrorism Getting Worse? In the West, Yes. In the World, No." *New York Times*, Aug. 16. http://www.nytimes.com/2016/08/16/upshot/is-terrorism-getting-worse-in-the-west-yes-in-the-world-no.html. Accessed January 2017.

Silver, Marisa. 2014. "The Walls are Closing In." *New York Times Book Review*, March 23. https://www.nytimes.com/2014/03/23/books/review/the-free-by-willy-vlautin .html?_r=0. Accessed November 2016.

Snyder, Rachel Louise. 2013. "A Raised Hand." *The New Yorker*, July 22. http://www .newyorker.com/magazine/2013/07/22/a-raised-hand. Accessed November 2016.

Solnit, Rebecca. 2014. "The Longest War." In *Men Explain Things to Me,* 19–38. Chicago: Haymarket.

Stafford, William. 2003. *Every War Has Two Losers: William Stafford on Peace and War*, edited by Kim Stafford. Minneapolis: Milkweed.

St. Clair, Justin. 2011. "Soundtracking the Novel: Willy Vlautin's *Northline* as Filmic Audiobook." In *Audiobooks, Literature, and Sound Studies*, edited by Matthew Rubery, 92–106. New York: Routledge.

Vlautin, Willy. 2006. *The Motel Life*. New York: Harper.

———. 2006a. "A Conversation with Willy Vlautin." In *The Motel Life,* 2–13. New York: Harper.

———. 2008. *Northline*. New York: Harper.

———. 2010. *Lean on Pete*. New York: Harper.

———. 2014. *The Free*. New York: Harper.

Žižek, Slavoj. 2008. *Violence: Six Sideways Reflections*. New York: Picador.

CHAPTER 7

POSTWESTERN ELSEWHERES

Mobility and Its Discontents in Willy Vlautin's *Lean on Pete*

by William V. Lombardi

Why Not Here

Willy Vlautin's ongoing fascination with landscape and the dispossessed positions his work as pivotal to postwestern studies, which began with Susan Kollin's edited collection, *Postwestern Cultures: Literature, Theory, Space* (2007). His novels bring into focus the proximal, substantial presence of class disparity in contemporary American life. As such, Vlautin's unyielding focus on minor tragedies, which by their very intimacy and particular locality seem to partition them from narratives of global inequity, forges an unmistakable link to "Others" worldwide. At the heart of Vlautin's work is a message of compassion across differences that exceeds the traditional parameters of the U.S. West as a cultural space. Still, Vlautin's novels illuminate a decidedly Western example of collective vulnerability and insistent worlding among his characters—not just being in the world as Heidegger suggests, but becoming visible or legible when they are otherwise forgotten or obscured. At present, interdisciplinary criticism recognizes unequally shared risk and the problems of visibility as key aesthetic and structural attributes of recent fiction written in response to, and as a result of, transnational precarity under late globalization.[1]

The class-specific crises that Vlautin depicts are small in the grand scheme of Ulrich Beck's sense of "risk society"—for example, when viewed independently—yet they are infinitely repeatable in their ubiquity across gender, race, and culture. The junkies dreaming of Mexico in *The Free* (2014); two veterans drinking themselves into a stupor of forgetfulness in the middle of the Great Basin in *Lean on Pete* (2010); the overt racism of *Northline* (2008); and even the train, as a symbol of regional and global connection, in *The Motel Life* (2006): each serves to remind Vlautin's readers that all spaces and predicaments preclude social or geocultural isolation, much as the language of critical regionalism, as forwarded by Neil Campbell and others, contends. Even seemingly provincial lives, Vlautin reminds us, are formed of imaginative as well as tangible planetary connections to people, things, problems, and ideas outside of our home places. Finally, these inter- or intra-actions subvert any supposed white hegemony attached to older narratives of masculine Western triumphalism. They form a rupture with bygone narratives of the U.S. West, the culture and landscape of which had been the purview of a singular and specific white, heteronormative desire. In effect, Vlautin's writing characterizes nuances of space and culture specific to writing of the late twentieth and early twenty-first centuries, in which inside and outside, real and imagined, and here and there have evolved from expressions of knowability into problems of being and finally into expressions of becoming. All told, Vlautin and his contemporaries express postwestern culture and geography in the language of the fluid and the blurred.[2]

Disenfranchisement is the central theme of Vlautin's body of work to this point. His people are those who are voiceless, overlooked, and at odds with themselves. Their emplacement is so unstable that mobility—coerced or otherwise—haunts their way of life. In this sense, Vlautin's novels contribute to a fundamental and evolving narrative of the U.S. West, where movement or the specter of it, by choice or circumstance and at their basest or most idealistic, underlie the Western master plot. The West as backdrop for such movement has consistently but not rigidly signified as *elsewhere*, as that *other place where things happen*; and, more importantly for Vlautin's people, it is the corollary: *not here*. In this way, the West-as-elsewhere connotes both utopian *and* speculative essences, wherein the utopian *no place* signifies an alternate geography but is also a means for understanding how the world works.[3] As I deploy the term "postwestern elsewheres" in this study of Vlautin's *Lean on Pete*, I mean those literal, figurative, or symbolic spaces that signify the established tropes of reinvention, escape, or retreat into the Western wilds, as received and enhanced by contemporary literature of the U.S. West since 1989.[4] *Elsewhere* has also, though, signaled exclusion, removal, or banishment to society's Others. The West has been the site of America's ugliest displacements. Always, deferral subtends the nature and character of escape, and so Vlautin's elsewheres maintain the traditional vibrancy, sacral nature, and utopic character of the West's other spaces, which are inherent to the escape narrative but complicate them in ways specific to his characters' class and the twenty-first-century West. I contend that imagining an elsewhere today is not solely an act of escapism but also an attempt to make sense of the world; or, more precisely, to imagine a world that makes sense (Tally 2013: xi). Robert T. Tally Jr. argues that we lack the collective imagination to act out this kind of "radical alterity" (2013: vii), but Vlautin's novels provide ample proof of individuals who, in their dreaming, exert the force of a deeply human everyday resilience that produces entire worlds they can at least *imaginatively, conditionally* inhabit with reasonable security.[5] In Vlautin's novels, even the West's most desperate people retain a belief in a separate, more hopeful space that is essential to their survival.

Elsewheres specific to the postwest, then, typified by those found in *Lean on Pete*, present us with a paradox of spatialized insecurity: for many, routes of relation are not equivalent to escape routes. On one hand, Vlautin's work insists on acknowledging the interconnectivity of the world's places and people, thus emphatically resisting disjunction; on the other, it forcefully underscores the desire to get away from, outrun, and disentangle oneself from immanent circumstances in the interest of survival. His characters' geographic and imaginative connections are thus elementally fraught. At this intersection lies the problem of self-preservation weighed against the promise of compassion. In a strategic, generalizable way, elsewheres of the postwest intend to support self-interest *and* compassion. Vlautin's postwestern elsewheres, in particular, indicate a latent logic of solidarity, in which escape from the circumstances of the present indicates a basic animal survival attuned to belonging, quite the opposite of the former meaning of *elsewhere* as the site of *retreat*. In this light, an articulation of the kind of space into which Vlautin's people seek to escape is crucial to realizing the nature and composition of postwestern geography and experience. The postwestern elsewhere is a field of self-preservation achieved *in and through* the desire for, and via acts of, compassion. It is equally a matter of *getting away from* and *getting back to*.

ELSEWHERES

In classic accounts, the Western lands were a certain but ineffable site toward which U.S. citizens were "impelled by the spirit of adventure and the temptations of gain," as Edwin Bryant put it in his overland narrative of 1848 (2001: 9). Even though practical intelligence regarding the Western lands was scarce in Bryant's day, as a singular and symbolic space the meaning of West-as-elsewhere was clear to the popular white imagination of the time. In the post-frontier literature of the late-nineteenth- and early-twentieth-century New West that followed, elsewhere served to valorize that past. "Virgin land" was the source of and proving ground for white masculinity, in much the same vein as in contemporaneous imperial romances set in Africa, India, or other hinterlands of the British empire operated in the interests of Mary Louise Pratt's "seeing man," in what John McClure calls the "late imperial romance" (McClure 1994).[6] Increasingly, though, the productions of the New West leading up to and in the three decades following World War II had, even when they were regularly steeped in nostalgia for that clean, direct, exceptionalism narrative, subverted the frontier mythos through narratives particular to race, gender, and class.[7] These late New Western narratives formed the basis for postwestern elsewheres expressed in contemporary literature.[8] While such deviations, substitutions, and heterodoxy undermined all traditional associations with the West's most cherished tropes, they nonetheless stabilized, even if indirectly, a singular geographic imaginary.

The line between this later New West and the postwest is less easily drawn. As Nina Baym explains, the difference between the Old West and the point of dissent at which the New West arrived was a movement from telling one story—that of triumphant white masculinity in the interests of nationalism—to telling the West's many stories (2006: 816-20). In effect, Western narrative had moved from an epistemological dominant to an ontological one (McHale 1986). That is, in characterizing New Western texts, we can locate a transformation from valorizing to subverting. As such, the New West as an aesthetic and cultural phenomenon participated in the decentering projects of postmodernism and postcolonialism at large.[9] New Westerns pluralized Western culture. This landscape became less a wilderness of mountains to conquer than the dangerous and high-stakes space of the subaltern's active insistence of selfhood. However, the postwest falls in that aesthetic period *after* this postmodern moment: post-postmodern, supermodern, cosmodern—call it what you will.[10] It falls along the axes of class, race, and gender suggested by leading Western scholars who situate the postwest among such critical movements as regionalism, globalism, and late feminism, but also adjacent to the aesthetics of speculative realism, to which Ramon Saldivar has recently drawn critical attention.[11] The postwest aligns most starkly with a post-racial, chthonic aesthetic articulated by Saldivar, Donna J. Haraway, Christian Moraru, and others, in which such representational projects collectively mark vast, but guarded solidarities characterized by complex relationships to strategic essentialism, trauma, and vulnerability.[12] In this regard, postwestern geography is a "paradoxically dynamic yet fixed space" (Tally 2011: vii). While much has been said about the postwest and "routes" or "relation," these critical terms still imply a legible and deliberate difference—parts distinct from each other constituting a whole—even as they address an accelerated connectivity. Thus, "routes" and "relation" rightly contend with the *inter*-actions of postmodernity in late New Western texts rather than with the strategic concerns and alliances articulated in postwesterns that respond to the problems of connection under twenty-first-century conditions. To my mind, the postwest, as it appears in Vlautin's work, contends with the optimistic space of entanglement in the sense that Karen Barad outlines, or that is manifested in Jane Bennett's expression of "vibrant matter." Thinking through things in relation, to borrow the language of critical regionalism, denotes copresence and contiguousness. However, "relation" does not ask us to collapse difference in the manner of Barad's agential realism or Bennett's vital materiality; entanglement connotes enmeshment and *mutual* constitution through meaning and materiality, or, in Bennett's terms, "distributive agency" or "confederation" (2010: 21). Entanglement in Vlautin's work, and in postwesterns generally, emphasizes how and to what or whom one is responsible. In effect, by their entangled nature, postwesterns address the mutual—if uneven—constitution of meaning surrounding things, ideas, nonhumans and humans alike, such that to care for another is to preserve oneself. Such entanglements signify a condition or worldview that supersedes relation. In other words, a postwest theorized as the result of *entanglements* rather than *relations* amends Edward W. Soja's concept of the real-and-imagined at the end of the twentieth and the beginning of the twenty-first century.[13] That is, to expose a particularly postwestern geography is to do the work of revealing its entanglements—of exposing the *responsibilities* of interdependency—even as our attention is drawn toward spaces that appear by turns either intimate, individual, or far away.

"Since It Was a Real House…"/"The House Scares Me"

It is no surprise that *Lean on Pete*, at face value the story of a boy escaping a troubled life in the city with a stolen horse, begins by accentuating an absent presence, and that the absent presence guiding his life acts as an antidote to the fear surrounding the instability of his material circumstances.[14] The boy, Charley Thompson, lives hand-to-mouth with his father Ray, moving from town to town across the Pacific Northwest, following job positions for unskilled laborers and outrunning angry women and their equally outraged husbands. Finally, upon Ray's death, Charley steals the racehorse Lean on Pete before the horse can be put down by its heartless owner. Charley has been caring for Pete, and he has forged a bond with him. Together they perform a contemporary version of "lighting out for the territories," but in reverse. Rather than running from Widow Douglas and Miss Watson as Huckleberry Finn had, Charley and Pete run toward Charley's aunt, who lives a quiet life in Wyoming. On the surface, a summary of *Lean on Pete* forecasts the traditional language of escape for a certain order of transient Americans. Yet these escapes belong to Ray, much as Huck had been at the mercy of Pap, for example, or Sarty's family had fled Abner's crimes in Faulkner's "Barn Burning," or Bruce Mason's life had been prey to Bo's schemes and dissatisfactions in Wallace Stegner's *The Big Rock Candy Mountain.*

Charley's private *elsewhere*, that of his waking reveries, is quite the contrary. From the moment he awakens, Charley allays his sense of desperate isolation by dreaming his way into a Polaroid that he keeps taped beside his bed, taken of him and his aunt beside a river in Wyoming. The elements contained in this banal image emblematize the entirety of Charley's desire: a place far away from where he is now—trapped in his father's wanderings—and a person with whom he can find happiness and safety—his Aunt Margy. Charley's escape is toward a domestic situation symbolized by the smiling figure of his aunt; his dream survives on the promise of a conventional life. Aunt Margy's presence in his life is powerful, hopeful, and sustaining, and yet it is precisely and only oneiric, preserved entirely in the photograph. Her absence, then, looms large in his life and throughout the novel, doubling as both a vacancy and the hope for something better. It allows him to believe he might someday live a settled existence. The inside and outside of Charley's predicament have been collapsed; elsewhere and here meet in the photograph, wherein the landscape of his desire overlaps with his day-to-day life. In practice, the precarity of his home life serves only to mandate the necessity of such a place as during an endless summer, on a river in Wyoming, with his aunt's arm around him. Though he lives in Portland, Wyoming is constantly, palpably near, both an agony and a private joy.

The paradoxically material absences contained in the world of the photo Charley holds so dear—a mother figure, a wild space, a smile—are contrasted by Vlautin with the transience and sparseness of Charley's lived experience. Charley, who narrates his own story, explains, "My dad and I had just moved to Portland, Oregon...We didn't know anybody...We brought our kitchen table and four chairs, dishes and pots and pans, our clothes and TV, and my dad's bed. We left all the rest" (Vlautin 2010: 1). Notable first because Vlautin gives Charley his own voice, the juxtaposition of the warmth of the photo with the cold composition of their new home, coupled with the Thompsons' dark mobility, casts a pall over Charley's story. Charley's *here* marks him as one of mobility's discontented. Leaving behind "all the rest" accesses old Western traditions, and yet, the fact that Vlautin, through Charley, is attentive to even the minimal trappings of domestic space suggests key details of the differences in this postwestern story. Charley's *here* is composed of promises and has little to do with comfort beyond the most essential transactions, which, in Charley's life, are only sporadically undertaken. He remarks without a hint of irony, for instance, that "since it was a real house my dad promised we'd get a barbecue and then a dog" (ibid.: 2). "Real," of course, in this line is the absolute pivot point around which the remainder of the narrative swings. Elsewhere, the imagined place of the photo, the not-here, simultaneously renders the "real" of his new home in Portland as a failed ideal and a material reality. Similarly, as Charley's memory of his afternoon on the river in Wyoming has grown dim, his extended imaginings about it have utterly revised the reality of that day, thus exposing it, too, as a kind of fake. Each space is markedly real—and interminably incomplete. Vlautin moves us beyond the fraught binary reckoning of authenticity, and even the language of simulacrum, that has been attached to Western studies; in their stead, Charley's predicament exemplifies the uncanny materiality of *imagined* space.

It is noteworthy that the dog and barbecue promised by Ray act as tangled symbols of failed domesticity that recur throughout Vlautin's novels. In *The Motel Life*, one of the last happy moments that Frank and Jerry Lee Flannigan spend with their mother before she dies involves home-cooked barbecue. Later in that novel, Frank rescues a cold dog tied on a short leash, which then becomes his companion as he walks the streets of Reno, Nevada. More concretely, though, the barbecue and the dog indicate food security and security from outside threats in each of Vlautin's first three novels. In *Northline*, no one uses the barbecue at Allison's house except Allison herself, as a place to burn letters she has written detailing her self-hate. She burns innumerable such notes as the dog her mother had bought to protect the house watches silently (Vlautin 2008: 14, 22). In effect, both the promise of the barbecue and the dog for Charley, and the realization of the barbecue and the dog for Allison, illustrate that each is but an empty totem for those without models to show them what the care and use of dogs and barbecues look like in practice. As symbols, the dog and barbecue drive home the point that, for all their desire, kids like Charley and Allison understand only secondhand the terms of family and compassion. However disastrous this proves in their daily lives, and in the lives of so many of Vlautin's characters, it nonetheless establishes the impetus for their most audacious acts of selfhood. Their escapes are rooted in the completely speculative nature of their inventions, launched by the instability of their daily lives. Their imaginations compensate them in dangerous ways, but in the end are the most trustworthy aspects of their existence.

Failed domesticity finally compels Charley to act. Ray dies in a Portland hospital from complications after being beaten and thrown through the front window of their home by his girlfriend's husband. Having kept few of his promises, he has left Charley to fend for himself in a place which, with its shattered window and spare furnishings, recalls global peril. The would-be "real" house is an abject failure, literally deconstructed. After Ray's fight, leading up to his death, Charley flees the scene before the police can put him into protective custody. Animal-like, he hides in nearby bushes. Charley's animality is cemented repeatedly in scenes such as this, where he finds some small space and burrows in for the night. This first time, though, he is as open and vulnerable as he has ever been. Still, he returns to the house much later and blankets the broken window with an old sleeping bag. Truly wretched and afraid, he later finds Ray lying in intensive care. Charley attempts to stay with his dad in the hospital because, he tells him, "The house scares me" (ibid.: 61). Though Charley's reasons are clear, there remains an incalculable distress implicit in this compact, heart-wrenching line. Plainly, those elements which Charley needs—a house, food, security, someone to love him—are shown to be wholly beyond his reach. Fearing the house, the symbol of his basic needs, the tragedy inherent to his life is that he dreads in practice what he most desires in his dreams. The broken window makes the house frightening, but so does Ray's absence from it. In life, Ray had been a reckless, inconsistent father, but he was all that had stood between Charley and destitution. His presence for a time precluded catastrophe, if not tragedy and dejection, in Charley's life. On one hand, the broken window signifies an opening to the world beyond. It functions as the stimulus for escape, even if Charley doesn't see it that way. On the other, it marks a breach that leaves Charley open to the world's hazards. In every sense, though, it is a symbol of permeability, of exchanges both wanted and unwanted. In the absence of hard borders, Charley's world is porous, susceptible to danger, and makeshift.

Charley's fear of the dangerous world, however, is felt most forcefully when he returns to the house after Ray's first night in the hospital. Walking miles through unfamiliar neighborhoods, he finally locates the house, moves the TV into his bedroom, and locks himself in. He recalls: "I hammered nails into the floor by the door to keep it shut and I slept in my clothes" (ibid.: 61). At once, Charley attempts a rough version of secure confinement even as he is prepared for a quick getaway. He performs riturals of the cyclical model of home and flight Ray has taught him. Nailing himself into an ever-smaller space is his most immediate recourse, and it is redolent of the situation so many of Vlautin's characters find themselves in. Staying dressed represents Charley's sublimated desire for escape. The room with the door nailed shut is a reduction of the house itself, as well as a space that mirrors Charley's sense of his own smallness; it mitigates the enormity of the forces aligned against him.

On the second day of Ray's hospitalization, prior to his death, Charley returns to the house again. He remarks that "even in the daylight it made me nervous" (ibid.: 65). He calls inside first, then checks each room to make sure they are empty and secure. He locks himself in the bathroom to shower, and then he says, "After that I left." For the second time at a critical moment in the novel, leaving is dealt with offhandedly and yet it is preeminent. Charley can't stay without thinking of leaving, and he can't leave without wishing for permanence. *Here* and *elsewhere* exceed mere dialectic, and their enmeshment is in excess of in-betweenness. As if to reinforce this situation, the intervening scene describes Charley's early attempts to find his aunt in the phone book, suggesting the further imbrication of *here* and *elsewhere*, and making doubly evident the hazards of staying put. The photo/elsewhere and the real/fearsome house disclose this commonality: they are equal parts substantial and ephemeral in their compositions. The nature of postwestern geography is such that its entanglements prevent epistemological renderings. Charley's "real" and "fictional," albeit dramatically different, are each constitutive parts of the other. This inability to know anything with certainty is no small point in Vlautin's work, which agonizes over the conditions, affect, and substance of *here* and *there* to the point of fetishism. Vlautin's obsession with geography signals his characters' search for something constant or material amid instability.

Wyoming Is Far

In Portland, Wyoming is always already nearby, but as the novel turns toward Charley's escape, Wyoming joins the known world, with its hard borders and measured distances. Wyoming is demonstrable in a way it clearly hadn't been in Charley's reveries. Charley's agency, however dubious, transforms the substance of his elsewhere. While his emotional needs remain static, preserving the form of Charley's elsewhere, the material composition of a now glaringly remote Wyoming changes dramatically. It becomes truly situated, identified by its correspondence to other sites as Charley takes to the road with Pete. Prior to his leaving, Charley's elsewhere had little to do with actual flight and more to do with the promise of being there. Acute instability had produced an unlooked-for isolation that Charley simply couldn't abide, but which sheltered him, however inadequately, when his father precipitated their moves. Moving now for his own sake, the physical geography Charley must traverse asserts itself in unimagined ways, incommensurate with the landscape in his mind.

Initially, upon escaping with Lean on Pete, Charley experiences a version of elsewhere that accesses the earlier Old and New Western modes of that trope. Charley dreams of someday "just disappear[ing]" with Pete. He dreams that they "could live in a place where there was no one else around and it would be warm with miles of grass for [Pete] to eat and no one would ever make him run. There would be a barn and a house and the house would be lined with food from floor to ceiling and there would be a TV and a huge swimming pool" (ibid.: 64). This passage marks Charley's evolving sense of his need to break free of his present circumstances. For instance, this fantasy reflects Charley's constant hunger, resulting from life with a father who often leaves him alone for days at a time without sufficient means to feed himself. It also underlines Charley's desire for companionship; Charley has so few human confidantes that he imagines Pete as a kind of nonhuman coconspirator, an equal in animality and shared circumstances.[15] Upon meeting Pete, in fact, Charley recognizes a kindred spirit, suffering all the same daily indecencies. Charley's sympathies reveal the basic animality at the heart of his own existence, so that the horse becomes the only trustworthy figure Charley chooses to include in his most cherished dreamscapes besides his aunt. Charley's dreamscapes are replete with modern desires like oversized televisions and pools. His *elsewhere* with Pete is clearly an update of the conventional, pastoral, labor-less vision.

His elsewhere with Pete indicates that Charley actually inhabits two versions of elsewhere at the outset of the novel, which, when he finally leaves, coalesce into one. The foremost of his elsewheres is the space of the river in Wyoming, the clearly postwestern space. The second is the elsewhere Charley imagines for Pete and himself as he daydreams at the racetrack where Pete is boarded, the clearly traditional elsewhere. Life with his aunt and life with Pete satisfy separate impulses. That life in the photo satisfies his desire for love and comfort; the dream life with Pete answers his need for a comrade. Because stability and fellowship are to be found elsewhere, they stamp the sites of his redemption. If the elsewhere his aunt inhabits denotes his desire for domesticity, it more significantly suggests that he wants to become a participant, to be part of a stable and sustainable whole. His elsewhere with Pete, his buddy-dream, is far more plastic. In the orthodox Western sense, it portrays separation rather than participation, and it demands constant movement, shadowing disappointment. Charley does, after all, tell Pete that their ranch will be a place where there is no one else, with miles of grass for Pete to graze upon—it is a dream absolutely unattainable for a destitute boy. This space is circular, or cyclical, in that it repeats the usual aim of running *from* rather than *toward*.

Significantly, when it becomes Charley's turn to leave Portland in the timeworn Western tradition—a moment that is unavoidable—it is this buddy-dream that finally compels him to act. He becomes the

Western man of action and not a dreamer in a city. Though it is out of character, the movement innate in Western sidekick narratives authorizes Charley to default to habit and impulse, and thus to escape, even if these are not his natural inclinations. The precise moment of his departure affirms this. Charley explains: "I could have gone either way, but there was more traffic heading north" (ibid.: 138). In essence, the act precedes intent, and his *going* overshadows the significance of *arriving*. Still, Charley expresses guilt about leaving with Pete, which is in part a marker of a fresh paradigm. But in standard Western fashion, he sidesteps responsibility at that exact point when he is most culpable: "I didn't mean for all of it to happen like that, I really didn't," he says, agonistically (ibid.: 136). Although his pretext for leaving is that he is saving Pete from slaughter, it is apparent in this scene that the sidekick's existence is always, and only, in service of the protagonist. At its core, then, the obvious, traditional elsewhere enables the realization of the new paradigm. If it is to materialize at all, it seems, the postwestern elsewhere must make disconcerting sacrifices to formula. In effect, Vlautin underscores the troubling fact of precarity: while the elsewhere of kinship preserves Charley's humanity, his agency and survival often depend on the broken script of constant escape, staying one step ahead of forced displacement.

The postwestern moment, then, that transformative point of radical alterity that revises the formulaic attributes of *Lean on Pete*'s narrative, occurs when Charley's conventional retreat is subsumed into his dream of belonging. It happens just as inadvertently, but perhaps more surprisingly. While we expect him to escape, a drive of "more than a thousand miles" to Wyoming seems absurd for a fifteen-year-old boy to make (ibid.: 139). Yet, forced to choose between two unviable options, he decides upon impracticable distance—Wyoming and his aunt— rather than impossible solitude with Pete. He opts for the elsewhere of belonging rather than a space apart. It turns out that however far away Wyoming certainly is, it is nevertheless more significantly real than houses full of food and acres of pasturage will ever be for either the boy or the horse. If Vlautin is concerned with the others in our midst, it is because he recognizes that their place is, and will always be, among us. Here, Vlautin finally and wholly changes the Western prototype:

Charley and Pete will belong together, if at all, not in a separate space away from others, because there is no such space. The map of the Western states that Charley steals from a gas station confirms this fact. It invokes geographies of nowhere, of anywhere, of complete and awful anonymity beyond any scale of suffering Charley has the skills to comprehend, but which he can intuit. He flees, but ultimately with a purpose other than fulfilling a transient idyll. Vlautin's reader understands that Charley realizes he can go anywhere but is welcome nowhere, and that random retreat would only restart the cycle of flight. Put simply, Charley must find his place in all of it. Saying, "I looked at the map for a long time and decided I'd go to Wyoming and try to find my aunt for real," Charley officially foregoes the big rock candy mountain for Rock Springs (ibid.: 138-9). His is an epistemological move, certainly—he means to "find his aunt for real"—yet it occurs in the context of kinship and of becoming.

Despite the onerous task before Charley, the manner in which Wyoming signifies, even after Charley leaves with Pete, runs contrary to its inherited resonance. Wyoming the state, in life and in fiction, is incommensurably freighted with the Treaty of Fort Laramie; seminal narratives by Roosevelt, Remington, and Wister; Gretel Ehrlich's *The Solace of Open Spaces*; the more recent, abominable atrocity committed against Matthew Shepard; and the intentional reclamations sought by Annie Proulx, Larry McMurtry, and Ang Lee with *Brokeback Mountain*, among other things. Wyoming is today one of Western culture's most contentious real-and-imagined landscapes. It is conspicuous, then, that Vlautin has positioned it in his storyworld as Charley's promised land. Charley possesses none of the aforementioned cultural reference points, yet as readers and critics we can't help but understand them as the troubled legacy with which Vlautin is grappling, with the state's duplicitous policies in the interests of settler colonialism, its cowboy ethos, its hate crimes and random violence, and its diminishing aesthetic of authenticity. In this regard, Wyoming-as-elsewhere serves metonymically as a last western outpost in the reader's consciousness while, in Charley's world, it is only a place where he once lived, and a place where he thinks he will be happy again. Vlautin's reader is left with a lingering dread that, even if Charley makes it to his aunt's, his life might yet entail some other, unspecified-but-ubiquitous suffering. In part, this is what makes Vlautin's novels so profound: the unthinkable is revealed too often to be intrinsic to everyday life. Vlautin captures the dread of the expected. In Charley's case, herein dramatically transformed Wyoming—as the proving ground for white masculinity—has caved in on itself; the old signifiers supporting it have rusted clear through. Charley doesn't want to go to Wyoming to be a cowboy, to be unfettered—he wants a mom.

Charley's travels with Pete are redolent of the chance encounters associated with literature of the frontier. The cast of characters Charley meets with Pete, and then on his own after Pete is killed on the highway due to Charley's negligence, forces the reader to acknowledge the vast numbers of those who are lost or losing against their will and/or by their own hands throughout Western space. This procession of cast-offs suggests who Charley might have been or could still become if he doesn't first perish because of their ill treatment. Yet this assemblage of the Western dispossessed does include characters of the kind readers would wish for Charley to become. For instance, early in Charley and Pete's odyssey, Charley is awakened by an old Mexican man who has pulled to the side of the road to check on him. The man appears almost saint-like. In this scene, Charley is already exhausted, sleeping in the dirt near the highway, with Pete tied to him so the horse doesn't wander off. The man questions Charley, speaking to him in both Spanish and English. Without malice, he articulates Charley's medial predicament succinctly. Having heard where Charley is from, the man responds, simply but almost uncomprehendingly, "Portland?" and "Far" (ibid.: 178). Bookended by a similar comment, their exchange ends in almost identical fashion. As he leaves Charley, the man informs him, in equally spare terms, "Wyoming is far" (ibid.: 180). Epigrammatic and pithy, his assessment summarizes the absolute bind of "here" for the West's disenfranchised: they are caught in between incomprehensible forces beyond their control; they are bound for many places; they are bound for nowhere; they are bound for somewhere else. Charley is equidistant from that which he is escaping and that which he is escaping into; in half-understood language, Charley's predicament is one he himself only half understands. Guillermo, the Mexican guardian angel, encompasses the entire thrust of the novel in this tersely spoken phrase, which connotes a sense of complete disbelief limning the border between here and elsewhere.

An interstitial figure himself, the Mexican man finds Charley and Pete inconceivable in their audacity and desperation. Teaching Charley the basic principle that tying oneself to a horse is dangerous, he laughs incredulously and shrugs when Charley tells him he is coming from Portland, and shakes his head when Charley tells him he is traveling without money. In Spanish, the man tells Charley he is crazy, that this is a man's world, so take care (my translation, ibid.: 179). And yet the man's words are a benediction of sorts, not the expected warning. Contained in his disbelief is sympathy and compassion for the boy out there on his own, if not a degree of admiration for him. Having fed him before they part ways, the man wishes Charley good luck and, no longer hungry, Charley reflects that "for the first time I felt that [Pete and me] weren't cursed" (180). Telling Charley that he has entered the world of men bestows not just manhood but personhood on him, even if, by some reckoning, Guillermo himself is subaltern and has no authority to do so. Effectively, by performing his own enfranchisement, Guillermo lifts the curse upon the "here" of Charley's existence. By taking his fate into his own hands, Charley has challenged his abjection and, in so doing, in the eyes of other marginalized Westerners, he emerges small but fit. If Guillermo's comment doesn't relay confidence in Charley's quest, it at least shows a respect for Charley's guts. It gives Charley not just a passing *feeling* of independence, but the genuine article. The curse of Charley's past is lifted, even as he recognizes the certainty of his plight and all the complications manhood entails.

The same kindness toward Charley, inflected with disbelief, is expressed in a later scene by another working-class Mexican mentor/donor figure when Charley reaches Denver. He gets a job doing yard maintenance with a man named Santiago, whose own family gives Charley perhaps his first glimpse of a stable home life. Although Santiago is dubious when Charley tells him he has no identification with which to cash his paycheck, Santiago nevertheless drives him to a bank where he knows how to get Charley's pay. Santiago waits in line with Charley, making sure to get a teller with whom he is familiar. Santiago and the teller "spoke in Mexican and she cashed his and then mine" (ibid.: 250). When Charley offers to pay Santiago for helping him, Santiago tells him, "'Don't worry, I was coming here anyway.'" In effect, without knowing Charley's actual circumstances, Santiago is willing to help him in a manner that few people Charley has encountered have. Captured in the lightness of Santiago's reply, as in the previous scene, is an implicit sense of shared or similarly risky circumstances. His "I was coming here anyway" suggests a parallel course through postwestern geography, inflected with latent empathy. More to the point, his aid is only possible because it is racially coded: without the subterfuge of Spanish spoken between him and the teller, Santiago's help would not have been possible. Too many witnesses would have been aware that the teller was cashing Charley's check illegally. Help comes again to Charley in a language he can't understand, yet one that is deeply embedded in Western space and history. Implied in Santiago's assistance is the notion that those pushed to the margins, despite their differences, might be of service to one another, even if they may never understand fully the details of each other's problems. Such alliances are necessarily and productively subversive for the plain reason that they indicate a widening web of unaffiliated agents operating periodically in concert, from below, against structural and institutional inequality.

The following week, Santiago is forced to shake his head in disbelief again when he finally realizes that Charley is homeless (ibid.: 254). In response, he invites Charley for a home-cooked meal. Santiago's household is multigenerational, and his empathy seems to stem from his devotion to his blood relatives. His sense of compassion is expansive precisely because he has the good fortune of being in one place with all of them, in a situation very different from Charley's previous experience with a "real" home. Still, Vlautin refuses to stereotype Santiago or his home life. Neither Santiago nor the anonymous man on the highway are cartoonish in their habits or kindness; rather, it is their essential willingness to provide some help to Charley that Vlautin's narrative suggests we should find admirable. In fact, Charley ultimately rushes away from Santiago's home, refusing this more substantial overture of tangible relief. Upon leaving, Charley reflects:

"When I left there I was pretty down. I never understand why seeing something nice can get you so down but it can" (ibid.: 255). Santiago's awareness of family engenders a wider sense of caring, even as Charley's troubled relationship to kin and kindness is too complex for him to accept it wholly. Santiago's home is just as unreal to Charley as the house in Portland proved to be. Charley, after all, senses that he doesn't want a clichéd version of family. He simply wants the family he has imagined, however it might be composed. Santiago's family, in Charley's eyes, is too good to be true, too much to wish for.

An oddly parallel scene in *The Motel Life*, which finds Frank Flannigan walking the streets of downtown Reno under similar circumstances, imparts an equally suggestive tone of inexplicability. Frank reflects, "Casinos always make me feel better, and I can't really even explain why. 'Cause when you look at it…mostly all they cause is misery" (ibid.: 85). In both scenes, our expectations are overturned. Whereas Charley feels down after his brush with normalcy, Frank feels composed after walking among the garish lights of Virginia Street. The reader's expectation is that Charley would feel relieved in the presence of Santiago's family, while one expects Frank to be overcome by the mass of strangers. Neither character is able to respond appropriately to his immediate surroundings. Both find their feelings relating to private and public spaces discordant and ineffable. Vlautin spatializes their separate traumas, depicting proximity as confusing, his characters' responses to it incongruous, and the intimacy of it unnerving. Something feral pervades each scene, in which both Frank and Charley are tightly wound yet introspective, each bent on his own private survival yet circling the boundaries of normalcy. Vlautin plays these moments of transgression slantedly: orthodox domesticity is not repudiated, nor is it entirely abandoned. Vlautin shows kinship and isolation to be fluid things, ill-defined by an ethics of hearth and home.

Conclusion
"A Rundown Mustard-Yellow Apartment Building"
A clear and direct correlation between conditions of uncertainty and distant places is lacking in Vlautin's narratives. Here and elsewhere, dangerous and safe are never clearly depicted in Vlautin's geographies.

Uncertainty is their common theme. Risk is located both proximally and far away in equal measure, whether it is obvious to his characters or not. Elsewhere, therefore, is a solution for Vlautin's characters, but not in the usual sense. Wyoming is far only inasmuch as it is literally at a great distance from where Charley begins; it is always with him figuratively, raising its own questions, causing its own problems. That which is uncertain is more often than not that which is known: Portland, the racetrack, the other Western towns Ray had escaped to with Charley in tow. Charley's overactive imagination preserves him through his life with Ray and propels him onto the road after Ray is gone. His imagination is what allows him to transgress borders and exceed expectations. Yet it engenders disbelief or incomprehension in those who mean to help him and, as the scenes above reveal, it stamps Charley, personally, with incomprehension as well.

Finally, Charley's quest ends with a want of recognition when he and Aunt Margy meet. In this regard, Vlautin suggests the postwest as a place of constant ambiguity even as he locates imagination as the key to optimism. Yet doubt and optimism are at last reconciled anticlimactically, in the most ordinary way. Upon reaching Laramie, with his aunt's address in hand, Charley recalls, "At the end of the street I came to a rundown mustard-yellow apartment building" (ibid.: 269). What Charley describes is a far cry from that home he had imagined for himself and Pete; also, it hardly resembles the long-loved photo he had kept with him. The apartment at the end of the street resonates with Vlautin's reader as a dead end, as a site of mean compromise if not outright mediocrity. Further, the nondescript building suggests the repeatability and banality of the lives it contains. Still, in Charley's world, these denote the privilege of an ordinary life. In effect, Charley arrives, fearful but relieved, at a place many would hope someday to leave behind if they could. He opens the door on the opportunity to succeed or fail in the usual ways. The transcendence of this scene lies in the remarkable *averageness* of his aunt's apartment building, the commonness, in the act of *arriving at all*. We are meant to reevaluate our most basic aspirational conceits in the face of the true ordinariness of Charley's, Aunt Margy's, and so many others' situations.

Aunt Margy's building is nothing like the river of his dreams, cherished in the photograph, and Aunt Margy, likewise, barely resembles the woman she once had been. They meet again as strangers after having been so familiar in Charley's dreams. He says that she "stood there and it took me a while to realize who it was. She was much heavier than when I knew her and she hadn't aged well" (ibid.: 269). Aunt Margy speaks first, unbelieving and then believing: "'Oh, Charley, it's you, isn't it?'…We sat there staring at each other, and then finally I told her about the Samoan and my dad and Del and Lean on Pete and some of the things I'd seen to get to her" (ibid.: 270). Charley's postwestern elsewhere is definitively this apartment building and this woman, neither of which are what he expected, but which do provide the shelter of a "real" home as well as the love he requires. Aunt Margy plans to help Charley face the things he has tried to outrun, she wants him to obey the law, and she promises to fulfill her responsibilities to him (ibid.: 272-3). It is also apparent that she needs him, too. Still, habitual doubt shadows Charley, largely because elsewhere looks so much like Portland—or any other town Ray had taken him to. This, of course, is Vlautin's point. Through his perceptive depictions of common circumstance shared by his characters in *Lean on Pete* and the other novels, Vlautin's characterization of vulnerability suggests new keywords to critics and helps cement the transnational accord between literatures of the U.S. West and other contemporary literatures. In *Lean on Pete*, entanglement is manifested in trust; it is expressed through active, affinitive kinship and nontraditional family bonds; it marks a consequential willingness to share responsibility across and beyond difference.

Place-making entails our everyday bodily reckonings as they are represented to us, as we represent them to ourselves, and as we relay them to others. In every case, places are contingent upon the dynamics of mobility, where movement and stillness are impelled by personal desire, force, or chance. Place-making, in this light, is not only an individual act but is simultaneously suggested, interpreted, and enforced from above and within the many social spheres in which we participate. The places we inhabit are ours circumstantially, but are also the result of "embodied mobile practices [with] complex histories and geographies" (Cresswell and Merriman 2013: 5). Grasping the meaning of postwestern elsewheres, therefore, requires exposing the ways in which marginalization is countermanded by resistance and manipulation in everyday practice. Thinking about postwestern elsewheres involves apprehending what Tim Cresswell and Peter Merriman, after Michel de Certeau, designate as "tactics of the weak" (ibid.: 5). In this case, to dream of and/or pursue elsewhere in Vlautin's novels is one of a limited set of maneuvers available to the West's most vulnerable people in order to allay insecurity or evade trauma. The stories that Vlautin's characters tell themselves—their elsewheres—make up for their lacks or losses.

The common element postwestern elsewheres share with previous spaces of escape is that the characters running toward them counteract their disposability with transience, with moving on as responsibility catches up with them. As indicative of a fresh paradigm, however, *Lean on Pete*—and the body of Vlautin's work, as it stands for texts presenting similarly othered spaces—furnishes a continued narrative of being *caught up with*. *Lean on Pete* recommends a world in which consequences refuse to be outrun. For this reason, the sometimes tragic beauty of Vlautin's novel reminds us, to our dismay, that the pathologies blanketing *Lean on Pete* refuse to be resolved and are emblematic of new genre conventions. Privileging the everyday over the monolithic or triumphalist event, postwestern elsewheres qualify whom we should care for and recalibrate why we should care for them. They increase—and increase the visibility of—our Western subjects.

NOTES

1. The language of postcolonial and globalization studies—"Other," "alterity," "risk," "vulnerability," "precarity"—as received from Spivak, Beck, Nixon, Butler, and others, is elemental to my reading of Vlautin's work. These terms articulate the relationships among difference, subjectivity, and enfranchisement. They speak to both social and ecological deferrals by the wealthiest people and to casualties among the world's poorest. As such, these terms establish the parameters of the "unequal burdens," to borrow Rob Nixon's phrase, carried by the world's poor in the interests of the world's most powerful. I argue that Vlautin's narratives impart a localized variation, which helps to expand our portrait of global inequality. In sum, these critical moves gain traction by emphasizing shared risk and mutual constitution as the sources for empathy and solidarity among marginalized people locally and globally.

2. I am thinking specifically of other texts I consider to be postwesterns. An incomplete list follows: Mukherjee's *Jasmine* (1989), Kingsolver's *Bean Trees* (1989), Pynchon's *Vineland* (1990), Sarris's *Grand Street* (1992), Butler's *Parable of the Sower*

(1994), Everett's *Watershed* (1996), Alexie's *Indian Killer* (1998), Yamashita's *Tropic of Orange* (1999), Boyle's *Friend of the Earth* (2001), Ondaatje's *Divisidero* (2006), Watkins's *Battleborn* (2010), and Hassmann's Girlchild (2013).

3. Elsewhere also is, and has been, exclusionary, whereby we dispose of our unwanted people, things, and ideas by sending them away, either literally or figuratively, as in Indian Removal. This shadow meaning increases visibly in Vlautin's novels. This elsewhere, especially, is in our midst. It represents the cultural margins to which whole sections of vernacular existence have been exiled. As such, it signifies more correctly as *nowhere*; that is, the present state of affairs Vlautin's characters seek to escape. See Chisum's chapter in this collection. See also Robert Tally Jr.'s treatment of utopia in contemporary literature (2013: vii-x).

4. I suggest this year to mark the postwestern moment, after certain studies in postmodernism and the period that follows it by Moraru, Brian McHale, and others—such as Francis Fukuyama, who posited the end of history from this point—and studies in post-racial aesthetics by Ramon Saldivar.

5. Elsewhere, in this case, is clearly exclusionary, such that it is to be displaced or left out. See also Jeffrey Chisum's contribution to this collection (chapter 4) on these ideas.

6. The same might be said of New Western geographies by Willa Cather, Mary Austin, Mari Sandoz, and Mildred Walker. Examples from this period range from the easily identifiable—*The Virginian* (1902), and *Riders of the Purple Sage* (1912)—to the less obvious, such as Jack London's *Valley of the Moon* (1913) and Upton Sinclair's *Oil!* (1927).

7. This period might be traced to texts as varied as *The Day of the Locust* (1939), *The Grapes of Wrath* (1939), *The Oxbow Incident* (1940), and *The Big Rock Candy Mountain* (1943). Coinciding with the advent of postmodernism, New West texts such as *Run River* (1963), *The Crying of Lot 49* (1965), and *The Last Picture Show* (1966) set the tone for the high-water mark of the period that followed, represented partially by *House Made of Dawn* (1968), *Yellow Back Radio Broke-Down* (1969), *Revolt of the Cockroach People* (1973), *The Monkey Wrench Gang* (1975), and *Housekeeping* (1980). This is also the period recognized for the New Western history.

8. See Krista Comer's discussion of the global cultural movements of 1968 and their relationship to the New West ("New West, Urban and Suburban Spaces, Post-west" 246), and her more recent rearticulation of post-civil rights literature, "Western Literature at Century's End: Sketches in Generation X, Los Angeles, and the Post-Civil Rights Novel."

9. For examples, see Richard W. Etulain's *Telling Western Stories*, Comer's *Landscapes of the New West*, and Neil Campbell's *The Cultures of the American New West*.

10. The term "postpostmodernism" comes into regular use during the early 2000s; Marc Augé describes "supermodernity" in 1995, and Moraru's term gives his book its title in 2011. These are only a few of the names for our present cultural era and its aesthetic productions.

11. The clearest and most suggestive examples of these critical positions in Western literary studies are to be found in works by Campbell, Comer, Susan Kollin, and Stephen Tatum.

12. The phrase "vaster solidarities" is Moraru's; recall here, also, Appiah's language of the "global tribe," and Saldivar's main argument that although we do not belong to a post-racial society, the confluence of postmodernism and postcolonialism has produced historical fantasies predicated on postrace alliance. For Saldivar, in this respect, postrace aesthetics are not big-tentism or pluralism in the melting-pot sense, but rather the space of fictional solidarity across race among marginalized subjects. For Haraway's part, such alliances are evinced in forms of "kinship," "in lines of inventive connection as a practice of learning to live and die well with each other in a thick present" (1). Barad's term for our present era is "Chthulucene," which she suggests is defined by "response-ability on a damaged earth" and "active trust in each other in working and playing for a resurgent world," specifically, in "becoming-with" (2; 3). All told, such critical work responds to the redefinition of borders or boundaries, emphasizing human and nonhuman bonds rather than those aspects that separate us.

13. Barad's keywords point to the both/and nature of meaning and materiality, a move that I feel expresses the main current of with-ness in contemporary multicultural literature: entanglement, "intra-action," and "agential realism" describe an enlarged perspective on the mutual constitution of agency beyond causality and before *interactions* (33). Bennett argues similarly, imagining a world of assemblages including and in excess of human meaning-making (vii-viii). Both Bennett and Barad's work signify an extension of Edward W. Soja's articulation of real-and-imagined places, wherein geography and culture are mutually formed, and people, places, and things are likewise inscribed. Finally, see Robert T. Tally Jr.'s language in his introduction to Bertrand Westphal's *Geocriticism: Real and Fictional Spaces*. Tally argues that we "understand 'real' places by understanding their fundamental fictionality" (x), and that "fiction may be as reliable as any form of understanding the world" (xi).

14. I borrow the term "absent presence" from poststructuralist mobilities studies, where it is deployed as a way to reveal the producers of global products whose labors are present in the things they make that circulate globally, though their personhood is erased or elided by distance. Here, I mean for it to signify the stable home that is-but-is-not-present in Charley's life, emblematized in the form of his half-forgotten and almost mythologized Aunt Margy.

15. The phrase "non-human coconspirator" is borrowed willfully from Matthias Klestil, from his talk on animals and slavery at the 2015 ASLE conference in Moscow, Idaho. In my reading, I intend for the phrase to evoke the trope of the white Western hero and his other-sidekick, revised and updated in the postwest by Vlautin's non-human sidekick Pete.

WORKS CITED

Augé, Marc. 1995. *Non-places: An Introduction to Supermodernity.* London & New York: Verso.

Barad, Karen Michelle. 2007. *Meeting the Universe Halfway: Quantum Physics and the Entanglement of Matter And Meaning.* Durham: Duke University Press.

Baym, Nina. 2006. "Old West, New West, Postwest, Real West." *American Literary History*, Vol. 18, 4: 814–828.

Bennett, Jane. 2010. *Vibrant Matter: A Political Ecology of Things*. Durham: Duke University Press.

Bryant, Edwin. 1848 [2001] *What I Saw in California*. Santa Barbara, CA: The Narrative Press.

Campbell, Neil. 2008. *The Rhizomatic West: Representing the American West in a Transnational, Global, Media Age*. Lincoln & London: University of Nebraska Press.

———. 2013. *Post-Westerns: Cinema, Region, West*. Lincoln and London: University of Nebraska Press.

Comer, Krista. 2013. "Introduction: Assessing the Postwestern." *Western American Literature*, vol. 48, nos. 1 & 2: 3–15.

Cresswell, Tim, and Peter Merriman. 2012. *Geographies of Mobilities: Practices, Spaces, Subjects*. Farnham and Burlington: Ashgate.

Haraway, Donna J. 2016. *Staying with the Trouble: Making Kin in the Chthulucene*. Durham: Duke University Press.

Kollin, Susan. 2007. *Postwestern Cultures: Literature, Theory, Space*. Lincoln & London: University of Nebraska Press.

McClure, J. 1994. *Late Imperial Romance*. London and New York: Verso.

McHale, Brian. 1986. "Change of Dominant from Modernist to Postmodernist Writing." In *Approaching Postmodernism*, papers presented at a Workshop on Postmodernism, September 21–23, 1984, University of Utrecht, edited by Douwe W. Fokkema and Hans Bertens (Amsterdam: John Benjamins).

Moraru, Christian. 2011. *Cosmodernism: American Narrative, Late Globalization, and the New Cultural Imaginary*. Ann Arbor: University of Michigan Press.

Saldivar, Ramon. 2011. "Historical Fantasy, Speculative Realism, and Postrace Aesthetics in Contemporary American Fiction." *American Literary History*, Vol. 23, 3: 574–599.

Soja, Edward. 1996. *Thirdspace: Journeys to Los Angeles and Other Real-And-Imagined Places*. Oxford: Blackwell.

Tally, Robert T., Jr. (ed.) 2011. *Geocritical Explorations: Space, Place, and Mapping in Literary and Cultural Studies*. New York: Palgrave Macmillan.

———. 2013. *Utopia in the Age of Globalization: Space, Representation, and the World System*. New York: Palgrave Macmillan.

Tatum, Stephen. 2007. "Spectrality and the Postregional Interface." In *Postwestern Cultures*, edited by Susan Kollin, 3–29. Lincoln & London: University of Nebraska Press.

Vlautin, Willy. 2006. *The Motel Life*. New York: HarperCollins.

———. 2008. *Northline*. New York: HarperCollins.

———. 2010. *Lean on Pete*. New York: HarperCollins.

———. 2014. *The Free*. New York: HarperCollins.

Westphal, B. 2011. *Geocriticism: Real and Fictional Spaces*. New York: Palgrave Macmillan.

CHAPTER 8

THE FREE AND THE FALLEN IN WILLY VLAUTIN'S WESTERN FICTION

by SUSAN KOLLIN

In the wake of the 2016 elections, as many Americans struggle to confront the realities of a divided nation, there could hardly be a better time to examine the Western fiction of Nevada-born author Willy Vlautin. In his four novels—*The Motel Life* (2007), *Northline* (2008), *Lean on Pete* (2010), and *The Free* (2014)—Vlautin focuses on problems facing the white underclass as they seek out meaningful attachments in communities trying to recover from an economic downturn that seems never-ending, and as they find themselves sacrificed on the global frontiers of America's "forever wars" (Filkins 2009). Attuned to lives on the margins, Vlautin offers stories about broken families, discarded kids, diminished communities, and abandoned dreams, while showing possible alternatives and solutions to the concerns facing these characters.

Chronicling the experiences of vulnerable populations left behind by the neoliberal economies of post-9/11 America, Vlautin's work mirrors the emerging southern tradition of Grit Lit, extending another region's literary form into the West through a raw, edgy, localist aesthetic (Carpenter 2016; Bengal 2013). In doing so, Vlautin is in the company of other recent authors such as Claire Vaye Watkins, Zach Falcon, and Smith Henderson, whose fictions about Nevada (*Battleborn*, 2012), Alaska (*Cabin, Clearing, Forest*, 2015), and Montana (*Fourth of July Creek*, 2015) also highlight the economic, social, and political struggles facing alienated and marginalized white communities across the region. Brian Carpenter notes the ways in which Grit Lit writers in the South are redefining the literary traditions that often "treated them and their kind with contempt," by engaging a "ruthless self-scrutiny" (ibid.: xviii) that doesn't let them or their characters off the hook (ibid.: xxii). Such attention to "small scale," "ordinary," or "everyday" regionalisms may enable the development of what Neil Campbell calls a "renewed cultural politics" in the American West, one that is attuned both to how people "interact with space and place" and how they are "defined by it" (Campbell, 2016: 148).

What is noteworthy about Vlautin's fiction is his keen understanding of these deeply troubled and at times dangerously compromised characters, many of whom are caught up in frightening and pointless situations of hatred, abuse, and violence. In his astute fictional portraits, the author manages to scale what Arlie Russell Hochschild has recently called "empathy walls," or persistent emotional obstacles that impede "deep understanding of another person" and "make us feel indifferent or even hostile to those who hold different beliefs or whose childhood is rooted in different circumstances" (Hochschild 2016: 5). Although Vlautin shows compassion for his characters, he does not present them as blameless or without power. Instead, he recognizes the depths of their anger, noting what drives their resentment while pointing to the limitations and hazards these sentiments pose for them and their fellow human beings. Even as some of his white working-class characters settle for despair, violence, and racial hatred, there are always ethical holdouts in Vlautin's literary worlds, characters who choose otherwise and who decide to forge different paths for themselves in the West.

At the center of Vlautin's novels are young castoffs from families struggling with intergenerational poverty who cannot claim the celebrated freedoms of the mythic West. Many of his characters are instead damaged American Adams and Eves who yearn for community, connection, and attachment (Lewis 1955: 5). The fictional worlds Vlautin creates reveal the dire economies of down-and-out white people struggling against class humiliations while fighting for self-esteem and dignity. Katherine Newman outlines similar concerns among urban poor and minority populations in her book, *No Shame in My Game: The Working Poor in the Inner City.* Newman's study addresses the risks and limits facing hardworking communities of color in urban America. Focusing on groups who have no chance of promotion, no means of upward mobility, no shot at affordable college tuition, and no hope of good-paying jobs with benefits or security, her findings reveal people who nevertheless work hard to maintain dignity and meaning in their everyday lives, trying to overcome the visible and hidden injuries of class (Newman 2000: 147; Sennett and Cobb 1993).

Many of the white characters in Vlautin's Western fiction face similar struggles, even as some of them also display hostility and resentment toward people of color and women in general. In a recent article in the *New Yorker*, Toni Morrison described how—with the perceived loss of their racial superiority—"a number of white Americans are sacrificing themselves" (Morrison 2016: 54). They are beginning "*to do things they clearly don't really want to be doing*" and in turn are "abandoning their sense of human dignity" (ibid.). While some whites "may hate their behavior and know full well how craven it is," they have taken up acts of violence, surrendering their humanity as a way of countering the "horror of lost status" (ibid.). For these white Americans, the "comfort" of claiming oneself superior to someone from another race, of never "having to struggle or demand civil treatment," often proves quite "hard to give up" (ibid.).

In a similar way, historian Nancy Isenberg notes an irony in the way many white working-class Americans are often "taught to hate," though not "those who are keeping them in line" (Isenberg 2016: 315). In Vlautin's literature, there are important lessons to learn about how misplaced antagonism leaves many victims in its wake. The white characters in *Northline*, for instance, do not unite along class interests, but typically divide along racial and gender lines. The novel features marginalized and alienated white working-class Westerners, including Jimmy Bodie, a hyper-masculine misfit and abusive boyfriend who crosses paths with white supremacist groups, brands his unsuspecting white girlfriend with neo-Nazi tattoos, and gets into fights with his

Mexican coworkers (Vlautin 2008). Masculinity and whiteness are indeed fragile in Vlautin's fictional worlds and must be shored up with violence.

Carol Anderson describes the particular form of racial hatred and antagonism expressed by Jimmy Bodie as "white rage." Questioning why political activism after Ferguson and the emergence of Black Lives Matter is labeled "black rage," she draws attention instead to a misdirected white anger or rage whose main trigger turns out to be "black advancement" (2016: 3). As Anderson points out, it is "not the mere presence of black people that is the problem; rather it is blackness with ambition, with drive, with purpose, with aspirations, and with demands for full and equal citizenship. It is blackness that refuses to accept subjugation, to give up" (ibid.: 3–4). In other words, it is rage triggered by a winner-take-all belief that groups that were once behind are now getting ahead and are doing so precisely at the expense of white working-class communities. In Vlautin's work, misplaced rage and resentment appear in full force where they are directed toward a broad range of people—Mexicans, Samoans, women, and children. In cases where brute force doesn't work, mobility offers false hopes. Refining the classic move West to greater freedom, as frequently depicted in popular stories of the region, many of Vlautin's white working-class characters yearn for a retreat to the North or Northwest, to remote red (and purple) states like Alaska, Idaho, and Montana, those rural holdouts thought to be the last, best strongholds for economic redemption and frontier freedom. In doing so, the characters seek an escape that often leaves them more isolated, disempowered, and vulnerable than they were before.

I focus in this essay on Vlautin's most recent novels, *Lean on Pete* and *The Free*, for the ways they bring into sharp relief ideas about white working-class freedom and gendered agency. Published in 2010, *Lean on Pete* has been adapted for the screen by British director Andrew Haigh with an expected release in 2017 and a cast including Steve Buscemi and Chloë Sevigny. The novel has been reviewed favorably, with one writer in *The Independent* aptly describing it as "Huck Finn for the crystal meth generation" (Williams 2010). Offering an ironic take on Mark Twain's famous boy narrator, *Lean on Pete* features a white teenager who is reluctantly propelled into the world of adults and struggles to find attachment and belonging. Unlike Huck Finn, the young protagonist Charley Thompson in Vlautin's novel seeks a solution to his abandonment and forced mobility by searching for an "Aunt Sally"—in this case his Aunt Margy—the only family member who may be able to provide him with a home and care for him until he grows up.

The author's 2014 novel, *The Free*, is also about the yearning to belong, and like *Lean on Pete*, debates freedom as a cherished Western and American ideal. Set against the backdrop of 9/11, the novel highlights the burdens placed on a white working-class community as its members suffer from poverty-related illnesses, work at dead-end jobs, and are sacrificed as the first casualties in America's war on terror. No doubt his most ironically titled novel, *The Free* tracks the dangers of social isolation, especially when it mixes with authoritarian cultures and a lack of opportunity. In doing so, the novel portrays the traumas of military service, crushing debt, and drug abuse, particularly as these forces prevent the characters from building meaningful lives in the West. Recently, Angela Davis has warned about forms of freedom that are "shrouded in unfreedom" (Davis 2012: 139). Vlautin's novel bypasses solutions that emphasize hyper-individualism or that require social hierarchy, in favor of a freedom built on deeper community attachments, greater obligations, and collective responsibilities. In this way, the larger task in Vlautin's novel involves locating a more inclusive freedom that, to borrow from Angela Davis, "does not need enemies for its sustenance" (ibid.: 149).

ON WESTERN BELONGING

Lean on Pete features 15-year-old Charley Thompson, whose journey takes him from Washington to Oregon and finally to Wyoming as he searches for a long-lost aunt he hopes will provide him with a home and a sense of belonging. Charley's world is a down-and-out West that features dive bars, shabby homes, strip malls, lonely highways, and few opportunities for getting ahead. When the novel opens, Charley's mother is already long gone. He and his father Ray soon pack up and leave for Portland for ominous reasons the older man won't explain, other than that "he'd rather go to prison and get the shit kicked out of him every day than spend any more time in a dump" (Vlautin 2010: 2). In Portland, they do not see much improvement in their lives. The two live in a rundown hotel for the first few days until they find a roach-infested house to rent. Charley later tries to attend the local high school, not an easy task with an absent father who doesn't buy food or provide much parenting. With Ray often gone for long periods, the boy is left to his own devices. Because of the mean and rough neighborhood they live in, Charley is afraid to go out by himself, except during the day when he should be in classes. The teenager instead passes the time watching hours of TV, shoplifting cans of chili and SpaghettiOs from the local grocery, and lying about his age so he can get a job.

Even when Ray manages to be home, he is not much of a role model, passing on his less-than-exemplary attitudes toward women along with his longstanding racial resentments. One morning over breakfast, he brags to Charley about his latest girlfriend, a woman who's married to a Samoan. "He'll probably chop my head off with a machete," the father whispers to the son (ibid.: 6). Ray takes pleasure in thinking he's sexually besting a man he's never met, but one he imagines to be a physically imposing racial competitor. "Samoans are big fuckers. They play football sometimes.... They're tough and they love to fight.... They're the size of mountains," Ray brags (ibid.). Putting one over on the Pacific Islander heightens the excitement of the affair by challenging the racial threat posed by the other man. Ray eventually does get in a fight with the Samoan and sustains serious injuries that land him in the hospital, where he later dies.

With his father out of the picture, Charley ends up at a horse track on the outskirts of Portland. There he meets Del Montgomery, a damaged and corrupt horse owner who races drugged-up and injured horses that he passes off to unsuspecting buyers. Although the boy finds a certain connection to Del and this community, Charley soon learns that the tracks are a tough and mean world, where animals are wasted by their owners, bosses don't pay their workers, whites cheat Mexicans, and almost no one has your back. Here, however, Charley meets Lean on Pete, a horse owned and abused by Del, an animal that soon becomes his closest confidante and eventually his means of escape to what he hopes will be a better life. After Del is caught in one of his many cheating schemes, Charley makes his break, rescuing the horse and going off on a desperate and dangerous search for his Aunt Margy who lives somewhere in Wyoming.

Vlautin's portrait of this white working-class community helps make visible a world often overlooked or stigmatized. In *White Trash: The 400-Year Untold History of Class in America*, Nancy Isenberg notes that many people in the United States prefer to forget about the white underclass, in part because their existence threatens to undo the meanings of America as a place of promise and uplift (Isenberg 2016: xv). They are instead shunted to the margins, with each era creating a means of explaining them away, often by racializing them, naturalizing their condition, or considering them subhuman (ibid.: 2). Thus, at various moments in American history, poor whites have been depicted as a separate breed of their own (ibid.: xv), treated as a diseased population, denigrated as inferior animals (ibid.: xvi), or deemed to be worthless "trash," "rubbish," or "waste" (ibid.: xv).

Shunted to the edges of society, Vlautin's white characters struggle against their status as "waste people" (ibid.: 5), a marginalization that is often reflected in the Western spaces they inhabit. Frequently, the novel's landscapes appear as blighted and diminished places, a far cry from the mythic frontier typically featured in regional writing. The closest the characters get to the celebrated spaces of the West are through their connections to such lingering reminders of the past as the worn-out cowboy boots and hats they wear, the horses they train, the jokes they make about bank robbers, and the Westerns they watch on TV. The tattoo that Lynn, one of Ray's girlfriends, wears perhaps best sums this up. On her ankle is the image of a flower and, as Charley notes, coming out of it is "some sort of snake" (ibid.: 5). The tattoo is significant, pointing to the ways that the West in the novel does not embody a hopeful geography for these American Adams and Eves but instead serves as a fallen place, where redemption is not guaranteed in advance but is a hard-fought achievement.

Here the author connects with other postwestern writers in recasting the meanings of Western spaces. Neil Campbell describes Vlautin's imagined West as a space "uncoupled from the optimism contained in the traditional myth of Manifest Destiny" (Campbell 2015: 381). While landscape in America's frontier myth is meant to be a place for expanded opportunities and positive character-building challenges for the white hero, or what David Rio describes as a glorified terrain for a "free western society unburdened by social barriers," in Vlautin's postwestern writings there are numerous obstacles in the way (Rio 2014: 221). In *Lean on Pete*, the West is often a blighted and unpromising space, its built and natural environments frequently depleted or exhausted. After he escapes Portland and the racetracks, Charley's journey through the West to Wyoming takes place along an empty, lonely highway where danger and death constantly lurk. Likewise, in the case of Del, who works with damaged animals at the tracks, close proximity to nonhuman nature is not ennobling but, shaped by abuse and corruption. The character, it turns out, is not a steward or a caretaker of the more-than-human world but someone who exploits and mistreats the animals for his own economic gain.

Critic Mark Busby points out problems in popular frontier discourses about Western landscapes, noting that because nature is frequently elevated in regional culture as "our best teacher," it often follows that "the only valuable learning comes from a life of action in the natural world," which implies that "any other education lacks worth" (Busby 1995: 77). This idea leaves Westerners unable to "cope with a changing world," or to deal with a landscape that is developing or becoming urbanized and that may require other forms of education to thrive in it (ibid.: 78). The frontier ideas that circulate in Vlautin's world prove especially disempowering to the white working-class characters and often lead to larger misunderstandings and a dangerous anti-intellectualism (ibid.: 77). Indeed, many of the adults in his novels face limitations, disappointments, and unexpected setbacks that they are unable to understand fully and that they often transform into racial resentment and hostility.

Charley, however, remains a thoughtful character who realizes there is more to life than anger, hatred, and distrust of others. He frequently makes efforts to welcome new people into his world, and they in turn often help him on his journey, including Guillermo, who finds Charley sleeping on the side of the road one morning and asks, "Eres un fugitivo?" (ibid.: 178). Realizing the boy is traveling alone and may be hungry, he offers to buy him breakfast. "Wyoming is far," Guillermo gently warns Charley as he leaves. "Good luck" (ibid.: 180). Abandoned by most of the adults in his life, Charley nevertheless holds out for family and community, eventually finding a nonhuman companion in Lean on Pete. As they travel east, the boy and the horse are left to their own devices, forced to journey along a paved road because every property they encounter is "lined with barbed-wire fences" (ibid.: 181). Cars slow down when they pass by, but none of the drivers stop or roll down their window to offer help. Charley trudges on, taking care of and confiding secrets to his animal companion along the way until a terrible accident leads to the horse's death.

After a number of other setbacks—including a confrontation with the police, who pick him up and bring him to a group home for teens, an incident in which he is framed for having drugs and is forced to run away, and another encounter during which he is beaten and robbed— Charley manages to find his Aunt Margy at the end of the novel. Rather than celebrating experiences of isolation and independence, *Lean on Pete* shows what happens if we take the iconic figure of the American Adam to its logical conclusion. As critic William Bevis has argued, when carried to their extreme, popular beliefs about the freedom and independence of the West may quickly devolve into antisocial behaviors that are debilitating rather than heroic (Bevis 1990: 102). As seen in Vlautin's writings, these behaviors may also result in identities that reveal less-attractive, even dangerous, qualities of mind, including loneliness, social isolation, misplaced rage, and despair. *Lean on Pete* holds out for a different meaning of place, however, one that reconfigures ideas of Western freedom and identity in order to include more sustainable opportunities for belonging and attachment.

FREEDOM AND ITS BURDENS

Vlautin's fourth novel, *The Free*, offers a haunting portrait of the American West in the post-9/11 era. It centers on Leroy Kervin, a 24-year-old returning vet from the National Guard who is barely surviving injuries sustained in Iraq during a roadside explosion, and whose struggles foreground problems in American self-perceptions in the early twenty-first century. Following 9/11, the United States launched its

war on terror by rallying around popular national ideas about freedom, independence, liberty, and democracy. In *The Intimacies of Four
Continents*, Lisa Lowe notes that these broad ideas frequently appear
at the foundation of many Western nations' conceptions of identity. As
she explains, such self-understandings typically rely on "a spatializa-
tion of the 'unfree'" as that which is always exterior to liberal humanism and is necessarily projected onto a distant Other (Lowe 2015: 39).
Acts of forgetting underwrite this collective national project, which
operates by way of "displacement and elision," through an amnesia
that buries previous and ongoing projects such as settler colonialism, slavery, and indentured labor (ibid.). Lowe argues that modern
humanism often "translates the world through an economy of affir-
mation and forgetting within a regime of desiring freedom. The affir-
mation of the desire for freedom is so inhabited by the forgetting of its
condition of possibility that every narrative articulation of freedom is
haunted by its burial, by the violence of forgetting" (ibid.).

Similar narratives of freedom often appear alongside experiences
of abandonment and loss in Vlautin's work. Throughout his novels,
Westerns often play on television in an endless loop of action, violence,
mobility, and promise that challenge and taunt the struggling characters. *The Motel Life*, for instance, features lost and confused Westerners
who discuss the character that Clint Eastwood played in *The Outlaw
Josey Wales* and who devour narratives of mobility and adventure by
popular Western writers such as Jack London and Larry McMurtry
(Vlautin 2007: 24, 66, 45). Throughout *Northline*, the protagonist, Allison Johnson, converses with an imagined Western hero in the form of
Paul Newman, whose dependable cowboy persona is a source of inspiration and a model for an honorable masculinity that is sorely lacking
in her world. Vlautin once described his early encounters with Westerns during childhood visits to his uncle's house, where they played
day and night on TV. The author noted how much he admired the characters that Paul Newman typically played on screen because they were
usually polite and respectful toward women (Vlautin 2015).

Westerns likewise appear in *Lean on Pete*, in particular in a scene in
which Charley watches a show featuring a mountain man who adopts
a mute white boy after his family is killed by Indians. The protagonist

later marries an Indian woman who is also murdered. The mountain man then spends the rest of the movie seeking revenge for her death by killing all Indians in his path. When the Western ends, Charley thinks it's a "horribly sad movie" about people who just wanted to "start a family together" but were undermined by violence, retribution, and death. The film haunts Charley, who is kept awake at night pondering the events and their meanings as he struggles to fall asleep (Vlautin 2010: 55).[1]

In *The Free*, the Iraq war vet Leroy also comes into consciousness as a Western plays on TV, "showing a kid…AWOL from the cavalry… killing Indians" (ibid.: 25). The sounds drifting across the room seem especially haunting given the character's own debilitating injuries, a reminder of the connections linking the Indian wars of the nation's past with the "forever wars" of the new post-9/11 global frontiers (Filkins). Although popular Westerns, even in their classic form, often deal with the problems of racism, the consequences of dispossession, and the violence of American nation building, as Stephen Tatum argues, these elements have frequently fallen out of our collective memories of the genre. This, in turn, has caused Westerns to emerge as shorthand for celebrations of an exceptionalist United States and its freedom-loving institutions (Tatum 1998: 164).

While Westerns appear endlessly on television in Vlautin's literature, right-wing radio also carries authoritarian messages about strong male leaders who are able to provide clear and simple answers to the problems haunting the white working class in times of crisis and confusion. In *The Free*, Dr. James Dobson's popular evangelical program, *Focus on the Family*, plays on the radio. Based in Colorado Springs, the show petitions listeners to "remain true" to the religious principles that have "guided this great nation since the days of its founding" (Vlautin 2014: 148). As the radio host explains, the answers to the nation's problems are simple. Now is not the time to "stand by idly" while the "social order is destroyed" and the family "as it has been understood for millennia" threatens to collapse (ibid.: 149). Nothing less than "chaos such as the world has never seen" will befall our nation if we fail to act, Dobson tells his listeners (ibid.). Offering hope, order, and authoritarian solutions, the *Focus on the Family* host promises to fulfill the thwarted dreams of the white working class by returning America to a mythical past, a world that never existed.

The radio show announces that this is not the moment for the "Christian people" or true Americans to "throw up their hands in despair" instead, they should do all they can to shore up the political authority of the heteronormative patriarchal family (ibid.). The radio show makes its case through fear-mongering and dire warnings about the chaos of the end times. More particularly, it makes its case through what Ian Haney López in *Dog Whistle Politics* describes as a carefully coded racial appeal, often used by elites in order to exploit collective fears for their own advantage and socially regressive ends (López 2014: 48, xii). As López points out, rather than disappearing in our allegedly post-racial society, racial patterns are able to adapt such that racism is transformed into a new model for new strategic purposes (ibid.: xii). While it still causes real and serious damage to nonwhites, this "ferocious" racism is not about race on a fundamental level but rather about amassing "power, money, and/or status" (ibid.: xi, 48). Political leaders pander with regard to race and promise to "protect supposedly embattled whites, when in reality" they are working to protect the "interests of the very affluent" (ibid.: 2). If "other means of gaining these ends are ready at hand," such as by exploiting fears about women, sexual minorities, or religious organizations, then calculating actors will traffic in cultural panics and "use those instead or in addition to race" to stir up new forms of moral panic and collective hysteria (ibid.: 48).

Such calls for freedom, which require "unfree" Others to sustain them, are precisely what Angela Davis warns us to avoid (Davis 2012: 139). These forms of freedom certainly do not help the fallen vet Leroy, who remains bed-bound throughout the novel, having suffered on the front lines of a war meant to liberate another struggling nation. Existing in a state of near death in a "second-rate group home for disabled men" in a small town in Washington State, Leroy at one point experiences either a profound sense of clarity or a horrific hallucination that leads him to attempt suicide (Vlautin 2014: 2). From there, he escapes deep into his mind, where he undergoes an imagined adventure that takes him far from his physical and emotional plight.

Other characters in the novel also struggle with the consequences of freedom, including Leroy's mother, who occupies a lonely, isolated world, watching *Star Trek* reruns, working at Safeway, living "alone in a small house in a failing neighborhood," and driving a "twenty-year-old car" (ibid.: 8). The nurse, Pauline Hawkins, likewise grapples with freedom and its discontents, with her shopping cart full of twenty-four cans of chicken noodle soup, fat-free coffee creamer, and glazed donuts, and who is kept company by a caged rabbit that provides a certain level of comfort and companionship. Pauline cares for her ailing father, who camps out on a military cot in his living room, wearing six-day-old stubble and urine-soaked long underwear, and stays warm under an electric blanket and a sleeping bag, because the hot water heater at his house has gone out (ibid.: 20).

Pauline moves through life making fleeting and momentary connections with other characters, including a man from Alabama named Ford. One night after work, she gets drunk and goes to a Red Lion motel with him. They have sex. His plan doesn't involve staying in town too long. He enjoys Pauline's company and invites her to drive to Utah with him, but she graciously declines the offer and instead goes back to her job. There she meets a 16-year-old runaway girl named Jo, who is bedridden with infections she received from used needles, having kept company with deadbeat druggies who abused her in unimaginable ways. Part of the novel centers on what happens when women reach out to help other struggling women. In Pauline's case, the task of enabling the girl to get back on track helps her as well, and while the "rescue" mission may be limited in its success, it is motivated in part by memories of Pauline's own youthful struggles as a wayward and abandoned teenager. As such, the older woman becomes a nonjudgmental female mentor for the girl, something the younger character sorely needs in these circumstances.

In her recent book on "the possibility of life in capitalist ruins," anthropologist Anna Lowenhaupt Tsing writes about "forms of haunted freedom" that often arise out of our present-day conditions of economic and environmental abandonment in ways that speak meaningfully to the fictional struggles in Vlautin's novels (Tsing 2015: 85). Tsing's project in *The Mushroom at the End of the World* involves chronicling unexpected developments that arise out of ecological disturbance, and the manner in which such forces may go either way, potentially leading to renewal or destruction. Survival "always involves others," she writes (ibid.: 29). It frequently entails collaboration, or what she calls "work across difference" (ibid.) As Tsing usefully points out in her study of ecological disturbance, the "evolution of our 'selves' is already polluted by histories of encounter; we are mixed up with others before we even begin any new collaboration" (ibid.). Such "work across difference" indeed may be needed now more than ever. As Arlie Russell Hochschild argues, in a time of deep social divisions and great uncertainty such as this, we often "grasp for quick certainties" and "settle for knowing our opposite numbers from the outside" (Hochschild 2016: 5). Yet Hochshild wonders if it is possible and preferable in this political climate to get to "know others from the inside" without compromising our core beliefs, "to see reality through their eyes, to understand the links between life, feeling, and politics" in order to better move forward together as a less divided nation (ibid.).

Vlautin's novel examines our collective survival and the potential for learning from each other, even as these possibilities are often presented as unstable, insecure, and uncertain. The characters in *The Free* are indeed free, at times painfully so. They are free from useful or healthy entanglements, free from the security of communities, and free from a much-needed sense of regional and national belonging. Yet, in an interesting way, the war that Leroy fights is in fact based on these ideals. From its beginnings, the war on terror was framed as a project to ensure that America would become, as Neil Campbell and Alasdair Kean point out, "more secure and the world freer and more peaceful" (Campbell and Kean 2016: 296). The critics sum up motivations framing the American global war on terror as an extension of the nation's age-old "special mission," which in previous times was marked by a "strong religious, economic or racial gloss" and which gained "renewed vigor" with the development of the United States' post–Cold War identity as the "leader of the free world" (Campbell and Kean 2016: 4). While the post-9/11 era saw global freedom as an American value requiring a strong collective commitment, the ideals underpinning the war on terror were themselves badly lacking at home.

In this way, the freedoms that Leroy and the other white working-class characters in the novel are fighting for overseas are in short supply in their own lives. As a result, they do not seem like particularly sure things to offer others, but instead as empty ideals often devoid of meaning for the characters themselves. As the story progresses and Leroy does not recover, and as other figures in the novel struggle to maintain a minimal existence, Vlautin draws attention to the larger failures underpinning U.S. wars in the twenty-first century. The novel eventually becomes a story about the struggle to connect across borders, the desire to fit in somewhere, and the search to create much-needed bonds with others. By turning freedom on its head and investigating the problems of rugged individualism in the twenty-first-century West, Vlautin's novel becomes an important and welcome exploration of the numerous poverties shaping white working-class Western lives and the possibility for hope, an element that may save these people if they are able to recognize that their freedoms are illusions.

Andrew Bacevich, a Boston University history professor, U.S. army vet, and West Point graduate, outlines similar concerns about freedom. In his book *Breach of Trust: How Americans Failed Their Soldiers and Their Country*, the author notes that the meaning of modern war in the United States is typically tied to ideas of freedom and democracy; yet he points out that the nation has recently altered the relationship between the military and the populace, in effect freeing the American people from the responsibilities they once maintained in the face of battle. As the nation sought resolution after the unpopular Vietnam War, the army "desperately needed to free itself" from the past. Looking for an escape from the disasters posed by the draft and "those compelled to serve against their will," the U.S. military searched for another way (Bacevich 2013: 11). The task involved creating distance between the army and the rest of America. By leaving behind the draft and freeing itself from its responsibilities to the nation as a whole, the U.S. military hoped to avoid repeating some of the mistakes of Vietnam.

For Bacevich, the result was that "war became the exclusive province of the state" (ibid.: 13). Washington could now wage war whenever it wanted, which Bacevich argues resulted in "something akin to perpetual war," making ongoing military conflict "the new normal" (ibid.: 14). By no longer requiring the American people to involve themselves meaningfully in war, the U.S. military brought forth what he calls a "great decoupling" between the armed forces and the public and a greater use of empty symbols and false assurances regarding what soldiers will be sent to do or what the consequences might be (ibid.: 28). Thus, even while waging a forever war, Americans can now be liberated from their responsibilities and largely able to behave as if they are at peace. The nation is now no longer called on to change its collective behavior, with the result being that most of its citizens believe that they neither have to pay nor "bleed" for war (ibid.: 31–2). Even as financial costs mount, "actual participation in war became entirely a matter of personal choice," as collective sacrifice becomes something entirely voluntary, shunted off onto a small percentage of the population (ibid.: 32, 35). For Bacevich, the economic problems we now face as a nation are intimately tied to this decoupling. "As much as or more than Big Government or Big Business," he argues, "popular attitudes toward war, combining detachment, neglect, and inattention, helped create the crisis in which the United States is mired" (ibid.: 40).

In answering who is actually paying the price for war, *The Free* makes visible which Americans are being called on to serve on the front lines of battle. In Vlautin's novel, the character Freddie McCall, who works on the night crew at Leroy's group home, references this larger history in painting a huge diorama of the Battle of Gettysburg, which he stores in a back room of his house. At one point, Freddie shares the image with his friend, Lowell Price, a Yakima Indian. Hundreds of dead soldiers are scattered across the diorama, a scene that prompts a comment from Lowell: "Serves them right to kill each other after killing the Indians for so long," he tells the other man (ibid.: 78). Freddie gets it, but points out something else to his friend. "Fifty-seven thousand men got hurt or killed during this one battle. More people than live in our entire town. And it was summer and they were left in the sun to die," Freddie notes (ibid.). "And what did it get them? Most of them were kids, hadn't even kissed a girl. Most of them were dirt poor. All that death and destruction and I'm here a hundred and fifty years later painting fake blood on them like it's a game" (ibid.). As the two men note the human losses suffered by the raced and classed bodies featured on Freddie's bloody battlefield, the identity of the nation's fallen becomes evident and it is clear which groups have paid the biggest price for American wars past and present.

Perpetual Freedoms

Vlautin's Western novels do not always make for easy reading. His work frequently portrays characters who are endangered by brutal forms of white male power, including vulnerable white working-class women who try to forge their own sexual identities and yet encounter men's violence and anger in the process. Yet his efforts to depict the contradictions facing these female characters are often noteworthy. Vlautin was born in the early years of Gen X, and one wonders if perhaps he experienced second-wave feminism in the groundwater of his boyhood, or maybe crossed paths with unapologetic Third Wavers— perhaps in the form of sisters, lovers, or coworkers—along the way. Often his stories tackle the intersections of gender, sexuality, class, and race with deeper insights than those of his literary male predecessors were able to do. Women's bodies and the possibilities of their sexual agency face complicated negotiations in his literary world. Some of the female characters want casual or at times rough sex, but always on their own terms. Others want something else. For instance, in trying to recover from a violent sexual past, the character Pauline is shown working hard to prevent a younger female from experiencing the same abuses she once faced.

Ultimately, Vlautin's novels may serve as vehicles for reflecting on the broader connotations of what it means to be free, what Americans in general and Westerners in particular are willing to sacrifice in the name of freedom, and what the relationship of Western American literature might be to this larger project. It is useful to recall Angela Davis's argument about rethinking the forms of freedom and democracy our nation is presently advancing in its perpetual wars. In *The Meaning of Freedom and Other Difficult Dialogues*, Davis points out how "the democracy that the U.S. military is fighting to protect in places like Iraq and Afghanistan sees the free market as the paradigm for freedom and sees competition as the paradigm for freedom" (Davis 2012: 145–6). This understanding favors a "neoliberal conception of economic freedom" that "requires the government to withdraw from virtually all social services," surely something that promises to greatly compound the problems that are already destroying the economically challenged communities Vlautin describes in his Western novels (ibid.: 146).

Immediately after the November 2016 election, a number of American authors began weighing in on what the election might mean for a divided nation and what it reveals about white working-class despair. Novelist Richard Russo, who often centers his work on small towns and white working-class communities in the Northeast, noted that many Americans who now find themselves in economically challenged circumstances are beginning to express anxiety and fear about their lack of opportunities and a new "sense of not belonging anymore" (2016). While he understands these responses, the author also suggests that greater historical and social contexts need to be restored to the larger discussion. While the white working class in America may indeed feel "undervalued, denigrated, ignored," Russo points out that such sentiments are actually not new to America. They are just new to the recently fallen. "Black people in America have felt that way for a long time. So have Latinos," he reminds us (ibid.)

Even as contemporary American writers recognize the limits and dangers of this white rage, the author Atul Gawande argues that now is a good time to figure out how not to make "the lives of those left out meaner and harder" (Gawande 2016: 50). In this way, Vlautin's writings may be helpful for understanding the anguish of living in a disconnected world, and how misplaced resentment, anger, and hatred often flow out of these brutalizing conditions. Even as he opens up this world to readers, Vlautin's Western fiction is carefully attuned to the fact that there's always another way, always the possibility of reaching out to others and questioning borders in order to build affinities across cultural differences. Against the American West's atomized identities and its celebrated anti-intellectualism, and against the larger U.S. pull toward racial anger, despair, and authoritarianism, Vlautin offers alternative visions in his complicated portraits of white working-class people and the struggles and hopes shaping their worlds in the twenty-first century.

ACKNOWLEDGMENTS

I wish to thank the Center for Western Lands and Peoples at Montana State University for research support while writing this essay. I also thank Dan Flory and audience members at the 2015 WLA meeting in Reno for useful comments on earlier versions of this essay.

NOTES

1. The film is *Jeremiah Johnson* (directed by Sydney Pollack, 1972), starring Robert Redford.

WORKS CITED

Anderson, Carol. 2016. *White Rage: The Unspoken Truth about Our Racial Divide.* New York: Bloomsbury.

Bacevich, Andrew J. 2013. *Breach of Trust: How Americans Failed Their Soldiers and Their Country.* New York: Metropolitan Books.

Bengal, Rebecca. 2013. "Nevada Gothic: An Interview with Claire Vaye Watkins." *The New Yorker*, May 20. <http://www.newyorker.com/books/page-turner/nevada-gothic-an-interview-with-claire-vaye-watkins>. Accessed January 26, 2016.

Bevis, William. 1990. *Ten Tough Trips: Montana Writers and the West.* Seattle: University of Washington Press.

Busby, Mark. 1995. *Larry McMurtry and the West: An Ambivalent Relationship.* Denton: University of North Texas Press.

Campbell, Neil. 2015. "Postwestern Literature and Criticism." In Susan Kollin, *A History of Western American Literature*, edited by Susan Kollin, 374–388. Cambridge: Cambridge University Press.

———. 2016. *Affective Critical Regionality.* London: Rowman & Littlefield.

Campbell, Neil, and Alasdair Kean. 2016. *American Cultural Studies: An Introduction to American Culture.* 4th Edition. New York: Routledge.

Carpenter, Brian. 2016, "Introduction: Blood and Bone." In *Grit Lit: A Rough South Reader*, edited by Brian Carpenter and Tom Franklin, xiii–xxxii. Columbia: University of South Carolina Press.

Davis, Angela. 2012. *The Meaning of Freedom and Other Difficult Dialogues.* San Francisco: City Lights Press.

Falcon, Zach. 2015. *Cabin, Clearing, Forest.* Fairbanks: University of Alaska Press.

Filkins, Dexter. 2009. *The Forever War.* New York: Vintage.

Franklin, Tom. 2012. "Preface: What's Grit Lit?" In *Grit Lit: A Rough South Reader*, vii–vii. Columbia: University of South Carolina Press.

Gawande, Atul. 2016. "Health of the Nation." *The New Yorker*, November 21.

Henderson, Smith. 2015. *Fourth of July Creek.* New York: Ecco.

Hochschild, Arlie Russell. 2016. *Strangers in Their Own Land: Anger and Mourning on the American Right.* New York: The New Press.

Isenberg, Nancy. 2016. *White Trash: The 400-Year Untold History of Class in America.* New York: Viking.

Lewis, R. W. B. 1955. *The American Adam: Innocence, Tragedy, and Tradition in the Nineteenth Century*. Chicago: University of Chicago Press.

López, Ian Haney. 2014. *Dog Whistle Politics: How Coded Racial Appeals Have Reinvented Racism and Wrecked the Middle Class*. Oxford: Oxford University Press.

Lowe, Lisa. 2015. *The Intimacies of Four Continents*. Durham: Duke University Press.

Morrison, Toni. 2016. "Mourning for Whiteness." *The New Yorker*, November 21.

Newman, Katherine S. 2000. *No Shame in My Game: The Working Poor in the Inner City*. New York: Vintage.

Rio, David. 2014. *New Literary Portraits of the American West: Contemporary Nevada Fiction*. Bern: Peter Lang.

Russo, Richard. 2016. "Author Richard Russo Ponders What the Presidential Election Was Really About." National Public Radio, *Morning Edition*, November 10. http://www.npr.org/2016/11/10/501537293/author-richard-russo-ponders-what-the-presidential-election-was-reallyabout?utm_medium=RSS&utmcampaign=nprnews. Accessed 11 November 11, 2016.

Sennett, Richard and Jonathan Cobb. 1993. *The Hidden Injuries of Class*. New York: W. W. Norton.

Tatum, Stephen. 1998. "The Problem of the Popular in the New Western History." In *The New Western History: The Territory Ahead*, edited by Forrest G. Robinson, 153–190. Tucson: University of Arizona Press.

Tsing, Anna Lowenhaupt. 2015. *The Mushroom at the End of the World: On the Possibility of Life in Capitalist Ruins*. Princeton: Princeton University Press.

Vlautin, Willy. 2008. *Northline*. New York: Harper Perennial.

———. 2010. *Lean on Pete*. New York: Harper Perennial.

———. 2014. "A Conversation with Willy Vlautin." In *The Free*. New York: Harper Perennial.

———. 2014a. *The Free*. New York: Harper Perennial.

———. 2015. "Author Comments." Roundtable Panel on "Reading Willie Vlautin's West," Western Literature Association, Reno, Nevada, October 16.

Watkins, Claire Vaye. 2013. *Battleborn*. New York: Riverhead.

Williams, John. 2010. "*Lean on Pete*, by Willy Vlautin." *The Independent*, February 3. http://www.independent.co.uk/arts-entertainment/books/reviews/lean-on-pete-by-willy-vlautin-1888692.html. Accessed 6 October 6, 2015.

CHAPTER 9

INTERVIEW WITH WILLY VLAUTIN

This interview was conducted with Willy Vlautin via email, with questions drawn from all the authors in this collection. We have, however, allowed Willy's unique "voice" to come through in these comments and so have not adjusted his expressions or sentence structure.

Tell me about some of your favorite movies and why they matter to you. I note the "sample" from Gas Food Lodging *as important on* Winnemucca, *for example.*

You're right, *Gas Food Lodging* meant a lot to me. My brother called me up one night and told me I had to see the movie, that it was close to our own lives. And he was right, it really was, and I'd never seen a movie that paralleled my own life. The dynamics between the mother and the daughters was similar to ours. Especially for me. The younger daughter and her relationship to her mother and part-time father was a lot like mine. It really was strange to see. I have always loved movies. Even now just the idea of a movie theater eases my mind. Right now, today, I think about *Fat City*, the John Huston film. There's a slowness and a desperation to it I really like. And Jesus, Susan Tyrrell (who plays Oma), is the best. Maybe the worst girlfriend of all time. *Hud* and *The Last Picture Show* are both movies I think about. Also *Repo Man*. When I was in my early twenties I loved *Repo Man* so much that I tried to get a job as a repo man, but the owner of this place asked me if I was tough, and I told him I wasn't. He asked if I minded getting into fistfights. I told him I didn't like fighting. He just laughed and told me he couldn't hire me. But for a kid, man, that movie was the best. Also, right this moment, I think about *Paris, Texas*, *Blue Velvet*, and *Ride the High Country*. They all influenced me.

You have spoken often in interviews of the music you love. Can I probe some more?

Willie Nelson's *Greatest Hits and Some That Will Be* is the one record my mother always had. From when I first can remember until her death it was there. I grew up listening to it and it's always been a friend of mine. Willie Nelson was the longhaired hippy who made it into my house. He somehow got a free pass. My mom grew more and more conservative the older she got; she was tough. But regardless, Willie never got kicked out. That record was always loved. It gave me hope, hope for myself. So Willie's always my man because of it. Tom Waits' music has also been a great pal to me most of my life. He's a classic songwriter, up there with Irving Berlin, the Gershwins, Cole Porter. If you took those guys and put them in a blender with dirt and gasoline and tequila, maybe that would be Tom Waits. I love classic songwriters who take left turns or get wild or dark. He does all that and then he breaks your heart. I love ballads and for me, he writes the best ones. Randy Newman does too. I love a lot of Bruce Springsteen as well. When I was a kid I used to wear his records out. He was cocky and insecure, a loser but not going to stay a loser. He was a romantic and tough and dented and weak all at the same time. I put his records on and I was transported to a different world and I was always looking for a different world. As for my own music I was ruined by the Replacements. The king of the losers. I bought into them like they were the ones with the key to life. My cousin and I used to drink in old man bars from when we were kids just to be like the Replacements. I loved them and all the cowpunk stuff out of LA: X, the Blasters, Rank and File, Green on Red, and Los Lobos. All that stuff really influenced the way I write songs.

I know you have said Northline *is your favorite novel. What about a Richmond Fontaine album you like most? Say why if you can.*

Ah, that's a hard one. I guess I'd choose *Post to Wire* because that's the record where I finally got to give something back to the band. Those guys had stuck with me for years and had gotten nothing more than a hangover and long drives in an old van. With that record people started noticing RF, and man oh man that was great. I suddenly felt all right about myself. Those guys had stuck with Richmond Fontaine and finally we got to play decent gigs and travel overseas. I finally felt like an asset, not the weird depressed guy who wrote too many songs and got too drunk. That era was one of the great breaks of my life.

I was intrigued by your liking for Charles Willeford's Pick Up *and would be interested in why you found this such an important book.*
I do go through fits of loving Jim Thompson, David Goodis, and Charles Willeford. I don't know if those guys actually wrote crime novels. To me they wrote about psychologically damaged people becoming unhinged. Or maybe their stories were just normal but the authors themselves were psychologically damaged. I did relate to them and still do. There's such a mania to them, a working-class defeatism. The idea of just putting a wrench in the middle of your already failing life. About giving up and waking up the next day and living inside the life you've given up. There were a few things I really liked about *Pick Up*. And it's not even the ending. The ending is a huge hook, very interesting and a great trick. But I identified with the self-hatred, the self-destruction. Harry is a failed painter who quits painting, who works as a short-order cook and is an alcoholic. He quit painting because he knew he was good but not great, that he'd never be great. But then he falls in love with Helen, an alcoholic depressive, and she inspires him to try once more to be great. He sobers up some and paints and paints and gets back to where he realizes he's never going to be great. It's so heart-breaking but real. A failed artist. I read all those Black Lizard books when they came out in my twenties. I used to collect them. They used to keep me up at night. I could read one a day and I would. When I began writing I wanted to write books that were raw like that, short and full of emotion. Stories where the people were hanging on by a thread and that's okay. Stories where it's normal to be dented and failed and emotionally ruined. It's okay to be a freak. In a weird way those books gave me great comfort, and really they were the only books my male friends would read when I'd give them a novel. And my goal, early on, was always to write books that working-class guys could get through and get something out of.

Hope often surfaces in your work despite its apparent bleakness. Kindness is often its vehicle. Say something about hope and kindness in your work and about why it matters to you so much.

At its very root life is meaningless without hope. Hope that you'll wake up in the morning, that you'll get through school, that a woman might like you enough to go out with you, that you won't end up a bum, that if you have kids that they'll live longer than you, that you'll make the right decisions more often than not. Throughout my life I've gotten myself in jams that I didn't think I could get out of. Sometimes I'd be too tired to do anything about it but hope and dream that someday I wouldn't be in the situation I was in. Without that hope, what do you have? So in most of my stories I try to talk about the idea of putting one foot in front of the other even when you don't want to or don't think you can. The idea that if you try and make small chess moves you'll break the confines that you've found yourself in. As far as kindness, when I've been on the rocks and found myself down I've been helped. I'm lucky that way. I've often been shown kindness when I'm at my worst. I've sought out that kindness, but I've been lucky to get it. In a different way when you go into a restaurant and a waitress is nice to you, it makes the world seem all right for at least that moment in time. That means something, at least to me. Kindness, even on the smallest level, eases a person's load. But if you've ever been down just to have someone take advantage of you, step on you, then you realize the brutality that's also there. That makes kindness and decency the most valuable things we have. Man, it's rough when it's the other way.

I was raised with the idea that in America you have the ability to do anything you want. It's just up to you to get it or do it. As a kid I'd never seen a bad economy. Before the rise of the Indian casinos I don't think Reno really had a bad economy. There were always jobs. Maybe not high-paying jobs, but okay jobs. My mom said to get a job in Reno all you needed was to be sober and wear a clean shirt. So I grew up with that hopefulness. Throughout America's short history there's always been the idea of heading West to start again. The idea of the West as a place to change who you've been, who you were. The opportunity to become the better you. In many cases that happened. But as it always is, it's also been rough on the working class and minorities. Humanity never changes, just the West had free land, the promise of quick money, and the opportunity or the idea that you might break free of your class or prior situation. Along the way Native people, vulnerable working-class people, and the natural resources were abused, used, and then cast aside. But again that's happened everywhere on earth. That's humanity.

So many of the characters in your fiction seem doomed—their hopefulness, as you have explained, is a counter to this. How does the notion of "fate" or "luck" figure into your worldview?

I mean luck has a lot to do with everything. There's a story I heard where kids are hunting. They are shooting rifles and they get bored and start shooting at a tree on a ridge. Three boys. One of their bullets kills a guy driving in his car a half a mile away. Random. Life can be like that. Or it can run the other way. A broke mom with a dead-end job meets a man in a parking lot who helps change her flat tire. The man runs a business and needs a secretary. The mom doesn't know anything about that kind of work but she's smart. He likes her and gives her a chance. Suddenly she has a good job with benefits. Her kids are better fed and clothed. They are around a mom who is proud of herself. A mom who can afford a new water heater and can buy new clothes for work. She got lucky but she made the most of the luck she was given. There's a huge distinction there. The idea of getting luck and then being smart enough to make it work for you. I thought a lot about that in *The Motel Life*. The Flannigan brothers were scared of being helped, scared of being lucky 'cause then they would have had to stand up and be men. They'd have to be responsible. For some people that's hard to do. In general most people have to make their own breaks. Create their own luck. And the only way to do that is to work hard and try to make things break your way. In regards to hope, hell, when you're in bed late at night to daydream with hope in mind is always more fun than to think of the worst. So I always side with hope, 'cause hope gets you out of bed in the morning and when you get out of bed and try once in a while something good happens.

The song "Allison Johnson" on Post to Wire *(2003) comes before the novel* Northline *(2008) and yet seems to be a "coda" in a way. How do you "marry" these two? How do they relate?*

Northline was a hard book because I truly worried about Allison Johnson. She was a combination of my grandmother, mother, and myself. It was the sort of book where if she makes it I'll make it. There were times when writing it that I would pull out big parts of it where she gets hurt or gets herself in a situation that turns ugly. I'd replace those scenes with a fake truth, an easier life. I'd have her move in with the trucker, T. J. Watson and his wife, I'd have her go to college and be less self-destructive, and I'd write her a song like "Allison Johnson." A song where someone's in love with her, someone's telling her not to give up, that if she keeps trying someday she'll have a place with a cottonwood tree in the backyard and her kids will play there and things will be okay. I'd write all that to ease my mind and then I'd have to pull it out because she wouldn't ever call T. J. Watson, she wasn't ready to go back to school, and she's not quite ready to like herself or take care of herself. I wrote more songs for that book than all my others combined. Mostly I think because that story felt dipped in melancholy, like a sad song you put on repeat. That story felt like a wrecked romantic ballad. But really all my books start as songs. Certain songs don't solve the story, they don't end the idea. Usually when I finish a song I'm finished with that certain idea but sometimes not. Then I write a few more songs about it, and then usually it makes its way into a story. *Lean on Pete* started as a song, *The Free* did, *Northline* did, and *The Motel Life* started as a series of songs. I always say this, but I feel my songs and stories live in the same building, live on the same block. They are connected. My songs are the soundtrack to my novels.

What do you believe parents owe their children?
I guess more than anything they just need to not leave. They need to show up and try the best they can for whoever they are that day. It would be hard to ask for more than that.

Say something about violence in your novels and how you see it socially/ politically?
Violence is in the fabric of humanity. There haven't been many years in the recorded history of mankind where a major military conflict wasn't

going on. Racism and violence have always been there, but I think as a society it's our duty to make a concerted effort to push against violence and racism. It's a never-ending ongoing struggle but to not fight it, to give in to it, brings nothing but pain, heartache, destruction, and hopelessness. Both personally and in society. In my own novels, I use violence only where I think it is necessary. Violence in movies and books is so often used flippantly. If you've ever seen violence in real life you realize how disturbing and frightening it is. How one punch can change people's lives. How one act of rage can ruin families. I try to remember that when I have violence in my books. There's a real cost to it and I'm interested in it only in terms of that.

I feel like a great many of the people in your books would be Donald Trump voters. I'm curious for your insights about this new state of affairs in the USA.

I was as surprised as anyone by the results of the election and I grew up in a conservative home. I grew up in a home that called the *New York Times* nothing more than a socialist rag. But still I would have bet my house that Trump would have lost. So I had no idea. In my novel *Northline* I touched on the ideas of white identity, white power, and the fear of a changing West, both in terms of ethnicity as well as the effects of population growth. But to see these ideas become more mainstream wasn't something I thought would happen. That being said I would see it all around me and hear people talk, but still I believed Americans were more tolerant and more forward thinking. But I was wrong. I guess more than anything it shows how disenfranchised and left out a large segment of society feels. That's something to take seriously. But I've never understood how working-class people can vote against their own self-interests. It's crazy to me. In terms of my novels, in general, my major characters are wounded. People with scars and dents. But mostly they help other people who are in similar situations. They don't try and exploit people's weaknesses for their own benefit. Maybe that's fantasy. Maybe I write that to save my mind and to give me hope. I know the world runs the other way so in my writing I make sure it runs my way too.

I'm curious what you think of the casting of Steve Buscemi as Del in director Andrew Haigh's film adaptation of Lean on Pete. *Did you have much say in the movie?*

I've always been a huge fan of Steve Buscemi. *Trees Lounge* is one of my favorite movies. So I was relieved as hell when I heard he was going to be in it and really he looks like he could work out there, so it was all great luck for me. I haven't seen the movie yet but I really respect and like the director, Andrew Haigh. So I'm hoping for the best. He's had a tough job as he's had to pick which characters to stay with and which to discard. I've always been a huge fan of movies so the whole process is very interesting to me. But in general I've decided to stay away from getting too involved. I love and believe in the novel and the movie industry has chewed up much better and smarter writers than me. So I've decided just to hide out at my place and sell the rights if there is any interest.

How do different forms of creativity, such as writing a novel or playing in a band, feed into each other, and possibly even impede or compete with each other?

Juggling being in a band and writing fiction has always been a struggle for me. You're right, there's only so much time, and both take up a lot of it. Novels take the day-after-day hours. You just have to sit in a room and do the work. Being in a band is different. So much of it is about gigs, trying to get to gigs and lining up tours. It is also about recording dates and rehearsals and doing artwork and the business side. Man, all that stuff just chews up the days, especially when you're a mom-and-pop outfit. But as art forms they really do help each other out. One is all soul and feel and the other is having the discipline to articulate the soul and feel in a longer piece. Writing fiction is so much about just showing up and putting in the hours. Music is too, but with songs sometimes melodies just come to you. And where from? Why does a good melody fall in your lap one day when for the previous month you couldn't write a decent melody to save your life? It's magic at times. Where they help the most is in ideas. I'm a story-oriented songwriter and like I said earlier, oftentimes the story in a song is the seed of a future novel. All my novels started as songs. So they help each other that way quite a bit. I've always written songs, since I was a little kid. I've tried over and over to quit but I haven't been able to yet. I'm just not cut out for the performing aspect of being in a band. It's always wrecked me. But the camaraderie of band life and writing songs is always what brings me back. Writing fiction, however, is something I always love. I might not be the best at it, but I love the process. I love the work ethic, of showing up every day and grinding it out and hopefully fixing a story to the point where it actually runs, where it actually has its own life. And really in the end the two forms take pressure off each other. I always say when I'm writing bad songs it's because I'm really a writer, and when I'm writing bad fiction I always say, well what do you expect, I'm just a musician.

In a recent interview for an online magazine, you put "Harold's Club" among your favorite songs. That's one of the first songs, still with that cowpunk sound of the beginning. Do you recognize yourself on that punk sound when you look back now? Is it difficult to play those songs now?
I always liked the song "Harold's Club." It was one of the first times I thought I got the right mix of cowpunk-garage rock and storytelling. There are certain songs that I never forget writing and that's one of them. It was written as a stab at a lot of the good ol' boys of Reno. Where my mom worked she had to deal with a lot of rich old Reno men. When she'd get home she'd tell me stories about them, the sexism she had to deal with and the elitism she had to be around. That song came from that and from a live pigeon shoot they used to have outside of town. On the last record I put the Harolds Club glass in as a nod to where the band was at the beginning. As the last real record I wanted the lyrics to end where they started, in Reno. As far as the band's changing sound I guess age has something to do with it. Also I just finally accepted that I like writing ballads and that most of the songs I write are ballads. But when you're first starting out and playing punk-rock clubs and dive bars it's hard to play ballads because people just talk over them. So in the early years my answer was to just speed up my ballads and buy a distortion pedal. Some of those old songs will fall by the wayside, more

because I can't get behind the lyrics anymore or the guys are tired of them, but a song like "Harold's Club" or "Saviour of Time" or "43" I never get tired of playing.[1]

I heard you talking about Paul Kelly when you were asked about inspiration or models when writing songs. You also talked about Tom Waits, Shane MacGowan, and many others—even about how literary writers influenced the way you write songs. But, who do you listen to when you want to write a melody, when you want to choose the bars?

Tom Waits and Shane MacGowan have great melodies. Both lean hard on classic melodies, especially MacGowan who seems to grab old Irish melodies and mold and morph them to his lyric ideas. Paul Kelly has great natural melodies. But where do melodies come from? I guess that's where the magic of music is. I'm not sure you can teach someone how to write a heartbreaking melody. You can teach them the chords, the ideas behind how to write one, but why do some writers break your heart and others don't? How can some of the best melodies lie over a simple progression that a kid who's played guitar only a week can figure out? It's the soul of the person maybe. Their blood and heart and of course then skill. The Beatles probably have all the melodies a person could ever want, and they were only one band of working-class guys. How did that happen? So who knows. I just hope for myself that I write a few songs in my life that have great melody, that work both lyrically and melodically.

Did being in a band and touring Europe change who you are and how you write? Do you think sometimes about how and why it is that you are so welcomed in Europe?

I have no idea why people in Europe like the band. I'm just relieved as hell that they do. We have a good manager, that's probably a lot of it. To have someone who cares about the band and is a smart businessman is a huge asset. And we got lucky with the press. They happened to like us. Man oh man what luck. It was the best break I've ever had getting to travel to Europe so often and play so many gigs there. I don't think anyone would have ever thought that I would get to go to Europe and travel and see some of the sites of the world. Only one guy in Richmond

Fontaine had a passport before we started our run over there. We had a party just to celebrate the fact we were getting passports. What a great time. I'm not sure it's changed the way I write though. Still through it all I'm in love with the same things I've always been in love with and I'm still troubled by all the same things I've always been troubled with. But to be driving through Spain is like being in a movie. So hopefully that somehow makes its way into a song or two someday.

Is the final song on Richmond Fontaine's final album, You Can't Go Back If There's Nothing to Go Back To, *the last song you wanted to record? I have the feeling that it is the most Tom Waitsy of the songs that you put on record.* It wasn't the final song we recorded, but I had always thought of that one as the last track on the record. Even when I wrote it I did. And you're right, it does feel like it's dipped somehow in Tom Waits. It's the idea that maybe, after twenty-odd years, the characters in Richmond Fontaine find a place where they fit. Where they are welcomed and belong, where they have an easy run. I was thinking about it in terms of literary characters, too. There are nods to the Flannigan brothers and Annie James as well. I had first recorded it on guitar but then we had Jenny Conlee come in and she played it on piano and it seemed to work better. That's where the Tom Waits feel comes in. I wanted it to be a song that would be played at the party the people in the song are at. One of them would play that song in the late hours of the night to everyone there.

You seem to rework the traditional rock/pop/country song structure so as to jettison the verse-chorus-lead instrumental break-verse-chorus template. What has been the thinking when approaching arrangements to your songs? In the early years of Richmond Fontaine, and maybe to a lesser degree in the later records, I was solely focused on the story of the song. I never thought of people listening or if it made sense musically or was enjoyable. I was just in my own little world worrying that the story of the song wasn't right. I was young. I'm surprised the guys didn't kill me. Or at least quit. As the band grew, so did I. When we started playing with Sean Oldham and Paul Brainard I think the band became its own. Those two are jazz guys, schooled, and they helped reign in some of my ideas. They also gave me a vocabulary to talk about music. They made it a lot more fun. But still, even now, I think of the song as a soundtrack to the lyrics so I don't always follow the traditional path. I guess that can be seen as a good thing but probably a bad thing as well.

Dream/escape/freedom seems central to all of your novels. This is perhaps the most Western thing about them. Can you speak to an evolution in your thinking on this subject? How has your thinking regarding this developed over time?

Escapism, the idea of escape, is central I think to who I am. The idea of being stuck and seeing no way out brings a serious destructive side to me. A hopelessness. As a kid I dealt with that by daydreaming, with living inside week- and month-long daydreams. I could be talking to my mom or a teacher and at the same time living in another world. It was how I got through life. It's not the best thing, a pretty bad crutch, but a crutch I've used for as long I can remember. I try my best now not to indulge in it too much. It's like drinking, it doesn't give you anything concrete back but isolation and longing. But it's fun when you're doing it. When I began writing I did so purely for escape. To live in a world I wanted but couldn't find. None of my early stories and daydreams were dramatically different than my own life, I just added the things I wanted or needed. Frank Flannigan from *The Motel Life* is a lot like me in that sense. Unable to really change his life, make a stand for himself, he hides inside the comfort of stories. The stories are often tragic and hard, but they are his, where he can control things and he can bring into it and take out who and what he wants. I think a lot of people are stuck to the point where they feel they have little choice in their lives. If you add economic instability, lack of confidence, and a shaky home life, what else do you have but your mind? Your mind has everything in the world you could ever want, you just have to dream it. To me that's a seriously seductive idea. I spent a lot of years in dead-end jobs where my confidence to even be a warehouseman was tested. I wasn't much at all, but in my daydreams I was. I wasn't the greatest man who ever lived, but I was living a better life, a life I couldn't seem to get in reality.

One of the most difficult aspects of writing about your work lies along these lines: to escape is to create an absence in one place, and a presence in another;

and yet, characters like Frank, Allison, Charlie, Freddie, and Pauline are already invisible, so to disappear is the last thing one would expect of them. Comment on visibility and disappearance in your work?

I don't think Frank, Allison, Charley, or Pauline *are* invisible. They are just normal people who have been dented by life. Like all people, they have scars. Their scars, however, get in their way of living more normally. I don't put Freddie McCall in this group. Freddy is weighted by responsibility and familial obligations. But Frank, Jerry Lee, Allison, Charley, and Pauline are damaged. They aren't invisible at all. Every person you pass walking down the street or in a store, they all have scars and are trying to get by. They all have dreams and heartbreaks. They are important. I think for a lot of people there is a hopelessness in that they are stuck in nowhere jobs, in relationships they don't feel they can get out of, and all the while their own mind is telling them they are nothing. Not only society is saying that, they are as well. They are battling with self-worth while they are getting beat up in real life by their situations. In a lot of ways I wrote *The Motel Life* as a study in self-defeat. The idea of helping do yourself in. Giving up before you even try. That idea of thinking like a beaten man, thinking of yourself as a failure is one of the hard things about living in the lower working class. But it's also comforting in a way. You think you're nothing, so you don't try for more. Trying is hard, trying and failing is demoralizing and embarrassing so a lot of people don't put themselves in those situations. When we meet the Flannigan brothers they are living that life. I was trying to figure those issues and ideas when I wrote the book. To me Charley Thompson and Pauline Hawkins are heroes. As heroic as anyone. Charley for always staying true to himself and not giving up, and Pauline for always helping people even when no one really helps her. Allison Johnson and Frank Flannigan are survivors. Maybe in a way they too are heroic. They didn't give up. In that sense they aren't invisible but important.

What role does race play in your novels?

I don't address race too much in *The Motel Life*, as Reno at the time the novel takes place was mostly white. When Nevada's ethnic landscape began to change, I started noticing more skinheads around Reno. I started noticing guys I grew up with say more and more racist things.

Northline came from that. In that book I was interested in the changing West. How people adapt to change. In a lot of ways *Northline* is also about fear. Fear of change, fear of standing up on your own, and fear of immigrants. It's a book on how damaged people respond to fear. Being weak gets a person into a lot of bad situations. Most of the bad decisions I've made have been rooted in weakness. Either self-destructive because of self-hatred or being too scared to take a chance on something or not standing up for myself. Allison Johnson in *Northline* pays the price for being weak. She gets dealt a rough hand and then for a while gives in to it. But at her core she's resilient, and she finally finds that part of herself and survives. She's wounded but she's trying hard not to be wounded. In that sense I wrote her to give myself hope. In *Lean on Pete* I was interested in perseverance. I was interested in the idea of not giving up. Of trying to land somewhere safe, somewhere you might want to be. A place where you might be proud to be yourself. In *Lean on Pete* the two Mexican men Charley meets represent immigrants who have made it but understand the hard life. The first man we don't know much about, he just gives Charley his breakfast and gives him some money. He does this out of kindness, he does this because he knows how lonely and hard it is to have no home. To be out of the system, on the run with no power or rights. He knows the perils and difficulties of a person on the road. The second man, Santiago, represents stability. The reward of keeping your head down and fighting for your place, for your family's place. The idea that if you don't give in to self-destruction you can find a place for yourself. In many ways Santiago sees in Charley the illegal immigrant's life. Charley has no solid footing, no family, no roots, no legal power. He's truly alone. *The Free* is a book about nursing, and also in my own way a State of the Union address. The story takes place in a no-name city. Its focus isn't race but the working class in general. The book I'm working on now focuses more on race in the West.

To what extent does vulnerability provide points of contact between the dispossessed as a means for solidarity and redemption?
If I do write about the solidarity of the dispossessed, it's because I need that sorta idea just to survive in my own head. The idea of kindness

towards people who are in the same sorta pain you're in. When you're down on your luck and someone is decent to you, helps you, treats you with respect, it's a tremendous feeling. It can really help. It can save you. But people in pain all respond differently. Some hurt those they shouldn't, they act out on those who want to help. Bitterness and selfishness. Cornered people can be the ugliest. They often try to drown those who are trying to save them. In my novels I think we see both sides. The kind and the unkind. But I do tend to show the kind more. It's important for me to do so because I've been helped in my life and so I know kindness is real. Also, like I've mentioned before, I write for myself first and oftentimes I need to be around people like Pauline Hawkins or Charley Thompson. I need heroes. In general, disenfranchised people always suffer injustice because they have no power. They are at the bottom and it's always ugly at the bottom.

To what extent do you view your books as being distinctively "Nevadan"?
I'm not sure. I know I've been in love with Nevada. Like a woman that you fall for. I've been that way about Reno, Winnemucca, and Elko. I've been that way about central Nevada. I don't think I know any more than anyone else about the state, I just like it. It's always been good luck for me to think about it. And I've always had good times there. Adventures and near-misses. As a drinking man you can't have a bad time in Nevada unless you're prone to having a bad time. So I'm just a sucker. I fall for things and when I can't have them I dream them into my stories.

What about the relationship between fiction and the places it describes? In particular, the American West. More exactly, is it possible to know which has the greater influence on the other, the place on the writing or the writing on the place?
The West today is as it's always been since European arrival, ever changing and being pushed around. Pushed around in the sense of exploiting it for its limited natural resources. The future of a lot of the Southwest and California revolves around water and population growth and it'll be interesting how we address these issues. What I also find interesting is the relationship of the Bureau of Land Management

(BLM) and local Western communities. The federal government owns so much of the West and so many smaller communities don't agree with the way they handle things. I find their relationship interesting. The Bundy incidents in Oregon and Nevada are fascinating examples in that regard. Both in terms of the outcomes, but also in the deep-seated distrust and dislike so many local communities have for the BLM, even though in most small communities at least one family member works for the federal government and rural counties rely heavily on federal money and grants.

However, it takes me a long time to write a novel. I'm slow at it. I live inside the world of a book for literally years. So I want to make sure that it's a place I'm in love with. Life's too short for me to not write about a place I love. So for me to spend years in the parts of Reno I like or years at Portland Meadows horse track was easy. Every day I worked on those books I felt lucky to be in the world of the novel. It was a lot different for *The Free*. Besides Leroy's dream life, location meant very little. Location isn't a character. It's a novel that could be set anywhere. I wrote it as a novel that could take place in any U.S. city. Sadly this story does take place in most U.S. cities. It was the hardest book I've done because of that. Besides Leroy, none of the characters are free, and they are trapped in their jobs, in their situations, and their city. Writing that one about did me in.

So how romantic are you about places? Are there places you dislike?
I've always been drawn to the American West, the landscapes of the high desert. I was spoon-fed it since I was a kid and it stuck. I could write a thousand stories set in the West and never be bored. I guess I don't have a lot of spaces that I dislike. Maybe a crowded Walmart where some crazy lady is yelling at me or an office of some warehouse where I'm getting interviewed for a job by a manager who doesn't like me but is going to hire me. A traffic jam in the middle of some huge city is something I always dislike. I have a hard time with mass humanity.

I remember where I was when I fell in love with Reno. I was in my early twenties. I was day drinking in a bar called the Last Dollar Saloon. It was a rough alky bar, and a place I would only go to when

I did my laundry next door. An old lady dressed like a rancher's wife from the 1950s asked me to dance. She was living in a trailer behind the bar. She was missing teeth and was half-crying while we were dancing. We were both wrecks; different ages and situations but we were both struggling. Brenda Lee was on the jukebox and for that little bit of time the world seemed all right. That day I realized if I ended up like the people in that bar maybe it was okay. It wasn't as bad as I thought. I'd be all right. I left that day truly in love with that part of Reno. The part that houses the casualties of a gambling city. Where the gamble-holics and alcoholics live. My heart felt like that part of the city. So in a lot of ways I was born to the right place. It was only later on when I tried to escape that sorta world that I found that world didn't want me to escape. I spent my first thirty-five years running into alky bars and now I do my best just to stay out of them.

If landscape is your inspiration, the heart of your work seems to be the odd construction, resentments, and aspirations of and for Western families.
Fractured families interest me mostly because that's what I know. I never lived with my dad. My home was stable on one front, my mom had the same job for thirty years, but I always felt the home part could vanish. That I could get kicked out, that if I said the wrong thing I would be asked to leave. I think even as a young boy I had one foot out the door in case I was asked to for real. As a kid I used to spend a lot of my life dreaming about living in a motel. I was too young to know how to set up utilities or fill out an apartment application but I knew all you had to have was money and you had an instant home in a motel. I think that's why I've always loved motels. Just seeing them is a comfort and Reno, when I was a kid, had literally hundreds of old motels. So I might not be the right one to ask about families and the West. I do think that the U.S. can be very lonely in terms of family. Maybe freeing but maybe also lonely. Grandparents often live in different cities, uncles and aunts in another, siblings in yet others, mom in one city, and dad in the next. I think for a lot of people today there's not a family safety net to help when things go south. In my own life I grew up believing that no one would save me and that those closest to me would probably let

me down. That's just the way I was raised so I see the world through that lens even though I try my best not to. But obviously it comes out in my stories.

What makes you laugh out loud?
Well, I mentioned *Repo Man* earlier, and just thinking about it made me laugh out loud. Usually movies do the trick and I watch the same ones over and over and they always make me laugh. *Slap Shot, Used Cars.* Not highbrow stuff, but I want to live inside all those movies and wish I could.

Here are a few New York Times *"By the Book" questions. What books might readers be surprised to see on your bookshelves? What books are waiting to be read on your night table?*
I have all my favorite books by my bed. Books that bring me luck. *Cannery Row* by John Steinbeck, *Dirty Work* by Larry Brown, *Ironweed* by William Kennedy, *The Woman Who Walked into Doors* by Roddy Doyle, *Fat City* by Leonard Gardner, *Where I'm Calling From* by Raymond Carver, and Flannery O'Conner's collected short stories. As to books that might be surprising...I always have some sorta self-help/psychology book going for when my mind falls apart. Sadly, I never get through any of them. I always have a Western too, and it's the same with them. I get partway through and then give up. But it always eases my mind to see a Western by my bed.

In the work you've created, what are you most proud of?
That's hard to say, I guess it depends which day it is. I love all my books. They're friends of mine, they've helped me get through hard times. They are my saints. If they are good literature or not, I don't know, but their hearts are good. I write first to save myself; I worry about everyone else later. So Pauline Hawkins and Freddy McCall from *The Free* are my friends. They inspire me to try and be better than I am. The Flannigan brothers, from *The Motel Life*, are my drinking buddies. They're in my blood. So is Allison Johnson. Charley Thompson, from *Lean on Pete*, always reminds me to be tougher, to get out of bed and put one foot in front of the other. He's tough as hell where I'm not.

What would you like to be doing ten years from now?
Hopefully I'll be writing a novel and working on a record. Those are the things I like to do. I wouldn't mind doing that on a ranch in Nevada somewhere though.

NOTES

1. The song "Harold's Club" has an apostrophe as it appears on the album *Obliteration By Time*; however, the actual casino was Harolds Club (see Alicia Barber, *Reno's Big Gamble: Image and Reputation in the Biggest Little City*. [Lawrence: University Press of Kansas, 2008], 158).

CONCLUSION

"And from the West Hope and Repair"

by NEIL CAMPBELL

As the essays in this collection make clear, Willy Vlautin's characters, like Francis Phelan in *Ironweed*, are "apparencies in process," moving like vagabonds, searching for family, purpose, and home in an American West that has for so long denied them what was traditionally a presupposed right and the bedrock of its self-defined mythology and legacy of conquest. They are *in process*, struggling to gain a foothold in the world, to be honest with themselves, to make meaningful connections with others, and to resist the terrible temptations and "quiet violence" of everyday life in the American West. Perhaps with this in mind, Vlautin once referred cryptically to his own writing as "crime fiction without the crime," as if drawing attention to his work's fascination with the consequences and aftermath of trauma, violence, and failure, and how these forces might be tracked back to the past and their inevitable mythic relations in the American West. As Frederic Jameson has written of Raymond Chandler, "the underlying crime is always old, lying half-forgotten in the pasts of the characters" (2016: 86), waiting to be unearthed and brought to light. In an interview, Vlautin said,

> In many ways crime writers are the ones who address working-class issues and working-class lives. They also have more freedom to bring up bigger social issues…I've always wanted to write crime fiction without the crime. Have the intensity of a crime novel, the directness and roughness, but without the crime. I've

always wanted to write working-class stories that could keep you up in the middle of the night, but not rely on having a guy coming through the door with a gun.[1] (La Tray, 2016)

"Crime" in Vlautin's writing is deeply entangled in the everyday lives of his working-class characters, living in the shadow of the past. His work, as a result, like so much crime fiction, exposes the "bigger social issues" surrounding his "dangerously compromised characters" in a society tainted by disparities of power, vast economic and class differences, and shrinking opportunities to fulfil the central promise of the go-getting good life. As Jameson has written of Chandler, "his crimes do without villains; or if you prefer...the villains are social" (2016: 86). As Walter Benjamin famously noted of Eugène Atget's photography, with its interest in the "unremarked, forgotten, cast adrift," it had the impact of "the scene of a crime" because for him, "every square inch of our cities [are] the scene of a crime" and "every passer-by a culprit" (1997: 250, 256). In Vlautin's writing, *the scene of a crime* is equally of the everyday, located in the cities and the countryside of the West, in the social worlds his novels and songs explore. Thus the writing inevitably becomes deeply interrogative, as all crime writing is, probing this milieu with the "intensity...directness and roughness" he admires in "noir" writers like Jim Thompson, Charles Willeford, and George Pelecanos, but without resorting to generic clichés like "a guy coming through the door with a gun." Instead, Vlautin's work is atmospherically engaged with a "poetics of exposure", revealing the West as a "fallen place," as Kollin has it, where crime is "buried in that world's past" (Jameson 2016: 86). Both "social" and structural, it is built into the cruel optimism of everyday life, with its systemic violence, endless distortions of freedom, and relentless exploitation of aspiration.

Thus the myths of freedom Kollin discusses in Chapter 8 can no longer be taken for granted as ethical and life-affirming because they have, in truth, become dangerously distorted, in effect given a licence for xenophobia, racism, and sexual violence. Perhaps this is what Frederick Jackson Turner long ago predicted in "The Problem of the West," when he wrote, "The West was another name for opportunity... an open field, unchecked by restraints," producing a type of freedom in which capitalism flourished, further empowering "Western man" as the flag-bearer of "manifest destiny" (1961: 69). More recently, George Packer's *The Unwinding* sums up this danger:

> …The unwinding brings freedom, more than the world has ever granted, and to more kinds of people than ever before—freedom to go away, freedom to return, freedom to change your story, get your facts, get hired, get fired, get high, marry, divorce, go broke, begin again, start a business, have it both ways, take it to the limit, walk away from the ruins, succeed beyond your dreams and boast about it, fail abjectly and try again. And with freedom the unwinding brings its illusions, for all these pursuits are as fragile as thought balloons popping against circumstances. Winning and losing are all-American games, and in the unwinding winners win bigger than ever, floating away like bloated dirigibles, and losers have a long way to fall before they hit bottom, and sometimes they never do. (2013: 3-4)

Yet even as these myths buckle under the interrogative gaze of Vlautin's critical regionality, revealing the deep-seated social crimes intrinsic to the West, his characters, "losers" with a "long way to fall" despite their flawed and vulnerable existence, hold on to gestures of hope wherever they can be found; through storytelling, as Chisum argues, through the entanglements of "elsewhere," as Lombardi explains, or through simple acts of mutual inclusion and exchange, as discussed in many chapters throughout this book. If these people are lucky enough to find some care and, perhaps, even love or "affection," as Chaparro Sainz claims in Chapter 1, then, despite the troubling times in which they live, they may have some hope of flourishing. As Vlautin put it in an early song, when all the compass points turned to pain and despair, "from the West" comes "hope and repair" ("Hope and Repair," *Lost Son*, 2004). So, despite the association of the West with "blood guilt and national aggression" (Jameson 2016: 33), disappointment, failed expectations, and what Tatum calls "dread," Vlautin holds onto an unshakeable belief in humanity: "It's the idea that if you persevere, if you can overcome anxiety and fear, and you run towards kindness and decency and not bitterness and hate, that maybe, just maybe you'll be alright" (Vlautin and Campbell, 2013).

Such human flourishing, as David Hesmondhalgh terms it (2013: 5), emerges through the power of narrative in fiction and songs to engage us individually via our inner being, but more than that, to enable us to reach out to others' lives, to see and feel as they do rather than remain trapped inside the cage of our own anxieties. In Chapter 7, Lombardi calls this hard-won "active affinitive kinship," emerging through "unthinkable" struggles that seem "intrinsic to everyday life" in Vlautin's work. Both music and fiction are central to this process, driven as they inevitably are by engaged storytelling or carried by the power of sound to expand emotions and alter consciousness, taking us from wherever we are to somewhere else. Being stretched beyond ourselves and our immediate locality can realign us with others who have different views, and can produce a sense of commonality often erased by the assumed social focus on individual achievement and personal gain. Judith Butler, appropriately, describes something similar as the capacity for "hearing beyond what we are able to hear...being open to narration that decenters us from our supremacy" (2006: 18). Vlautin's fictional worlds rewrite individualism as a form of "supremacy" and strive instead for commonality of purpose, mutuality, and kindness based on "an apprehension of the precariousness of life" that depends upon an understanding of "the Other" (Butler 2006: xvii-xviii). Karen Barad, as Lombardi reminds us in Chapter 7, argues that "the entanglements we are a part of reconfigure our beings, our psyches, our imaginations, our institutions, our societies" (2007: 383), and it is this difficult journey Vlautin's characters so often undertake. For they are living in the aftermath of loss, to borrow a phrase once again from Stephen Tatum, or, as Vlautin might put it, they are "fuck-ups" and losers trying to make it through life in the best way they can, "trying to make heavy decisions when they shouldn't be making any decisions at all" (*No Depression*, 2003). Yet contained within this sense of loss, as Butler argues, is something potentially vital, since, "when one loses, one is faced with something enigmatic: *something is hiding in the loss*" (ibid.: 21-22—emphasis added). As Vlautin's people mourn their loss—of home, dignity, stability, and relationships—and struggle with the dread, fear, and anxiety this produces, "something about who [they] are is revealed, something that delineates the ties [they] have to others, that shows us that these ties constitute what [they] are, ties or bonds that compose [them]" (ibid.: 22). In other words, losing or being lost can return us to some sense of community's "relational ties," challenging our "self-conscious account of ourselves" as autonomous individuals so as to face up to the reality that, ultimately, we live *with* and *through* others and, as a consequence, are "undone by each other" (ibid.: 23). In moments of extremis, in grief, loss, and violence, but also in love and care, "one is beside oneself," "undone," and as such, is taken beyond a bounded being and, therefore, "implicated in lives that are not our own" (ibid.: 28).

So, as Lombardi and Kollin explain in their chapters, using the same example from *Lean on Pete*, Charley, at a low ebb, vulnerable, exhausted, and desperate, is shown kindness by a Mexican man, Guillermo, who asks him "Eres un fugitivo?" ("Are you a fugitive?"). He then feeds him and tells him he is crazy for making his perilous journey with such a tired horse in a man's world, and above all, that he should take care (2010: 179). Of course, referring back to the discussion above, it is "care" and compassion Guillermo offers Charley and, in his vulnerability, Charley is opened up ("undone") enough to accept this kindness with a knowing exchange of smiles (ibid.: 180). As he moves away, Charley feels different, even transformed by this recognition of help and support: "For the first time I felt that we weren't cursed" (ibid.). Under such conditions of hopefulness, the West for Vlautin cannot be static or unchanging, but rather is constantly adapting to the worlds it absorbs, its "vagabondage," as Tatum calls it, approaching what Kathleen Stewart terms "a live composition," "a thing made up of our itineraries shuttling back and forth across its surface" (2014: 551, 557).

In such moments of vulnerability throughout Vlautin's work, it is as if there were "a sudden address from elsewhere" (Butler 2006: 29), like Paul Newman speaking to Allison Johnson or Willie Nelson to the Flannigans, from which new and different relations might occur, entangling characters within forms of community with a renewed appreciation of "our collective responsibility" for all things (ibid.: 29-30). Precisely because Vlautin's characters are haunted, wounded, and vulnerable, like Allison Johnson, Pauline Hawkins, and Charley Thompson, they are opened to the world through others, and "the wound itself testifies to the fact that... [they are] impressionable, given over to the Other in ways that [they] cannot fully predict or control" (ibid.: 46). Through *opening up* to others and their lives, they move, however tentatively, toward compassion, empathy, and love. As Martha Nussbaum explains, this amounts to a universal human capability: "Being able to have attachments to things and people outside ourselves; to love those who love and care for us, to grieve at their absence; in general, to love, to grieve, to experience longing, gratitude, and justified anger. Not having one's emotional development blighted by fear and anxiety, or by traumatic events of abuse or neglect" (2000: 79).

So, at the end of *The Motel Life*, Vlautin seems to sketch out an agenda for much of his writing: "I hoped. Because it's better than having nothing at all" (Vlautin 2006: 206). His novels constantly reach through suffering, despair, bad luck, weakness, and insecurity to find some alternative economy, organized around a pattern of exchange and giving built not on the material of work, labor, wages, enterprise, and the dream of the good life, but on an affective economy of love, loyalty, care, kindness, mutuality, and hope. As Brian Massumi has written, "In affect, we are never alone," since it operates as process, exchange, or "transition": if "you affect something, you are at the same time opening yourself up to being affected" (2015: 6, 4). One of Vlautin's favorite characters, Earl Hurley, demonstrates many of these characteristics, which shine through his gritty, capitalist exterior, like several of the other minor characters within the novels who offer help, advice, or kindness: "I don't mean to offer you advice, kid, but I like you. It's your mind set, your whole way of thinking, what's bothering me. You're thinking like a beaten man.... My guess is you're still an all right kid...don't make decisions thinking that you're a low life, make decisions thinking you are a great man, at least a good man.... There's a world out there. If you don't open your eyes you ain't ever gonna see it" (Vlautin 2006: 155–56).

To survive in the post-West without simply repeating the myths of the past cannot, ultimately, be a solitary act, like that of some heroic movie cowboy, or as in crime fiction, like a guy coming through the door with a gun. It must be something closer to Anna Tsing's recent notion of "collaborative survival," born out of appreciating "entangled," interdependent ways of life often emerging precisely because of "precarity" and "disturbance" (2015: 4). Tatum refers to LaCapra's "empathic unsettlement" in this context as a necessary extension of the self (2001: 699). Vlautin's writing is filled with affective disturbance, with what Tsing calls "knots and pulses of patchiness" in which people, like Tsing's precious matsutake mushrooms, grow and flourish or, at least, survive, realizing that "to survive, we need help, and help is always the service of another" (2015: 29). In Karen Barad's extended discussion of related topics, she claims that "Responsibility entails an ongoing responsiveness to the entanglements of self and other, here and there, now and then" (2007: 394), and, similarly, Vlautin's characters learn, to varying degrees, that their lives have to include others, and can only flourish through exchange, encounter, and entanglements: e.g., Frank and Annie, Charley and Aunt Margy, Allison and Dan, and Freddie McCall and his children ("We have to stick together. There's no point if we're not nice to each other. Okay?" (Vlautin 2014: 260). Susan Kollin calls this a "more inclusive freedom" because it opens individual lives up to others for cooperation, communion, and love, understanding that, as Tsing puts it, "survival always involves others" and "collaboration is work across differences" (2015: 29). To achieve all this, one has to face, question, and critique "the simplifications of progress narratives" and the "expansion-conquest strategies of relentless individuals" (ibid.: 6, 29), like those long associated with and endlessly reproduced in narratives of the mythic American West. One must adopt alternative forms of critical regionality that exhort one to engage in "entangled ways of life," "curiosity," and "noticing" so that the nuances, details, and surprises of the local become uppermost; the goal is not to turn inward and close borders, but rather to "enlarge what is possible . . . [through] other kinds of stories" (ibid.: 4, 6, 37, 156). Vlautin understands the complex interrelations between the local events of Reno or Portland and the wider world of global wars, economic strain, and racist fears, for they are everywhere in his writing, and the stories he tells return us again and again to the conditions of human care and reciprocity. As Kathleen Stewart argues, "Regionality comes into view at a limit" where established "categories and representations" are questioned and one starts to pay attention to "the tactile compositionality of things" and how "strands of influence" stretch "from land to heart and habit" in a complex, multifaceted arrangement (2013: 277–78). So regionality, as in Vlautin's work, "is constituted in moves and encounters that continually re-set the self-world relationship" as people and places exchange, "shift or roll . . . accrue, sediment, unfold, wear out, or go flat" in an ever-changing assemblage (ibid.: 278). Such an affective sensitivity reminds us increasingly of "our angle of participation in processes larger than ourselves" and our "sense of embeddedness in a larger field of life" (Massumi 2015: 6).

Interestingly, in the context of this book's concern with the intersections of music, fiction, illustration, and soundtrack, Tsing explains her approach to writing new stories as creating "polyphonic assemblages" inspired by "music in which autonomous melodies intertwine" rather than simply follow unified, repetitive structures (2015: 157). Derived in part from Bakhtin's use of the term in *Problems of Dostoevsky's Poetics* (1984), can also describe Vlautin's writing, across all its forms, "polyphonic", in the sense that it too rejects a "single perspective" (ibid: 24). Assembling simultaneously a number of voices and sounds from "elsewhere," from below, from the "minor" or fugitive margins of American culture, it expresses postwestern regional worlds as "a plurality of consciousnesses...each with its own world [that] combine but are not merged" (Bakhtin 1997: 6). Think of Dan's plural response to the Harolds Club mural, with its mythic pioneer creation-story of the West, interrupted by his uncle's imagined tales of "all the people in it," of Dan's photographs and memories, and of his uncle's request for deeper information ("how many kids the lady in the wagon train had") (Vlautin 2008: 191). As Karen Barad explains,

> Remembering and re-cognizing do not take care of, or satisfy, or in any other way reduce one's responsibilities; rather, like all intra-actions, they extend the entanglements and responsibilities of which one is a part. The past is never finished. It cannot be wrapped up like a package, or a scrapbook, or an acknowledgment; we never leave it and it never leaves us behind. (Barad 2007: ix)

Through Dan's inclusiveness, multiple layers usurp the single perspectives of corporate myth to offer new and different, more-human
engagements with the world of the West, where the ongoing past becomes bound up with a lived and responsible sense of the present and
future.

Tsing's polyphony goes further, searching for "fugitive moments
of entanglement" (2015: 255) and, as many of these essays have shown,
Vlautin's writing moves in a similar direction, representing characters
from precariously unstable "worlds" quick to disappear, fleeting, and
elusive, wandering and roving like vagabonds, escaping captivity or
intolerable circumstances in search of some "elsewhere." It's a mood
captured brilliantly on Richmond Fontaine's final album: "I know what
you abandon dies/What you leave leaves you too/I know you can't go
back/If there's nothing to go back to" ("I Got Off the Bus"). These are
the voices that we hear in the songs and follow through the novels,
existing in fugitive environments and yet still able to survive, learn,
and even flourish since, as Simon O'Sullivan puts it, through "genuine
encounter...our typical ways of being in the world are challenged, our
systems of knowledge disrupted. We are forced to thought. The encounter then operates as a rupture in our habitual modes of being.... It
produces a cut, a crack" (2006: 1). And yet these cuts and cracks emerge
from within what Tatum calls the "phantasmagoria of the everyday",
as Vlautin's work testifies: "microshocks," providing "a rustle at the
periphery of vision... [a] shift of attention...an interruption, a momentary cut...," from which, as we "re-jig around the interruption...
the body braces for what will come...its potential for more of life to
come" (Massumi 2015: 53). Out of precarity's disruptive force, new directions may appear *for what will come.*

Perhaps, nonetheless, this polyphonic quality of drawing in influences and voices from elsewhere, to "crack" or "cut" into the established frames of thought, myth, and expectation, has its roots closer to
home, in the *experience* of belonging within Richmond Fontaine, which
Willy Vlautin has often spoken of as a communal process, collaborative, generative, and social (see O'Hagan, 2016). He often speaks of the
band as comrades and family members and the touring experience as
a productive, if entangled, journey where the individual encounters

others and a rich, artistic "contamination" accrues (Tsing 2015: 29).[2] Earlier, Tatum cited Greil Marcus's comment about how the Clash (another favorite band of Vlautin's) produced a type of politics "for community" from "an intensified eyes-open version of everyday life" that understood "the self-discovery of individuals as a means to solidarity" (1999: 29). Working with others, building songs out of differences and contradictions, is a type of polyphonic action standing in contrast to novel writing's often solitary creative process, achieved by retreating from the world for long periods of time. These differences return us to a central concern in Vlautin's writing, having to do with commonality, kindness, and care emerging not smoothly but through contestation and what Tsing calls "friction": "A wheel turns because of its encounter with the surface of the road; spinning in the air it goes nowhere" (Tsing 2005: 5). The West's mythic emphasis on the individual, often alienated and struggling against others to succeed, has morphed into a neoliberal order or "crime scene," emphasizing concepts of freedom and competitive individualism like those explored in Packer's *The Unwinding*. Under such regimes of representation, notions of commonality, community, mutual inclusion, and reciprocity appear remote and old-fashioned, even sentimental. However, one of Vlautin's favourite novels, John Steinbeck's *Cannery Row*, sums it up in a much more positive manner:

> "It has always seemed strange to me," said Doc. "The things we admire in men, kindness and generosity, openness, honesty, understanding and feeling are the concomitants of failure in our system. And those traits we detest, sharpness, greed, acquisitiveness, meanness, egotism and self-interest are the traits of success." (1947: 232)

The *community* of Richmond Fontaine, and of playing as part of a collective sociality, equates to the type of world Steinbeck creates in *Cannery Row*: of Mack and the boys living together in a diverse and contrary place, "a poem, a stink, a grating noise, a quality of light, a tone, a habit, a nostalgia, a dream" (1947: 121). Despite their poverty, they live cooperatively and productively, if "frictionally," within this affective landscape, exercising many of the "traits" Doc speaks of above, and providing, for Willy Vlautin, an analogical vision of a necessary and hopeful existence in the world of the West.

Regionality, with its mantra of "Being 'from here,'" argues Stewart, is not, in reality, a localized and isolating process, but one that "nests in concentric rings stretching out from encounters to tastes, bodies, neighborhoods, a valley, a state, a geographical region" (2013: 280). As in Steinbeck's *Cannery Row* or Vlautin's novels and music, regionality is an "edgy composite," alive and actively assembling itself through relations, encounters, entanglements, and conflicts (ibid.: 281). Again, Tsing expresses this nicely: "Rubbing two sticks together produces heat and light; one stick alone is just a stick" (2005: 5).

When Steinbeck asks at the opening of *Cannery Row*, "How can the poem and the stink and the grating noise—the quality of light, the tone, the habit and the dream—*be set down alive?*," he poses the issue of how everyday regionality can be conveyed in all its terrible, multiple beauties. His answer, like Vlautin's, is "to open the page and to let the stories crawl in by themselves" (1947: 122—emphasis added). Of course, for Vlautin, *to let the stories crawl in* demands an unflinching and cathartic confrontation with every aspect of life in the post-West, which, as in Anna Tsing's work, involves deliberately disturbing the ground and unsettling the past with "productive friction" because "hope begins in considering the possibility that tiny cracks might yet open the dam" (2005: 3, 267). As Jacques Rancière writes, the artist's job—in whatever medium—is to "crack open the unity of the given and the obviousness of the visible, in order to sketch a new topography of the possible" (2009: 49). As we crawl through the cracks in Vlautin's writing, through the scarred characters' lives and their melancholic relations, we do well to remember the words of another great writer of prose, poetry, and songs, Leonard Cohen, who famously sang, "There is a crack in everything.... That's how the light gets in" (Leonard Cohen, "Anthem," *The Future*, 1992).

NOTES

1. Vlautin contributed a "noir" story, "Bus Ticket to Phoenix," to *Crime Plus Music: Twenty Stories of Music-Themed Noir*, edited by Jim Fusilli (New York: Three Rooms Press, 2016). The story is about a band on tour whose amps, watches, and other items disappear, so a band member sets out to investigate. He also wrote "The Kill Switch"

The Highway Kind: Fast Cars, Desperate Drivers, and Dark Roads, edited by Patrick Millikin (New York: Mulholland Books, 2016).

2. "The guys have been the best family I could have asked for, the camaraderie of Fontaine is great. That was something I've always liked about being in a band, more than anything, is just the camaraderie." "The Fontaine Event: Interview with Willy Vlautin," http://www.hotpress.com/Richmond-Fontaine/music/interviews/The -Fontaine-Event-Interview-with-Willy-Vlautin/17220722.html. Accessed December 2016.

WORKS CITED

Bakhtin, Mikhail. 1984. *Problems of Dostoevsky's Poetics* (1997 edition). Minneapolis: University of Minnesota Press.

Barad, Karen. 2007. *Meeting the Universe Halfway: Quantum Physics and the Entanglement of Matter and Meaning*. Durham: Duke University Press.

Benjamin, Walter. 1997. *One-Way Street*. London: Verso.

Butler, Judith. 2006. *Precarious Life: The Powers of Mourning and Violence*. London: Verso.

Cohen, Leonard. 1992. *The Future*. Sony Music.

Hesmondhalgh, David. 2013. *Why Music Matters*. London: Wiley-Blackwell.

Jameson, Frederic. 2016. *The Detections of Totality*. London: Verso.

LaCapra, Dominick. 2001. *Writing History, Writing Trauma*. Baltimore: Johns Hopkins University Press.

La Tray, Chris. 2016. "The proper vehicle: Checking in with writer/musician Willy Vlautin, who reads from his latest, The Free, Shakespeare & Co." *Missoula Independent*, November 10. http://missoulanews.bigskypress.com/missoula/vehicles-for -songs/Content?oid=3228247. Accessed December 5, 2016.

Marcus, Greil. 1999. *In the Fascist Bathroom: Punk in Pop Music, 1977–1992*. Cambridge: Harvard University Press.

Massumi, Brian. 2015. *Politics of Affect*. Cambridge: Polity Press.

No Depression. 2003. "Richmond Fontaine-Willy and the Poor Boys." http://nodepres sion.com/article/richmond-fontaine-willy-and-poor-boys. Accessed September 28, 2017.

Nussbaum, Martha C. 2000. *Women and Human Development: The Capabilities Approach*. Cambridge: Cambridge University Press.

O'Sullivan, Simon. 2006. *Art Encounters/Deleuze and Guattari: Thought Beyond Representation*. London: Palgrave.

Rancière, Jacques. 2009. *The Emancipated Spectator*. London: Verso.

Steinbeck, John. 1947 (first 1937). *Two-In-One: Of Mice and Men and Cannery Row*. London: The Reprint Society.

Steininger, Alex. 1999. "Interview: Richmond Fontaine: Alt-Country? Rock 'n' Roll? Call Them Anything, Just Listen to the Music." *In Music We Trust*. http://www .inmusicwetrust.com/articles/26h03.html. Accessed December 2016.

Stewart, Kathleen. 2013. "Regionality" *Geographical Review*, vol. 103, no. 2: 275-84.

Tsing, Anna Lowenhaupt. 2015. *The Mushroom at the End of the World: On the Possibility of Living in Capitalist Ruins*. Princeton: Princeton University Press.

———. 2005. *Friction: An Ethnography of Global Connection.* Princeton: Princeton University Press.

Turner, Frederick Jackson. 1961. "The Problem of the West." In *Frontier and Section.* Englewood Cliffs: Prentice-Hall.

Vlautin, Willy, and Neil Campbell. 2013. Email Interview.

DISCOGRAPHY

Richmond Fontaine and Willy Vlautin Recordings

Safety, Cavity Search, 1996
Miles From, Cavity Search, 1997
Lost Son, El Cortez Records, 1999
Whiskey, Painkillers & Speed (Live On The Road), Cryptophonics, 2001
Winnemucca, El Cortez Records, 2002
Post to Wire, El Cortez Records, 2003
The Fitzgerald, El Cortez Records and Decor Records, 2005
Obliteration by Time, El Cortez Records, 2005
Live at the Doug Fir Lounge, El Cortez Records, 2005
Thirteen Cities, El Cortez Records and Decor Records, 2007
$87 and a Guilty Conscience That Gets Worse the Longer I Go, El Cortez Records and Decor Records, 2007
A Jockey's Christmas, El Cortez Records and Decor Records, 2008
Northline (Original Soundtrack), Faber and Faber/Harper Perennial (with *Northline* novel), 2008
We Used to Think the Freeway Sounded Like a River, El Cortez Records and Decor Records, 2009
Postcard from Portland: Live at Dante's, El Cortez Records and Decor Records, 2010
The High Country, El Cortez Records and Decor Records, 2011
Clearcuts, El Cortez Records and Decor Records, 2011
You Can't Go Back If There's Nothing to Go Back To, El Cortez and Fluff and Gravy Records, 2016

ABOUT THE EDITOR

NEIL CAMPBELL is Professor Emeritus of American Studies at the University of Derby, U.K. He has published widely in American Studies, including the books *American Cultural Studies* (with Alasdair Kean), *American Youth Cultures* (as editor), and *Issues on Americanisation and Culture* (as coeditor). He has edited the essay collections *Land and Identity*, *Photocinema*, and *Affective Landscapes in Literature, Art and Everyday Life*. His major research project has been an interdisciplinary trilogy of books on the postwar American West: *The Cultures of the American New West*, *The Rhizomatic West*, and *Post-Westerns: Cinema, Region, West*. He is coeditor of the book series *Place, Memory, Affect* and is the author of a volume within it, *Affective Critical Regionality*.

CONTRIBUTORS

Ángel Chaparro Sainz holds a degree in English Philology from the University of the Basque Country (UPV-EHU) and a PhD from that same university. He is presently teaching at the UPV-EHU in the Translation Studies program. His book *Parting the Veil: Phyllis Barber's Writing* was published in 2013 while, earlier in his career, his short stories were published in *Deia*, a Basque Country newspaper. In 2015, he coedited the volume *Transcontinental Reflections on the American West: Words, Images, Sounds beyond Borders*. His research deals mostly with Western American Literature, ecocriticism, feminist studies, popular music, minority literatures, and translation.

Jeffrey Chisum is an Associate Professor of Writing at the University of Southern California, where he teaches courses on composition and critical reasoning, technology and society, aesthetics, and the American West. Both a fiction writer and a literary scholar, he has published work in *The Mississippi Review*, *Western American Literature*, *L.A. Weekly*, and elsewhere.

Susan Kollin is a College of Letters and Science Distinguished Professor and Director of the Western Lands and Peoples Initiative at Montana State University. She recently edited *A History of Western American Literature* for Cambridge University Press, and authored *Captivating Westerns: The Middle East in the American West*, which won the Thomas J. Lyon Book Award from the Western Literature Association.

Lars Erik Larson is an Associate Professor at the University of Portland, where he teaches courses in twentieth-century American literature. His research explores the representation and circulation of material spaces, including systems of infrastructure, cities, and regions. He has published on issues of pedagogy, the interstate system in Kerouac's *On the Road*, and road-book scholarship. A 2014 Fulbright scholarship took him to India to teach and do research, which enabled him to publish articles on India's road films, dialectical culture, and conceptions of the subcontinent's literary space.

William V. Lombardi is Assistant Professor of English at Feather River College, where he teaches composition courses and nature writing with an eye toward place-based pedagogies. He specializes in literatures of the U.S. West and ecocriticism, and he has published essays on the natural history tradition and various aspects of the global West in the nineteenth, twentieth, and twenty-first centuries. His essay "It All Comes Together in…Reno" is the first published critical examination of Vlautin's work. His current book projects include a survey of place-making in California literature, and *Pioneering Families: Precarity, Solidarity, and the Postwest*, a study of affinitive kinship in twenty-first-century Western literature.

STEPHEN TATUM is Professor of English and Affiliated Faculty member of the Environmental Humanities Graduate Program at the University of Utah, where he teaches courses on the literatures and cultures of the U.S. West, critical theories of "the popular," and writing about the environment. His recent publications include "Urban New Wests" in *A History of Western American Literature* and the coauthored book (with Nathaniel Lewis) *Morta Las Vegas*. He is a two-time recipient of the Don D. Walker Prize for best article or essay in Western American literary studies.

INDEX